California Wine Country

Matt Villano, Sharron Wood, and John Doerper
Photography by Robert Holmes
and Charles O'Rear

COMPASS AMERICAN GUIDES
An imprint of Fodor's Travel Publications

Compass American Guides: California Wine Country

Editor: Laura M. Kidder
Designer: Fabrizio La Rocca
Compass Creative Director: Fabrizio La Rocca
Production Editors: Jennifer DePrima, Linda Schmidt
Production Manager: Angela L. McLean
Photo Editor and Archival Researcher: Melanie Marin
Map Design: Mark Stroud, Moon Street Cartography
Cover Design: Nora Rosansky
Cover photo (ballooning over Napa Valley): Robert Holmes

Sixth Edition
Copyright © 2011 Fodor's Travel, a division of Random House, Inc.
Maps copyright © 2011 Fodor's Travel, a division of Random House, Inc.

This book is available for special discounts for bulk purchases for sales promotions or premiums. Special
editions, including personalized covers, excerpts of existing books, and corporate imprints, can be created
in large quantities for special needs. For more information, write to Special Markets/Premium Sales,
1745 Broadway, MD 6-2, New York, New York 10019, or e-mail specialmarkets@randomhouse.com.

ISBN 978–1–4000–0492–8
ISSN 1547-7274

The details in this book are based on information supplied to us at press time, but changes
occur all the time, and the publisher cannot accept responsibility for facts that become
outdated or for inadvertent errors or omissions.

Compass American Guides, 1745 Broadway, New York, NY 10019
PRINTED IN SINGAPORE
10 9 8 7 6 5 4 3 2 1

To Nikki, the most patient wife in Wine Country,
and our beautiful daughter.
—Matt Villano

To David, my chosen lifelong travel companion, and to Ian,
my cherished culinary co-conspirator.
—Sharron Wood

C O N T E N T S

Maps

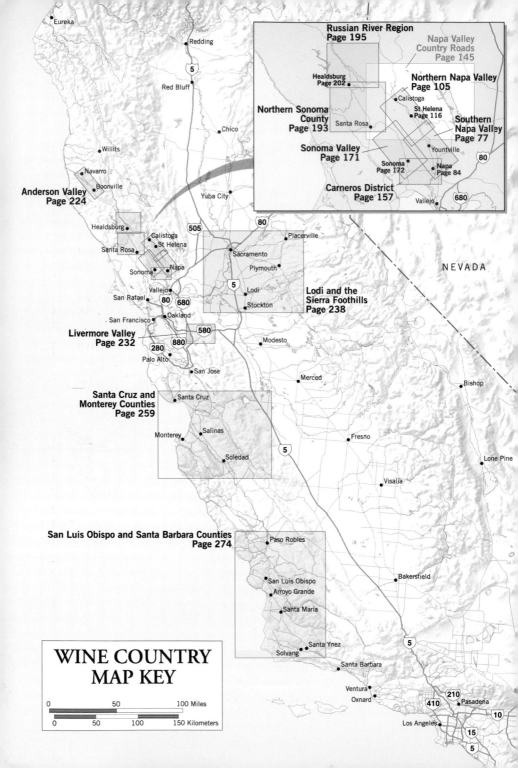

Eureka

Redding

Red Bluff

5

Chico

Willits

Navarro

Boonville

Anderson Valley
Page 224

Healdsburg

Calistoga
St Helena

Santa Rosa

Sonoma

Napa

Vallejo

San Rafael

80 680

San Francisco

Oakland

Livermore Valley
Page 232

280 880

580

Palo Alto

San Jose

Santa Cruz and
Monterey Counties
Page 259

Santa Cruz

Monterey

Salinas

Soledad

Russian River Region
Page 195

Napa Valley
Country Roads
Page 145

Healdsburg
Page 202

Northern Napa Valley
Page 105

Calistoga

St Helena
Page 116

Southern
Napa Valley
Page 77

Northern Sonoma
County
Page 193

Santa Rosa

Sonoma Valley
Page 171

Yountville

Sonoma
Page 172

Napa
Page 84

Carneros District
Page 157

Vallejo

80

680

Yuba City

505

80

Placerville

Sacramento

Plymouth

5

Lodi

Stockton

Lodi and the
Sierra Foothills
Page 238

NEVADA

Modesto

Merced

Bishop

Fresno

Lone Pine

Visalia

San Luis Obispo and Santa Barbara Counties
Page 274

Paso Robles

San Luis Obispo

Arroyo Grande

Santa Maria

Bakersfield

Santa Ynez

Solvang

Santa Barbara

Ventura

Oxnard

5

210

410

Pasadena

10

Los Angeles

15

5

WINE COUNTRY
MAP KEY

0   50   100 Miles

0   50   100   150 Kilometers

Sidebars

INTRODUCTION

There's never a dull moment in California's Wine County. Over the past 40 years, the state's winemakers have gone from shocking upstarts to world-renowned brands. Dusty agricultural backwaters have morphed into cradles of cult vintages. When driving among the imposing stone wineries, faux châteaux, and gleaming modern tasting rooms, it can be hard to believe that not long ago even Napa was little known. Now wine lovers carefully watch each hint of development, looking to catch the next up-and-comer. In the past couple of years, the Central Coast has been hailed as the hottest cutting-edge region, what *Wine Spectator* called a "winemaking frontier." Which region will be next? The very thought can make you thirsty.

Still, some things don't change. The countryside's beauty and the enthusiasm among visitors and locals are as potent as ever. At tasting rooms and wine shops, festivals and restaurants, the easy flow of conversation signals a happy curiosity and a welcoming spirit to these special areas. The discovery of wine is an experience to be shared and savored. This book aims to guide you to the best of these experiences.

■ How to Use This Book

Our guide begins with two important background chapters: one cultural and one practical. The first covers Wine Country's history, development, and current scene. The following chapter explains how wine is made and what to expect from a winery visit, including wine-tasting tips.

The regional chapters start with the long-established big guns, Napa and Sonoma. Next our coverage branches out into the backroads of those valleys and inland to the Sierra Foothills, before swooping south to the Central Coast. Each regional chapter sketches the key winemaking characteristics of its area and describes the best local wineries to visit.

Winery listings appear in geographical order, following the most common driving routes. Star icons highlight the wineries that are particularly outstanding for visitors. And each regional chapter includes a suggested day-long driving itinerary.

Following these chapters are our recommendations for the best places to eat and stay throughout Wine Country. Here too we star our top choices.

Hypnotic rows of vines at a Domaine Chandon vineyard in the southern Napa Valley.

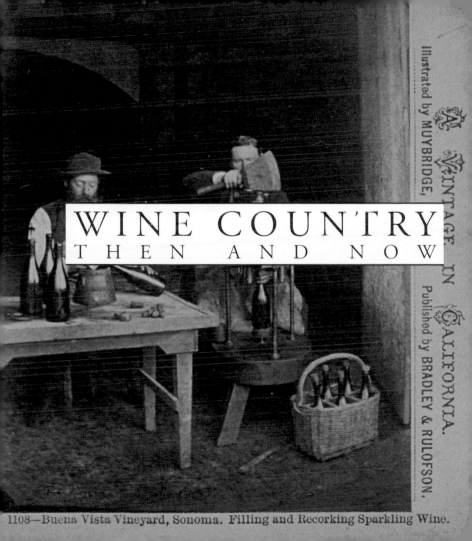

WINE COUNTRY
THEN AND NOW

1108—Buena Vista Vineyard, Sonoma. Filling and Recorking Sparkling Wine.

The afternoon sun blazes down on rough-hewn wooden steps that angle from the balcony to the dusty patio. Cut off from the outside world by thick, whitewashed adobe walls topped with red tiles, this is a courtyard that time forgot. An old cannon lurks in a gloomy passageway. A prickly pear cactus, as tall as a small tree, sprawls over the far wall of the courtyard.

In the 1830s, this humble courtyard was part of a great colonial fortress: the Sonoma *palacio* of the Mexican military commander General Mariano Guadalupe Vallejo. Now you'd hear only birdsong and rustling leaves, but the compound once echoed with the whinnying of horses and the creaking of leather saddles. Beneath this busy noise ran an undercurrent of grumbling from the Mexican soldiers frustrated by their posting at this remote northern station. More often than not, chasing the Wappo of the upper Napa Valley and the Wintun of the Suisun marshes on the lower Sacramento River proved fruitless. Were it not for the native tribes who refused to surrender their ancestral lands without a fight, they thought, the rolling, green Napa and Sonoma valleys would be paradise.

■ COLONIAL TIMES

Europeans did not settle north of the San Francisco Bay until they'd been in southern California for half a century. By the time they got here, Mexico had won its independence from Spain and taken California with it. In 1823 Father José Altimira, a headstrong Catalan, founded Mission San Francisco Solano, the last and northernmost of the Franciscan missions, at Sonoma. The newcomers had constant trouble with the native tribes, but the mission prospered and the Mexicans established ranchos around the Sonoma Valley, as well as in the Petaluma and lower Napa valleys. They raised cattle, planted olives and grapes, and made wine. Visitors reported that the wine was indifferent at best, but it was good enough to be served at Mass, and it made decent brandy.

Wine grapes came to California with Spanish colonization, spreading northward as padre Junipero Serra and his successors set up the mission system. Father Serra planted a Spanish *vitis vinifera* variety also known as *criolla*—the mission grape—at San Diego as early as 1769. Put to work by the Franciscans, Native Americans learned to press wine by foot in cowhide bags. Before long, Spanish soldiers and settlers also started making wine. General Pedro Fages planted one of California's earliest commercial vineyards alongside his orchards in 1783, not far from his residence in Monterey.

General Vallejo poses with his daughters and granddaughters, many of whom went on to marr
prominent Californians.

The Blue Wing Inn, built around 1840 by General Vallejo, stands across the street from the Sonoma Mission.

After Mexico broke away from New Spain in 1821, American- and European-born immigrants began arriving in California. Among them were Jean-Louis Vignes and Louis Bouchet, who brought along French vinifera varietals capable of producing wine much better than that made from mission grapes. They planted vineyards near Los Angeles in 1833.

General Vallejo, military commander of northern California and the first secular grape-grower in Sonoma, enthusiastically promoted viticulture. When the Mexicans dismantled the mission system in the 1830s, he parceled out to his relatives and friends much of the secularized land under his control, which included present-day Sonoma and Napa counties as far as the Dry Creek Valley, plus lower Lake County. Vallejo kept prime properties like the Petaluma Valley and the lower Napa Valley for himself, allotting the upper Napa Valley, which bordered tribal lands, to Anglo adventurers known to be at least as fierce as the indigenous people.

■ ANGLO ADVENTURERS

In 1834 Vallejo granted Rancho Caymus, in the heart of the Napa Valley, to George C. Yount, a former mountain man who had been performing odd jobs at the Sonoma Mission since the 1820s. Yount built himself a blockhouse—equipped with rifle ports—smack in the middle of an Indian *ranchéria,* and managed to keep his foothold. Edward T. Bale, an irascible British physician who had married one of Vallejo's nieces, was relegated to the upper Napa Valley after he tried to shoot the General's brother. Bale named his rancho *Carne Humana* ("Human Flesh"), a mangled version of its Wappo name, *Callajomanas* (meaning unknown). Both Yount and Bale planted some grapes, but only on a very modest scale.

In Sonoma, a ragtag band of American mountain men and adventurers captured Vallejo's adobe fortress on June 15, 1846. The rebels raised a makeshift flag decorated with a star, a badly painted bear, and a strip of red flannel, and under the command of William B. Ide declared California an independent republic—the Bear Republic. No one around knew that the United States and Mexico had been at war for more than a month, or that U.S. troops were about to arrive in California.

A U.S. supporter, Vallejo was released when the American troops took possession of California. The Mexican commander's Sonoma fortress became the U.S. Army barracks, and Vallejo's eldest daughter married its American commander. Not far away, Vallejo built himself an American-style mansion named Lachryma Montis, for the natural springs nearby; the well-preserved home is now part of Sonoma State Park. He continued making wine, which started to win competitions.

The 1848 discovery of gold in the Sierra Foothills, east of the Napa and Sonoma valleys, gave California's wine industry its real launch. As prospectors descended on the mountains and on San Francisco, the population of central California mushroomed. Within just a couple of years, the San Francisco Bay Area, Sacramento, and the Sierra Foothills were the most densely populated areas of the brand-new state. Many of the new arrivals immigrated from France and Italy, bringing with them a taste for wine and the know-how to make it. Some realized that they could make a bigger fortune selling scarce goods to miners in this wilderness than they could searching for gold. Vineyards, not only of mission grapes, but of zinfandel and barbera, appeared all over the foothills, and before long the Mother Lode had more wineries than any other region of California.

Wine boomed all the way across the Central Valley to the East Bay. English-born rancher Robert Livermore, who held a large tract in the valley that now bears his name, planted that area's first commercial grape crops. German immigrant Charles Weber, who founded the city of Stockton in 1849, established vineyards near present-day Lodi the following year. With cuttings from Weber's vines, American ex-prospector George West started growing zinfandel and flame tokay grapes. In 1858 he opened El Pinal Winery, the region's first. Lodi and Livermore would both become massive wine grape producers.

South of San Francisco Bay, a logging bonanza started in the Santa Cruz Mountains, clearing land that was snapped up by commercial grape growers. A Scotsman named John Burns established Ben Lomond vineyard in 1853, while the Jarvis brothers planted Vine Hill above Scotts Valley. Over the grade in the Santa Clara Valley, European immigrants such as Charles Lefranc found that the soil and climate were perfect for raising grapes. In 1857, Lefranc established Almaden Vineyards; soon, vintners with names like Cribari, Pellier, Wehner, and Delmas set up their own operations.

In the early days, commercial growers most often focused on productivity rather than quality, but the wine was not necessarily rotgut. Almost all the wine went to San Francisco, where it was either sold to locals or shipped to the major markets back east. To save on shipping costs, most wine was shipped in bulk, in tank cars and casks, and bottled at the destination.

The grist mill on the old Bale ranch, just north of St. Helena.

■ FINE WINE EMERGES

It took a Hungarian count to kick things up a notch. When Count Agoston Haraszthy arrived in Sonoma in 1857, he set out to make fine wine commercially. He planted European vinifera varietals rather than mission grapes and founded Buena Vista Winery the year he arrived. Things were also improving in the Napa Valley at about the same time, when growers George Beldon Crane and Sam Brannan introduced high-quality grapes to the rocky soils there.

Haraszthy deserves credit for two breakthroughs. At Buena Vista, he grew grapes on dry hillsides, instead of in the wetter lowlands, as had been customary in the mission and rancho periods. His success demonstrated that Sonoma's climate was moist enough to sustain grapes without irrigation. Haraszthy was also the first to try aging his wine in redwood barrels, which were much less expensive than oak barrels. More affordable barrels made it more feasible to ratchet up wine production. For almost 100 years, redwood barrels would be the California wine industry's most popular storage method (even though redwood can impart an odd flavor).

Bottling wine in the 1870s at Buena Vista.

California growers were slow to switch from the mission grape, which gives inferior wine but is very prolific, to better varieties of French, German, and Italian vinifera grapes, but Haraszthy's success began to make an impression. In the 1860s, most of the state's wines still came from mission grapes, which were widely used through the 1870s. But a new red-wine grape, the zinfandel, was becoming popular, both because it made excellent claret (as good red wine was then called) and because it had adapted to the area's climate.

The second half of the 19th century could be called Napa Valley's German age, because so many of its winemakers came from that country. German vintners such as Charles Krug and Jacob Schram heavily influenced the area's wine style and industry for years. Gustave Niebaum, who in the 1880s built a winery at Inglenook (in Rutherford), boosted the quality of his wines not only by planting prime vinifera grapes and practicing meticulously clean methods of vinification, but also by bottling at the winery. (The prevailing practice was to ship wine in barrels, or even railroad tank cars, to San Francisco, the Midwest, or the East Coast, where the wine would be aged and bottled.) J.J. Sigrist distinguished himself by making wines from

Zinfandel, a grape of mysterious European origin, adapted well to the climate in many California wine regions.

THE VINTAGE IN CALIFORNIA—AT WORK AT T

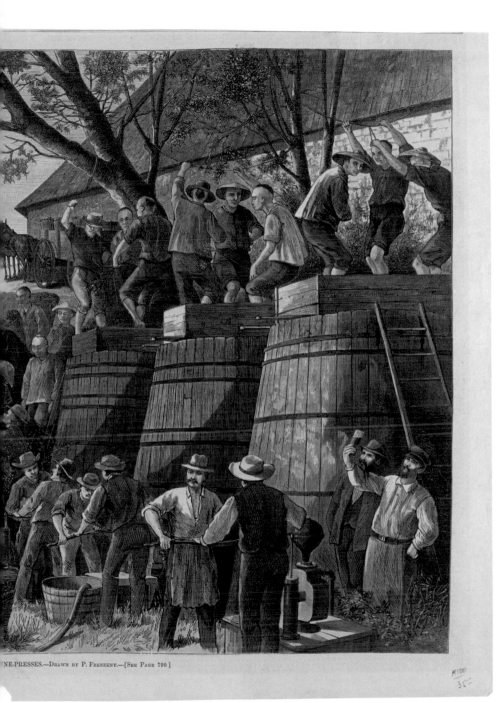

NE-PRESSES.—Drawn by P. Frenzeny.—[See Page 790]

single-grape varietals, as many winemakers do now. Germans such as Sigrist also pioneered a new style of architecture: most of the imposing stone wineries that still dominate hillsides in the Wine Country were built during this period.

■ A GROWING BUSINESS

California's Gold Rush prosperity and the completion of the Transcontinental Railroad in 1869 fueled a phenomenal population explosion. Along with everything else in the state, the wine industry got bigger. Napa and Sonoma, however, were not the leading producers. From the 1860s through the early 1880s Southern California grew more wine grapes than Northern California. In 1870 the four largest wine-producing counties were, in descending order: Los Angeles, Sonoma, El Dorado, and Calaveras (the latter two in the Sierra Foothills). Calaveras County alone had more wineries than Napa and Sonoma combined.

European immigrant farmers began arriving in San Luis Obispo County, about halfway between San Francisco and Los Angeles, in the 1860s. One wine-growing pioneer was Frenchman Pierre Hippolyte Dallidet, who purchased the neglected 18th-century vineyards at Mission San Luis Obispo de Tolosa and Mission San Miguel Arcangel. In 1879 English-born Henry Ditmas imported zinfandel and muscat grapes from France and Spain for his Rancho Saucelito near Arroyo Grande. York Mountain Winery, today the county's oldest operating winery, was started in 1882 by rancher Andrew York, from Indiana.

In Sonoma County, the Korbel brothers established a successful sparkling-wine operation in the Russian River Valley; the Kunde family became major grapegrowers; and Jacob Schram planted grapes in Knights Valley. The Dry Creek Valley filled with Italian family wineries. Napa vintners planted grapes in the nearby Conn, Pope, and Chiles valleys; on Howell Mountain; on the rolling green hills of the Carneros; and in Solano County.

Sonoma's Italian population initially made wine for home use but a few family operations became small businesses. They mostly concentrated on productive, cheap local grapes such as zinfandel, but they imported a few vines from the Old County as well. Cultural prejudice kept most of the Italian immigrants poor, and they did not build the grand wineries or homes that the Germans did in Napa. Before long, though, they formed a hugely influential wine-making enterprise.

(previous pages) Workers, many of them Chinese, crush grapes with their feet and work wine presses in a 19th-century engraving by French artist Paul Frenzeny.

The most successful of Sonoma's Italian enterprises was the Italian Swiss Colony in the northern part of the county. This cooperative winery was set up by Italian immigrants in 1881 to buy land, plant it to grapes, make wine, and turn a tidy profit. In its scale and success, if not its concept, the Colony was unique. The group bought land along the Russian River just south of Cloverdale, where the climate was similar to that of northern Italy, and classic Italian grapes such as charbono, mourvedre, and zinfandel were planted. The project earned a profit right from the start. By 1895 it turned out two million gallons; in 1902, it made 10 million gallons.

Profitably productive and yielding much better wine than the criollo, zinfandel and other hearty varieties steadily supplanted the old Spanish mission grape. C. H. Wente, James Concannon, and Charles Wetmore opened their Livermore Valley wineries in the early 1880s, and at the end of the decade a wine from that area took a gold medal at the Paris Exposition, making Livermore one of the first California wine regions to attract international attention.

Farther south, Paul Masson took charge of the Santa Clara Valley's Almaden Vineyards when founder Charles Lefranc died. Masson wasted no time releasing his first sparkling wine, and in 1896 the Paul Masson Champagne Company was born. In Santa Cruz County, Scottish Dr. John A. Stewart arrived in Scotts Valley in 1883 and established Etta Hill vineyard. He emulated the best French vineyards and achieved superior quality by blending wines in the French manner—a practice new to California. Wines from both the Santa Clara Valley and the Santa Cruz Mountains were soon winning national and international awards.

■ TROUBLED TIMES

California's fledgling wine industry hit substantial turbulence as the 19th century wound down. In the 1890s it faced upheavals in its workforce, its distribution, and in the vines themselves. Many of the workers who dug the caves, constructed the stone wineries, and built the stone fences that still snake across Wine Country hillsides were Chinese. The Chinese had come to the American West to help build the Transcontinental Railroad, and when that job was done they found other work. Not only did the Chinese help build the wineries, they also cleared the land, tilled the soil, harvested the grapes, and in some cases, made the wine. However, most Chinese settlers were driven out of California in the early 1890s because of anti-Asian agitation in San Francisco. Immigrant workers from Italy and other regions of southern Europe took over their jobs.

(left) Barrel making has changed little since Roman times.
(above) Howard C. Tibbetts, a San Francisco commercial photographer,
documented winemaking and bottling at a California winery in 1911.

Picking grapes in an Italian Swiss Colony vineyard in the 1880s.

Trouble also came from nature itself. During this period, some California vineyards were attacked by the pest phylloxera, a louse that eats vine roots. Phylloxera, which was native to America, had all but destroyed the French wine industry in the 1860s and 1870s before the problem was solved by importing phylloxera-resistant American root stocks. The only way to fight the bug was to graft the French vines onto the resistant root stocks. When the pest hit California vineyards, they had to undergo the same time-consuming and uncertain procedure, using root stocks brought over from France. Once this was accomplished, though, the vineyards continued to flourish. Luckily, the infestation wasn't as severe as it had been in France, and those vineyards that were hit were out of commission for only a few years.

California vintners interested in marketing their product as fine wine also had to battle a less-than-stellar reputation. The standard practice of shipping wine by the barrel or tank car—still in place despite Gustave Niebaum's earlier efforts at Inglenook—left it vulnerable to tampering before it reached the table. To boost profits, distributors sometimes blended cheaper wine with better wine as it made its way to market. Some distributors bottled the better California wines under fake European labels, only putting the California designation on inferior wines.

What's more, those who stored the wine at any point along the line set the purchase and sales prices and could speed up or delay the release of vintages to glut or starve the market. In 1894, powerful shippers formed the California Wine Association, a monopoly that would dominate the state's wine industry until Prohibition. The association's control of the market sharply brought down the price of grapes, and some growers had to sell below cost.

In an attempt to combat these problems, the Italian Swiss Colony saw that co-op members received fair prices for their grapes and began in 1904–05 to bottle wine in its San Francisco facilities before shipping. Vintners received support from the Pure Food and Drug Act of 1906, which discouraged alteration of wines by the shipper. Even then, almost no wine was shipped to the East Coast in the bottle; it still went by tank car and barrel as before.

■ PROHIBITION AND DEPRESSION

The National Prohibition Act, which passed in 1919 under the popular name of the Volstead Act, had far-reaching effects on California wineries. Some, particularly Napa operations such as Beaulieu Vineyards, Beringer, and the Christian Brothers, stayed in business by making sacramental wines. A few kept their inventories in bond, storing their wine in warehouses certified by the Department of Internal Revenue and guaranteed secure by bonding agencies. Magically, wine flowed out the back doors of the bonded warehouses into barrels and jugs brought by customers, and just as magically it seemed to replenish itself. Now and then a revenuer would crack down, but enforcement seems to have been lax at best.

Some consumers took matters into their own hands during Prohibition and started making wine at home. The demand for grape juice and grapes jumped, and by the end of the "Great Experiment" California growers were shipping more grapes than they had at its start. This was especially true around Lodi and Livermore. Unfortunately, quality declined. Growers had grafted over their vineyards to high-yielding red varieties such as the red-juiced alicante bouschet, which allowed home winemakers to get more gallons of wine per ton than they could from other grape varieties—especially if they spiked the juice with a generous helping of cane sugar.

Prohibition forced many wineries to shut down altogether. In Mendocino, Santa Clara, and Santa Cruz counties, few wineries survived. Operations in the Sierra Foothills, limping since the Gold Rush went bust late in the 19th century, collapsed, though many of the vineyards were abandoned rather than destroyed and simply lay dormant for decades. In richer agricultural areas such as Sonoma County, good soil allowed farmers to replant their vineyards with fruit and nut trees.

By contrast, family vineyards and wineries, many of them planted by Italian immigrants, multiplied around Paso Robles in northern San Luis Obispo County. In what may be the first documented instance of celebrity involvement in California wine culture, Polish concert pianist Ignace Paderewski purchased 2,000 acres when he visited Paso Robles in the early 1920s. He named his place Rancho San Ignacio and planted petite sirah and zinfandel.

After the repeal of Prohibition in 1933, rebooting legitimate winemaking in California proved difficult. Wineries had lost many of their customers to bathtub gin and cheap cocktails, and those still drinking wine now preferred sweet wines to dry ones. With the price of grapes and wine at a Depression-era low, it did not pay to replant grape acreage taken out of commission during Prohibition. In regions where vineyards had switched over to other crops or low-quality grapes, it made more financial sense to stick with the new regime than to go back to the old one.

Prohibition did less damage in the Napa Valley, where grapes thrive but fruit trees grow poorly on the rocky and gravelly slopes, bench lands, and alluvial fans. Fewer Napa growers had been able to convert to other crops, and more had been able to survive with sacramental wine, so more vineyards could be brought back to fine-wine production after repeal. Several major wineries survived Prohibition, including Inglenook, Louis M. Martini, and Charles Krug (acquired in the 1940s by the Cesare Mondavi family). Considering the all-time low demand for their product—and the state of the American palate—these wineries made some amazingly good wines during this period. Nevertheless, the wine industry would struggle to regain its customer base well into the 1960s.

■ STATE OF CONFUSION

California winemaking, in the period from the end of Prohibition to the wine renaissance of the 1960s, was marked by confusion. Drinkable wine was still made in the state, but much of it was shipped in bulk, to be blended and bottled as generic styles or in jug brands.

White wine came in three styles: dry, medium, and sweet. What passed as "white burgundy" or "sauterne" in California was more often than not a blend of any white wine grapes at hand, just like the latter-day California whites known as "chablis" or "Rhine wine." Red "burgundy" was blended in from all kinds of red-wine grapes except pinot noir, the noble grape of France's Bourgogne (Burgundy) wine-growing district. "Claret" and "chianti" could also be made from any convenient red wine grape. To overcome this anarchy of meaningless proprietary and generic names, some wineries began labeling their finer wines with the name of the grape: what was once called "sauterne" became "sauvignon blanc," and "claret" became "cabernet sauvignon."

One of the bright spots in this landscape was Moscow-born André Tchelistcheff, who in 1938 joined Beaulieu Vineyard in Napa Valley as vice president and chief winemaker. He set out to develop high-quality cabernet sauvignon, and created the "Georges de Latour Private Reserve" label, named for Beaulieu's founder. In the cab category, it became the standard that other California winemakers aimed for. Tchelistcheff introduced innovations such as barrel-aging in

The "baggypants vintners brigade" were the movers and shakers in the revival of Napa's wine industry. They included (left to right): Brother Timothy Diener of Christian Brothers; Charles B. Forni of Sunny St. Helena Co-op; Walter Sullivan and Aldo Fabrini of Beaulieu Vineyard; Michael Ahern of Freemark Abbey; Peter and Robert Mondavi of Krug; John Daniel Jr. of Inglenook; Louis M. Martini, Charlie Beringer, and Martin Stelling of Sunny St. Helena Co-op; and Fred Abruzzini of Beringer.

Old Vine *(1961), by Ansel Adams.*

Man Plowing Vineyard *(1961), by Ansel Adams.*

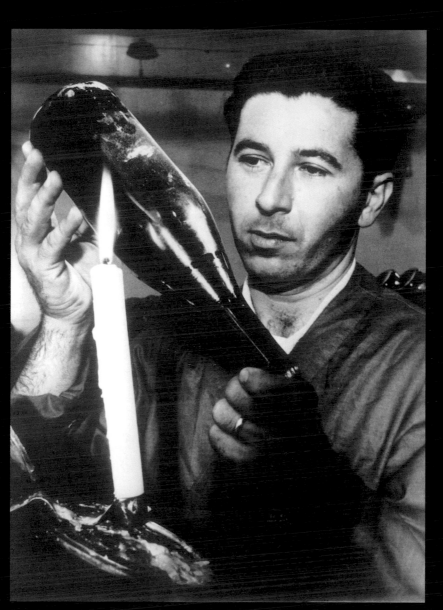

Man Looking at Bottle *(1961), by Ansel Adams.*

American oak and did much to advance wine-making technology, not to mention the reputation of California wine. Until his 1973 retirement, he remained at BV but also consulted for everyone from Joseph Heitz and Mike Grgich to Neibaum/ Coppola and Buena Vista Winery. Many winemakers who went on to success credited Tchelistcheff as a mentor.

■ RENAISSANCE

After World War II, California wine was poised for a comeback, as Americans started to get serious about wine. Between the thousands of U.S. soldiers returning from service in France and the droves of young people traveling on the Continent in the 1950s, more Americans were exposed to wine's role in European lifestyles— and they brought home a more appreciative attitude toward wine. A sign of real change appeared in 1952, when Eleanor and Fred McCrea released the first of their now legendary chardonnays from Stony Hill Vineyard, a gravelly patch of land high up Spring Mountain on Napa Valley's western slope. The wine set a new standard for California whites.

Tourists had been passing through the Napa Valley for decades, but their numbers increased in the 1950s after wineries started courting them by opening tasting rooms. These were initially modest affairs meant to sell wine to whomever stopped by, and the trend spread to other regions only slowly. Fascinated with wine, more and more "respectable" people got into the business. Millionaire James Zellerbach built Hanzell, a tiny Sonoma Valley winery dedicated to producing true Burgundian-style wines. Before he died in 1963, Zellerbach's winery had pioneered two methods that have become standard practice in California winemaking: fermentation in stainless steel tanks rather than redwood or oak tanks, and the aging of chardonnay in small French Limousin oak barrels (the same oak from which Burgundian wine barrels are traditionally made).

In 1965, Jack and Jamie Davies refurbished Jacob Schram's old cellars and began making first-rate sparkling wines from Napa Valley chardonnay grapes rather than from the colombard or riesling used by other local producers. In 1966, after a quarrel with his brother Peter, Robert Mondavi left Charles Krug, the family winery, and built a place of his own in Oakville—the first new winery built in the Napa Valley since the repeal of Prohibition. Mondavi popularized the use of stainless steel fermenting tanks and French oak barrels and made a number of clever marketing moves, such as giving barrel-fermented sauvignon blanc a user-friendly name, fumé blanc. He was soon a huge name.

It was the right move at the right time: demand for high-quality varietals was beginning to grow. Rising to the occasion, wineries were opened by ground-breakers such as Donn and Molly Chappellet on Pritchard Hill (1969), Charlie Wagner at Caymus in Rutherford (1972), David S. Stare at Sonoma County's Dry Creek Vineyard (1972), John and Janet Trefethen in Napa (1973), and Fred Fisher on the Sonoma side of the Mayacamas Range (1973). Napa Valley winemakers received a morale boost in the early 1970s, when the renowned French Champagne house of Moët & Chandon bought vineyards and platted a winery site to make French-style sparklers with Napa Valley grapes.

Winemakers started flexing the boundaries of California Wine Country. In the early 1960s, Monterey County got its first commercial wineries, including Mirassou, J. Lohr, and Chalone. Santa Barbara County also got on the wagon in the 1960s, when vineyards were planted in the Santa Ynez Valley. The first winery to operate in the Anderson Valley since Prohibition, Husch Vineyards started crushing chardonnay, gewürztraminer, pinot noir, and other varietals in 1971. Some of the abandoned Sierra Foothills vineyards were resurrected in the 1970s, and drew praise for their zinfandel in particular. Many winemakers throughout California bought grapes from Lodi and the Livermore Valley (as they still do today), but the two regions remained largely unknown to the public. Growers in these areas worked on a massive scale, developing vineyard technology such as overhead irrigation, mechanical harvesting, and roller crushing.

The 1970s were a pivotal decade for San Luis Obispo County. In Paso Robles, Dr. Stanley Hoffman planted cabernet sauvignon, pinot noir, and chardonnay with the help of André Tchelistcheff. Hoffman Mountain Ranch soon won international kudos. Also in Paso Robles, half-brothers Gary Eberle and Cliff Giacobine introduced syrah and established Estrella River Winery. Smaller operations, such as Chamisal Vineyard and Paragon Vineyard, started up in the Edna Valley, and in Arroyo Grande the 1879 vineyard at Rancho Saucelito was revived.

■ THE PARIS WINE TASTING OF 1976

The event that changed the California wine industry forever took place half a world away, in Paris. To celebrate the American Bicentennial, Steven Spurrier, a British wine merchant, sponsored a comparative blind tasting of California cabernet and chardonnay wines against Bordeaux cabernet blends and French chardonnays. The tasters were French and included journalists and producers. The 1973

Top row, from left: Robert Mondavi, Jacob Beringer, Frederick Beringer, Charles Krug.
Second row: Agoston Haraszthy, Jack Cakebread, Samuele Sebastiani, David Stare.
Third row: Zelma Long of Simi, Gustave Niebaum, Louis Kunde, Janet and John Trefethen.
Bottom row: Joe Heitz, Eleanor and Fred McCrea, Jim Bundschu.

Stag's Leap Wine Cellars cabernet sauvignon came in first among the reds, and the 1973 Chateau Montelena chardonnay edged out the French whites. The so-called Judgment of Paris stunned the wine establishment, as it was the first serious challenge to the supremacy of French wines.

When the shouting died down, the rush was on. Tourists and winemakers streamed into the Napa Valley. Wine prices rose so much that they helped revitalize the Sonoma County wine industry, at long last replacing the prune orchards with vineyards. California vintners' work really paid off in 1981, when Christian Moueix of Chateau Petrus tasted some well-aged Inglenook reds and decided to get involved in Napa's prestigious Dominus Estate.

To some degree, this recognition from the Old World reflected the success with which Napa and Sonoma vintners mimicked French wine styles. (In fact, judges at the infamous 1976 tasting often couldn't tell which wine came from which country.) Premium wineries focused on cabernet sauvignon and chardonnay and bottled them unblended. Managing their vineyards to yield grapes comparable to French grapes, growers harvested before the brilliant California sunshine fully developed the grapes' sugar content. Where French winemakers sometimes augment fermenting grapes just to reach the standard 12 percent alcohol content, California winemakers struggled to keep the alcohol level of their wines down. European yeasts were imported for use in the fermentation of wines styled after Burgundy whites, Bordeaux reds, and Champagne.

■ THE STATEWIDE BOOM

The unprecedented ascent of Napa and Sonoma wines had an enormous impact on lesser-known wine regions of California in the 1980s and 1990s. Hoping to replicate the success of the big boys and the good life that became synonymous with Wine Country, vineyards sprang up all over the state. As the price of Napa and Sonoma valley real estate soared to nose-bleed heights, a robust wine industry emerged in the nearby Anderson Valley. Handley Cellars, Pullman Vineyards, and Pepperwood Springs Vineyards were at the forefront. In 1982, when French Champagne maker Louis Roederer decided to start producing sparkling wine in the Anderson Valley, the region's prestige shot up.

Major wineries from around California purchased large tracts around Paso Robles and planted grapes mostly for use in mass-market bottlings. Smaller independent wineries also began to appear, and in the 1990s Paso Robles gained an

Barrels of aging wine are labeled in an old stone cellar.

international name for exceptional Rhône varietal vintages such as syrah, viognier, and roussanne. Meanwile, Santa Barbara wine country really flowered, with dozens of boutique and family wineries producing exceptional wine in the Santa Ynez and Santa Maria valleys. Between 1970 and 2002, wine in Santa Barbara County mushroomed from non-existent to a $360-million business pumping out a million cases a year.

Monterey County simultaneously experienced a similar phenomenon, planting over 45,000 acres of vineyards from the 1970s through 2005. Lodi and the Livermore Valley, long endowed with extensive and profitable vineyards, enjoyed a different sort of bonanza, finally gaining name recognition with mainstream wine drinkers. This allowed smaller wineries oriented to premium wine, especially zinfandel, to prosper. The situation has been more difficult in the Santa Clara Valley and Santa Cruz Mountains, where vineyards fell victim to the rapid expansion of Silicon Valley in the late 1990s. Still, some of the highest mountain vineyards have survived to supply the area's wineries.

Stainless steel vats (above, at Domaine Chandon) are also used to ferment wine.

■ BIG REDS, BIG WHITES, OAK BLUES

In the 1990s, California vintners started trying to forge a distinctively Californian wine style. Instead of imitating the French, growers experimented with later harvests that allowed grapes to develop greater fruitiness, complexity, and depth. Higher sugar content came hand-in-hand with longer growing seasons, often boosting alcohol levels to literally dizzying heights of 14.5 percent and beyond. New oak, and lots of it, came into style as vintners aged their wine in young barrels to maximize the toasty, buttery, and vanilla flavors preferred by the easy-drinking public. Influential wine critic Robert Parker, who favors gigantic, concentrated red wines, was instrumental in promoting the newly popular style.

Winemakers experimented to see which grape varietals grew best in their region. Unblended cabernet sauvignon and chardonnay, the warhorses of the 1970s and 1980s, were joined by other single varietals in the pantheon of high-end California wine. Rhône varietals, such as grenache, syrah, and viognier, and traditional Italian varieties, such as barbera, nebbiolo, and sangiovese, became popular. Blends made a big comeback, but this time around wineries carefully labeled their bottles with the names of the grapes that went into the wine.

However, California has not abandoned the grapes that made its name and its fortune. Makers of fine wine still have faith in the old standards, and some are turning away from the recently popular oaky, fruity styles to focus on more subtle wines. Meanwhile, there's strong evidence of the longevity of California's wines. In 2006, a recreation of the earth-shaking 1976 tasting took place in Napa Valley and London. A panel of American, English, and French experts unanimously voted a 1971 Ridge California Cabernet Sauvignon the best of all. In fact, Californian cabernet sauvignons from the early 1970s swept the top five places—happy proof that California's wines can age as well as French vintages.

Wine is big business in California, reaching beyond the vineyard to tourism and other industries. Admission to its college oenology programs, especially those at the University of California's Davis and Fresno branches, is highly competitive. (There are hundreds of vintners both here and abroad who've hit the books at these campuses.) Marketing groups such as the Rhône Rangers and ZAP (Zinfandel Advocates and Producers) spread the word about California wines, and consultants advise winemakers on everything from where to grow to how to navigate government regulation.

Recognizing the benefits wine can bring to their economy and their image, communities around California have embraced the industry and promoted it aggressively. Wherever you go in California Wine Country, and whatever your palate preferences, you will find tasting rooms to welcome you, restaurants to excite you, lodgings to pamper you, and, most important, wines to dazzle you.

Wooden vats for aging wine.

VISITING WINERIES
TASTING AND TOURING

Around the world and across the United States, California wine is more popular than ever before. The pull to visit the land that produces these magical vintages is no mystery. Travel magazines, television shows, epicurean memoirs, and gorgeously shot movies are saturated with lush, romantic images of California's Wine Country. If these make your mouth water, you won't be disappointed when you get here: The meandering back roads, vineyard-blanketed hills, and ivy-draped wineries—not to mention the luxurious restaurants, hotels, and spas—really *are* that beautiful.

Even if you don't yet know much about wine tasting or production, you can have a great time touring these areas. Most wineries welcome visitors, whether by appointment or on a walk-in basis. Your gateway to their world is the tasting room, where the staff (and occasionally even the actual winemaker) are almost always happy to chat with curious guests. Tasting rooms range from the grand to the humble, offering everything from a few sips of wine to an hours-long immersion in the winery's vision. Especially in the Napa and Sonoma valleys, wineries may give fun, illuminating tours of their facilities. Many host occasional events such as concerts and dinners, often held outdoors. Everywhere in Wine Country, independent operators offer van or bus tours that stop at wineries for tastings; on these, you can put away your maps and sit back as the scenery rolls by.

■ WHEN TO GO

In high season (April through October), and on weekends and holidays during much of the year, Wine Country roads can be busy and tasting rooms can be crowded. If you prefer less hustle and bustle, tour on a weekday. To avoid the frustration of a fruitless drive to the boonies, confirm in advance that the wineries that interest you will be open when you plan to stop by. (See the "Down on the Farm: Viticulture" section below for more info on the vines' seasonal stages. See "Festivals and Events" in the Practical Information chapter to find out when and where seasonal celebrations take place.)

Winter is a beautiful time to visit California's wineries: In January and February bright yellow mustard plants bloom between the bare spindly grapevines, and in March the first wildflowers spread beneath the oaks. While the vineyards lie dormant you're more likely to meet winemakers in their tasting rooms, for they have some time to discuss their work with visitors. The tasting rooms, wineries, and inns tend to be considerably less busy in winter than at other times of the year, although the pace picks up a bit between Christmas and New Year's Day.

Workers race to harvest grapes at the peak of ripeness.

Spring is another great time to visit the wine regions because it brings even more wildflowers: golden poppies; buttercups; blue and cream irises; and red, white, blue, and yellow lupines. Winemakers stick close to their work, because this is not only the season when they are bottling last year's vintages, but also a time of dubious weather, when late frosts can descend on the vineyards and kill the tender leaf buds. The crowds of visitors start to grow in late April, but you can still enjoy quiet moments. Wine festival season gets underway in May.

Summer days tend to be hot and dusty. The wineries get mobbed with visitors, and so do the hotel swimming pools. This is also prime time for wine festivals and county fairs. If the weather is favorable, the first of the grapes, those destined for crisp white wines and sparklers, will be harvested as early as August.

Fall is both the busiest and most exciting season to watch the wineries at work. This is the time when field hands and machinery comb the vineyards for ripe clusters, trucks groan with loaded fruit bins as they lumber along the roads, and winery workers dash about seeing to massive vats of fermenting juice. The air is heavy with the aroma of grapes. As October wears into November, the vineyards turn flaming red and burnished gold.

■ IN THE TASTING ROOM

Many California wineries have tasting rooms where you can sample their offerings. These are almost universally relaxed places where everyone is having a good time— so don't worry if you're new to tasting. A tasting room may be nothing more than a corner in a barrel room, with a table set up amid stacked boxes and idle equipment. Flashier wineries run elaborate visitor centers with art galleries, gift shops, restaurants, and opulent tasting rooms. Either way, tasting rooms are designed to introduce newcomers to the pleasures of wine and to inform visitors about the wines made at that winery.

In more heavily visited regions or at popular wineries you might have to pay for your tasting, anything from a nominal $5 fee to $30 and up for a tasting that includes a tour, a guided tasting, or perhaps a glass you can take home. This fee is often deducted from your tab if you buy some wine at the end of the tasting.

Start by describing to the person behind the bar what sort of wine—the house specialty, their whites or reds, the whole shebang—you'd like to try and he or she will suggest where to start on the list of wines being poured that day. Most often you'll find an assortment of different wines from the winery's most recently released vintages. There might also be a list of library wines (those aged somewhat longer) that you can taste for a separate fee. To create a more cohesive tasting experience, tasting rooms sometimes offer flights consisting of three or four particular wines selected to complement or contrast with each other. These might be vertical (several vintages of one wine), horizontal (several wines from one vintage), or more intuitively assembled.

Each taste consists of only an ounce or so. While you taste, ask any questions that come to mind; your pourer will do his or her best to answer. Other guests might join the conversation. Feel free to pour out whatever you don't want to finish into one of the dump buckets on the bar. There might be a plate of crackers on the bar; nibble them when you want to clear your palate of one wine's flavor before tasting the next.

Remember, those little sips add up, so pace yourself. If you plan to visit several wineries, try just a few wines at each so you don't hit sensory overload, when your mouth can no longer distinguish subtleties. (This is called palate fatigue.) Choose a

Signs point the way to some of Sonoma Valley's leading wineries.

Natural light is best when checking wine for clarity and color.

designated driver for the day: Wine Country roads are often narrow and curvy, and you may be sharing the road with bicyclists and wildlife as well as other wine tourists.

■ TASTING TIPS

Starting with the pop of the cork and the splashing of wine into a glass, all of your senses play a part in winetasting. Knowing the basic tasting steps and a few key quality guidelines can make your winery visit much more enjoyable. Follow your instincts at the tasting bar: there is no right or wrong way to describe wine.

Use your eyes. Before you taste it, take a good look at the wine in your glass. Holding the glass by the stem, let natural light flow through the wine. No matter whether it's white, rosé, or red, your wine should be clear, without cloudiness or sediments when you drink it. Some unfiltered wines may seem cloudy at first, but they will clear as the sediments settle.

In the natural light, place the glass in front of a white background such as a blank sheet of paper or a tablecloth. Check the color. Is it right for the wine? A California white should be golden: straw, medium, or deep, depending on the type. Rich, sweet, dessert wine will have more intense color, but chardonnay and sauvignon blanc will be paler. A rosé should be a clear pink, from pale to deep,

Sniff first, then sip.

without too much red or any orange. Reds may lean toward ruby or garnet coloring; some have a purple tinge. They shouldn't be pale (the exception is pinot noir, which can be quite pale yet still have character). In any color wine, a brownish tinge is a flaw that indicates the wine is too old, has been incorrectly stored, or has gone bad. If you see brown, try another bottle.

Breathe deep. Your nose may well be the most important wine-tasting tool you have, because aroma plays a huge role in wine's flavor. After you have looked at the wine's color, gently move your glass in a circular motion to swirl the wine around. As the wine releases its aromas, stick your nose into the glass and take a sniff.

Wine should smell good to you. You might pick up the scent of apricots, peaches, ripe melon, honey, and wildflowers in a white wine; black pepper, cherry, violets, and cedar in a red. Rosés (which are made from red wine grapes) smell something like red wine, but in a scaled-back way, with hints of raspberry, roses, or strawberries. You might encounter surprising smells, such as tar—which some people actually appreciate in certain (generally expensive, red) wines.

For the most part, though, wine's aroma should be clean and pleasing to you, not "off." If you find a wine's odor odd or unpleasant, there's probably something wrong.

THE WINE AROMA WHEEL

© COPYRIGHT 1990 A.C. NOBLE

WWW.WINEAROMAWHEEL.COM

Scan this wheel from the inner ring to the outer ring for specific descriptive terms used for wine aromas.

Watch out for hints of wet dog or skunk, or for moldy, horsey, mousy, or sweaty smells. Sniff for chemical faults such as sulfur, or excessive vanilla scents (picked up from oak barrels) that overwhelm the other aromas. A vinegar smell indicates that the wine has started to spoil. A soggy cardboard smell means the wine is corked—the cork has gone bad, ruining the wine. If the wine in your glass has any of these funky aromas—unlikely in a tasting room, since servers usually check for faults with each bottle opened—dump it and ask your server to open another bottle.

Just a sip. Once you've checked its appearance and aroma, take a sip—not a swig or a gulp—of the wine. As you sip wine, gently swish it around in your mouth—this releases more aromas for your nose to explore. Do the aroma and the flavor complement each other, improve each other? While moving the wine around in your mouth, also think about the way it feels: silky or crisp? Does it coat your tongue or is it thinner? This combination of weight and intensity is referred to as body: a good wine may be light-, medium-, or full-bodied.

Do you like it? If not, don't drink it. Even if there is nothing actually wrong with a wine, what's the point of drinking it if you don't like it? A wine can be technically perfect but nevertheless taste strange, unpleasant, or just boring. It's possible to learn to appreciate wine that doesn't appeal to your tastes, but unless you like a wine right off the bat, it probably won't become a favorite. In the tasting room, dump what you don't like and move on to the next sample.

The more complex a wine is, the more flavors you will detect in the course of tasting. You might taste different things when you first take a sip ("up front"), when you swish ("in the middle" or "at mid-palate"), and just before you swallow ("at the end" or "on the back-palate"). A good table wine should be neither too sweet nor too tart, and never bitter. Fruitiness, a subtle near-sweetness, should be balanced by acidity, but not to the point that the wine tastes sour or makes your mouth pucker. An astringent or drying quality is the mark of tannins, a somewhat mysterious wine element that comes from grape skins and oak barrels. In young reds this can taste almost bitter—but not quite. All these qualities, together with the wine's aroma, blend to evoke the flavors not only of fruit but of unlikely things such as leather, tobacco, or almonds.

Spit or Swallow? You may choose to spit out the wine (into the dump bucket or a plastic cup) or swallow it. Either way, pay attention to what happens after the wine leaves your mouth—this is the finish, and it can be spectacular. What flavors stay behind or appear? Does the flavor fade away quickly or linger pleasantly? A long finish is a sign of quality; wine with no perceptible finish is inferior.

BUYING AND SHIPPING WINE

Don't feel obliged to buy a bottle of wine just because the winery has given you a taste or two—especially if you paid a tasting fee. You're not required to make a purchase, though some of the large, more commercial wineries might apply a little pressure. Tasting room sales are a significant slice of revenues at many wineries, particularly small operations. At small wineries, courtesy suggests that you buy some wine if you spend more than a few minutes tasting and ask more than a few questions.

Small or large, in the tasting room you can stock up on hard-to-find wines, some of them sold only through the winery. If you find a particular winery exceptional, you can join their wine club, which will periodically send wine to you (except in some states), offer members-only releases, and give you a discount on all of your purchases.

If you're an out-of-region visitor, ask about the winery's direct-shipment program. Most wineries are happy to ship the wine you buy, as long as you live in a state that lets consumers receive California wine directly from the winery. The rules apply whether you make your purchase in the tasting room, join the wine club, or order online.

Sending wine home is getting easier, especially since the U.S. Supreme Court set a new precedent in 2005. The court found unconstitutional the discriminatory bans on interstate, direct-to-consumer wine shipments in New York and Michigan. More states are opening their borders to such shipments from California, but laws vary greatly from state to state. The penalties for noncompliance in some states can be severe, so if you're going to ship wine home, it is wise to do so either through the winery or a professional shipper. For up-to-date information, check www.wineinstitute.org/programs/shipwine/.

Many California producers turn out "big," or full-bodied, wine, with concentrated fruit flavors, a higher percentage of alcohol, and sometimes a whopping hit of oakiness. These often get high ratings, but more delicate wines can be just as worthwhile. The bottom line is that wine of any variety and style should have a nice balance of flavors and feel good in your mouth. You decide: if you like it, it's good wine.

Browsing the Bounty Hunter Wine Shop in Napa.

ALL WHITE, SPARKLING, & ROSE WINES ARE CHILLED AND READY TO DRINK

■ In the Winery

Even if you're not a devoted wine drinker, a winery can be fascinating, as you'll see how wine is made. Tours are most exciting during harvest, between August and October, when most of the grapes ripen and are crushed and fermented into wine. In harvest season you'll likely see workers picking in the vineyards and hauling fruit bins and barrels around with forklifts. At other times of the year, winery work consists of monitoring the wine, "racking" it (eliminating sediment by transferring it from one tank or barrel to another), and bottling and boxing the finished wine.

Depending on the size of the winery, a tour might consist of a few visitors or a large group, following the staff guide from vineyard to processing area and from barrel room to tasting room. The guide explains what happens at each stage of the wine-making process, usually emphasizing the winery's particular approach to growing and vinting. You'll find out the uses for all that complex machinery, stainless steel equipment, and plastic gadgetry; feel free to ask questions at any point in the tour. If it's harvest or bottling time, you might see and hear the facility at work. Otherwise, the scene is likely to be quiet, with a few workers tending the tanks and barrels.

Malbec grapes minutes from being crushed.

HOW FINE WINE IS MADE

Juice that flows from crushed grapes before pressing is called "free-run."

White wines are not fermented with pulp and skins. The grapes are pressed before fermentation. White wines may be fermented in barrels. They are often cool-fermented to preserve their fruitiness.

Red wines are fermented with pulp and skins. Some grapes are pressed after fermentation.

Stemmer-Crusher: Removes the grapes from their stems and pierces their skins so juice can flow off freely.

Wine Press: An inflatable bag that gently pushes the grape pulp against a perforated drum.

Fermentation: The process by which the natural fruit sugars of grapes are converted, with the aid of yeasts, into alcohol. Takes place in large vats or tanks or in oak barrels.

Racking: After fermentation, wine is racked, that is, moved to new, clean tanks or barrels, to aid clarification. It may be filtered or fined or allowed to settle naturally.

Aging: Many premium wines are aged in oak barrels. Keeping wine in oak too long, though, kills delicate grape flavors and may make the wine taste "woody."

Bottling: Very small wineries still bottle by hand, but most bottling is done by machine in a sterile environment to keep impurities out of the bottle.

Crushing grapes the old-fashioned way . . .

Some large wineries offer a choice of tours, from a general introduction to an exploration of the vineyard, to seated food-and-wine pairings. If you plan to go on a winery tour, wear shoes that will take you comfortably along dirt paths and on cement floors that may be wet.

■ THE CRUSH

The process of turning grapes into wine generally starts at the **crush pad**, where the grapes are brought in from the vineyards. Good winemakers carefully monitor their vineyards throughout the year. Their presence is especially critical at harvest, when regular checks of the grapes' ripeness determines the proper day for picking. Once that day arrives, the crush begins.

Wineries pick their grapes by machine or by hand, depending on the terrain and on the type of grape. Some varieties, especially whites, are harvested at night with the help of powerful floodlights. Why at night? Not only is it easier on those picking the grapes (late summer temps can easily exceed 100°F), but the fruit-acid content in the pulp and juice of the grapes peaks in the cool night air. The acids—an essential component during fermentation and aging, and an important part of

. . . and the newfangled way.

wine's flavor—plummet in the heat of the day. Red wine grapes, which carry their acid in their skins, don't have to be picked at night, because the heat doesn't have the same effect on them.

Grapes must be handled with care, so none of the juice is lost. They arrive at the crush pad in large containers called gondolas and drop gently onto a conveyor belt that deposits the grapes into a **stemmer-crusher**. A drum equipped with steel fingers knocks the grapes off their stems and pierces their skins, so the juice can flow off freely. The grapes and juice fall through a grate and are carried via stainless steel pipes to a press or vat. The stems and leaves drop out of the stemmer-crusher and are recycled to the vineyards as natural fertilizer. After this general first step, the production process goes one of three ways to make a white, red, or rosé wine.

■ Making White Wines
The juice of white wine grapes goes first to **settling tanks**, where the skins and grape solids sink to the bottom, separating from the clear **free-run juice** on top. The material in the settling tanks still contains a lot of juice, so after the free-run juice is pumped off the remains go into a **press**. A modern press consists of a perforated

The Fine Art of Barrel Making

Creating the oak barrels that age the wine is a craft in its own right. At Demptos Napa Cooperage, a French-owned company that employs French barrel-making techniques, the process involves several elaborate production phases. Below, the staves of oak are formed to the barrel shape using metal bands. At bottom left, semi-finishing smoothes the rough edges off the bound staves. Finally, the barrels are literally toasted (bottom right) to give the oak its characteristic flavor, which will in turn be imparted to the wine.

drum containing a Teflon-coated bag. As this bag is inflated slowly, like a balloon, it slowly pushes the grapes against the outside wall and the liquids are squeezed from the solids and flow off. Like the free-run juice, the **press juice** is pumped into a **fermenter**—either a stainless-steel tank (which may be insulated to keep the fermenting juice cool) or an oak barrel.

Press juice and free-run juice are fermented separately, but a little of the press juice may be added to the free-run juice for complexity. Because press juice tends to be strongly flavored and may contain undesirable flavor components, winemakers are careful not to add too much of it. White press juice is almost always fermented in stainless-steel tanks; free-run juice may be handled differently. Most white wines are fermented at 59°F to 68°F (15°C to 20°C). Cooler temperatures develop delicacy and fruit aromas and are especially important in fermentation of sauvignon blanc and riesling.

An enologist draws wine into a pipette to measure its acidity.

During fermentation, **yeast** feeds on the sugar in grape juice and converts it to alcohol and carbon dioxide. Wine yeast dies and fermentation naturally stops in two to four weeks, when the alcohol level reaches 15 percent. If there's not enough sugar in the grapes to reach the desired alcohol level, the winemaker can add extra sugar before or during fermentation, in a process called **chaptalization.**

To prevent oxidation, which damages wine's color and flavor, and to kill wild yeast and bacteria, which can produce off-flavors, winemakers almost always add **sulfur dioxide,** in the form of sulfites, before fermenting. A winemaker may also choose to encourage **malolactic fermentation** ("malo") to soften a wine's acidity or deepen its flavor and complexity. This is done by inoculating the wine with lactic bacteria soon after alcoholic fermentation begins or right after it ends, or by transferring the new wine to wooden vats that harbor the bacteria. Malo, which can also happen by accident, is undesirable in lighter-bodied wines meant to be drunk young.

Filling oak barrels at Kenwood Vineyards.

For richer results, free-run juice from chardonnay, and some from sauvignon blanc, might be fermented in oak barrels, in individual batches, with each vineyard and lot kept separate. **Barrel fermentation** creates more depth and complexity, as the wine picks up vanilla flavors and other harmonious traits from the wood. The barrels used by California winemakers may be imported from France or eastern Europe, or made domestically of American oak. They are very expensive and can be used for only a few years.

When the wine has finished fermenting, whether in a tank or barrel, it is generally **racked**—moved into a clean tank or barrel to separate it from the lees, the spent yeast and any grape solids that have dropped out of suspension. Sometimes chardonnay and special batches of sauvignon blanc are left on the lees for extended periods of time before being racked—at the winemaker's discretion—to pick up extra complexity. Wine may be racked several times as sediment continues to settle out.

After the first racking, especially if it is white, the wine may be **filtered** to take out solid particles that can cloud the wine and any stray yeast or bacteria that can spoil it. Wine may be filtered several times before bottling to help control its development during maturation. This is a common practice among commercial producers, but many fine winemakers resist filtering, as they believe it leads to less complex wines that don't age as well.

White wine may also be **fined** to clarify it and stabilize its color. In fining, agents such as a fine clay called bentonite or albumen from egg whites are mixed into the wine. As they settle out, they absorb undesirable substances that can cloud the wine. As with filtering, the process is more common with ordinary table wines than with fine wines.

Typically, winemakers blend several batches of new wine together to balance flavor. Careful **blending** gives the winemaker an extra chance to create a perfect single-varietal wine, or to combine several varietals that complement each other in a blend. Premium vintners also make unblended vineyard-designated wines that highlight the attributes of grapes from a single vineyard.

New wine is stored in stainless-steel or oak casks or barrels to rest and develop before bottling. This stage, called **maturation** or **aging,** may last anywhere from a few months to over a year for white wine. Barrel rooms are kept dark to protect the wine both from light and from heat, either of which can be damaging. Some wineries keep their wines in air-conditioned rooms or warehouses, others have bored tunnel-like **caves** (pronounced "kahvz," from the French) into hillsides, where the wine remains at an even temperature.

If wine is matured or aged for any length of time before bottling, it will be racked and perhaps filtered several times. Once it is bottled, the wine is stored for **bottle-aging**. This is done in a cool, dark space to prevent their corks from drying out; a shrunken cork allows oxygen to enter the bottle and spoil the wine. In a few months, most white wines will be ready for release.

For the scoop on making sparkling wines, see the "Champagne and Sparkling Wines" sidebar in the Northern Napa Valley chapter.

■ **MAKING RED WINES**

Red wine production differs slightly from that of white wine. Red wine grapes are crushed the same way white wine grapes are, but the juice is not separated from the grape skins and pulp before fermentation. This is what gives red wine its color. After crushing, the red wine **must**—the thick slurry of juice, pulp, and skins—is fermented in vats. The juice is "left on the skins" for varying periods of time, from five days to two weeks, depending on the grape variety and on how much color the winemaker wants to extract.

Fermentation also extracts flavors and chemical compounds such as **tannins** from the skins and seeds, making red wines more robust than whites. Tannin levels are kept down in a red designed for drinking soon after it is bottled; they should have a greater presence in wine meant for aging. In a young red not ready for drinking, tannins feel dry or coarse in your mouth, but they soften with age. Over time, a wine with well-balanced tannin will maintain its fruitiness and backbone as its flavor develops. Without adequate tannin, a wine will not age well.

Red wine fermentation occurs at a higher temperature than that for whites—reds ferment at about 70°F to 90°F (21°C to 32°C). As the grape sugars are converted into alcohol, carbon dioxide is generated. Carbon dioxide is lighter than wine but heavier than air, and it forms an **"aerobic cover"** that protects the wine from oxidation. As the wine ferments, grape skins rise to the top and are periodically mixed back in so the wine can extract the maximum amount of color and flavor. This is done either in the traditional fashion by punching them down with a large handheld tool, or by pumping the wine from the bottom of the vat and pouring it back in at the top. **Punching down** is generally considered preferable since it keeps the carbon dioxide cover intact and minimizes exposure of the wine to oxygen.

At the end of fermentation, the free-run wine is drained off. The grape skins and pulp are sent to a press where the remaining wine is extracted. As with the whites, the winemaker may choose to add a little of the press wine to the free-run wine—if he or she feels it will add complexity to the finished wine. Otherwise the press juice might go into bulk wine—the lower quality, less expensive stuff. The better wine is racked and maybe fined; some reds are left unfined for extra depth.

Next up is **oak-barrel aging,** which lasts for a year or longer. Unlike many of the barrels used for aging and fermenting chardonnay, the barrels used for aging red wine are not always new. They may already have been used to age chardonnay, which has extracted most of the wood's flavors. Oak, like grapes, contains natural tannins, and the wine extracts these tannins from the barrels. Oak also has countless tiny pores through which water in the wine slowly evaporates, making the wine more concentrated. To make sure the aging wine does not oxidize, the barrels have to be regularly **topped off** with wine from the same vintage.

The only way even the best winemaker can tell if a wine is finished is by tasting it. A winemaker constantly tastes wines during fermentation, while they are aging in barrels, and regularly, though less often, while they age in bottles. The wine is released for sale when the winemaker's palate and nose say it's ready.

Not just a pretty face: terroir largely dictates a wine's potential.

■ MAKING ROSÉ WINES

Rosé or blush wines are also made from red wine grapes; but the juicy pulp is left on the skins for a matter of hours—12 to 36—not days. When the winemaker decides that the juice has reached the desired color, it is drained off and filtered. Yeast is added, and the juice is left to ferment. Because the must stays on the skins for a shorter time than the must of red wines, fewer tannins are leached from the skins, and the resulting wine is not as full-flavored as a red. You might say that rosé is a lighter, fruitier version of red wine, not a pink version of white.

■ IN THE VINEYARD

Growers, winemakers, and wine-lovers who believe in the importance of *terroir* (a French term that encompasses the soil, the microclimate, and the growing conditions) argue that wine is really made in the vineyard. In this view, the quality of a wine is determined by what happens before the grapes are crushed. Even a small winery can produce spectacular wines from small vineyards if it has the right location and grows the grapes best suited to its soil and microclimate. (For a rundown on California's main grape varieties, see the list at the end of this chapter.)

When a region's terroir is unique in the U.S., the Alcohol and Tobacco Tax and Trade Bureau can designate it an American Viticultural Area (AVA), more commonly called an **appellation**. Different appellations—there are more than 100 AVAs in California, with 15 in the Napa Valley alone—are renowned for different wines.

Appellation always refers to the source of a wine's grapes, not to the place where the wine was made. Wineries can indicate the appellation on a bottle's label only if at least 85 percent of the grapes used in the wine were grown in that appellation. Many wineries buy grapes from outside their AVA (some do not even have vineyards of their own), so it is quite possible that they will label different wines with the names of different regions.

Grapes grown in particular areas diverge widely in quality, and when it is to their advantage winemakers make sure to mention prestigious appellations, and even specific vineyards, on their labels. If the grapes have come from multiple AVAs within a given region—say, the Sierra Foothills—the wine can be labeled with the name of the region. Wines simply labeled "California" are made of grapes from more than one region.

■ GEOLOGY 101

Wherever grapes are grown, geology matters. Grapevines are among the few plants that give their best fruit when they grow in poor, rocky soil. On the other hand, grapes just don't like wet feet. The ideal vineyard soil is easily permeable by water; this characteristic is even more crucial than its mineral content. Until the 1990s, California growers paid far more attention to climate than geology when deciding where to plant vineyards and how to manage them. As demand for premium wine has exploded, though, winemakers are paying much more attention to the soil part of the terroir equation. Geologists now do a brisk business advising growers on vineyard soil.

Different grape varieties thrive in different types of soil. For instance, cabernet sauvignon does best on well-drained, gravelly soils; soil that's too wet or contains too much heavy clay or organic matter will give the wine an obnoxious vegetative quality that even the best wine-making techniques cannot remove. Merlot grapes, however, can grow in soil with more clay and still be made into a delicious, rich wine. Sauvignon blanc grapes do quite well in heavy clay soils, but the grower must limit irrigation and use some viticultural muscle to keep the grapes from developing unacceptable flavors. Chardonnay likes well-drained vineyards but will also take heavy soil.

Napa's soils are extremely diverse, including loam, tuff (both left), and serpentine (the paler soil at right).

The soils below Napa Valley's crags and in the wine-growing valleys of Sonoma County are dizzyingly diverse. Some of the soils are composed of dense, heavy sedimentary clays washed from the mountains; others are very rocky clays, loams, or silts of alluvial fans. These fertile, well-drained soils cover much of the valleys' floors. Other areas have soil based on serpentine, a rock that rarely appears aboveground. In all, there are about 60 soil types in the Napa and Sonoma valleys, allowing a wide variety of grapes to be grown in a relatively small area.

The geology of the Central Coast is less complex: calcareous (calcium-rich) shale predominates at higher elevations, while loamy alluvial soils with fewer nutrients make up flatter land. Good rainfall, soaked up by rocky clay, makes the higher elevation areas prime spots for dry-farming without irrigation. The sandier, drier flatlands require more irrigation but are much easier to cultivate because of their topography. The light-colored granite of the Sierra Nevada, famed for its quartz-shot veins of gold, yields gold of another sort in the well-drained vineyards, where eons of weathering have turned the granite into gravelly soil.

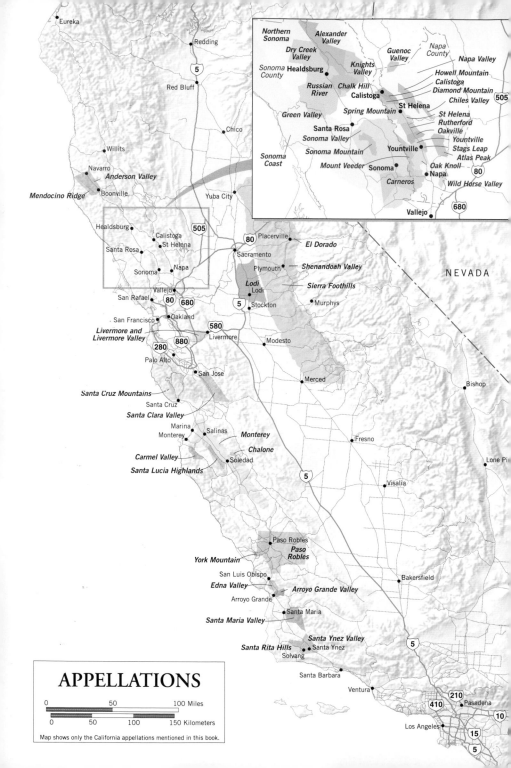

APPELLATIONS

| 0 | 50 | 100 Miles |
| 0 | 50 | 100 | 150 Kilometers |

Map shows only the California appellations mentioned in this book.

In Wine Country you'll hear a lot about limestone, a nutrient-rich rock in which grapevines thrive. Some California winemakers claim to be growing in limestone when in fact they are not. In fact, only small patches of California's Wine Country have significant amounts of limestone. The term is often used to describe the streak of light-colored, almost white soil that runs across the Napa Valley from the Palisades to St. Helena and through Sonoma County from the western flanks of the Mayacamas Mountains to Windsor. The band is actually composed of volcanic material that has no limestone content. The error is easily made on the Central Coast, where sea shells from a prehistoric ocean floor turned into calcareous shale. Limestone forms in much the same way.

■ DOWN ON THE FARM: VITICULTURE
Much like a fruit or nut orchard, a vineyard can produce excellent grapes for decades—even a century—if it's given the proper attention. The growing cycle starts in winter, when the vines are bare and dormant. While the plants rest, the grower works to enrich the soil and repair the trellising system (if there is one) that

A misty autumn morning on the Sonoma coast. (following pages) A medley of wine labels: the wines of Napa (top row), Sonoma (middle), and other regions (bottom).

HOW TO READ A WINE LABEL

Vintage: All the grapes in the wine were harvested in 2000.

AVA: At least 85 percent of the grapes were grown in the Napa Valley viticultural area.

Vineyard name: The grapes were grown in Mondavi's To Kalon Vineyard.

Varietal composition: At least 75 percent of the grapes in this wine are sauvignon blanc. (Robert Mondavi invented the fanciful name fumé blanc.)

Reserve: An inexact term meaning "special," this can refer to how or where the grapes were grown or how the wine was made.

Filtration: This wine has not been filtered to remove sediments and other elements; with this strategy a winemaker often achieves deeper color and richer flavors than with filtered wines.

Winery name

Alcohol content: By U.S. law, this must be listed.

2000
NAPA VALLEY
TO KALON VINEYARD
FUMÉ BLANC
RESERVE
UNFILTERED
ROBERT MONDAVI WINERY
ALCOHOL 13.5% BY VOLUME

Winery name

No vintage date: The grapes could have come from more than one year's harvest.

Wine name: "Le Mistral" is the winery's name for this red-wine blend.

AVA: The grapes could have come from anywhere in California.

Additional label terms
Estate grown: The grapes came from vineyards the winery owns or operates.

Estate bottled: The grapes were estate grown, and the wine was bottled at the winery, with both winery and vineyard in the same appellation.

JOSEPH PHELPS
Le Mistral
CALIFORNIA
A RED TABLE WINE
JOSEPH PHELPS VINEYARDS
ST. HELENA, CALIFORNIA
PRODUCED AND BOTTLED BY
POST OFFICE BOX 1031
ALC. 13.5% BY VOLUME

No varietal: No single grape made up 75 percent or more of the wine.

Production: Phelps did not grow the grapes; it bought them.

Alcohol content: Table wines can be between 7 and 14 percent alcohol.

holds up the vines. This is when **pruning** takes place to regulate the vine's growth and upcoming season's crop size.

In spring, the soil is aerated by plowing and new vines go in. The grower trains established vines so they grow, with or without trellising, in the shape most beneficial for the grapes. **Bud break** occurs when the first new bits of green emerge from the vines, and a pale green veil appears over the winter's gray-black vineyards. A late frost can be devastating at this time of year. Summer brings the flowering of the vines, when clusters of tiny green blossoms appear, and **fruit set,** when the grapes form from the blossoms. As the vineyards turn luxuriant and leafy, more pruning, along with leaf-pulling, keeps foliage in check so the vine directs nutrients to the grapes, and so the sun can reach the fruit. As summer advances the grower will **thin the fruit,** cutting off (or "dropping") some bunches so the remaining grapes intensify in flavor. A look at the vineyards reveals heavy clusters of green or purple grapes, some pea-size, others marble-size, depending on variety.

Fall is the busiest season in the vineyard. Growers and winemakers carefully monitor the ripeness of the grapes, sometimes with equipment that tests sugar and acid levels and sometimes simply by tasting them. As soon as the grapes are ripe **harvest** begins amid the lush foliage. In California, this generally happens in September and October, but sometimes a bit earlier or later depending on the type of grape and the climatic conditions. Picking must be done as quickly as possible, within just a day or two, to keep the grapes from passing their peak. Most California grapes are harvested mechanically, but some are picked by hand (see The Crush, above). After harvest, the vines start to regenerate for next year.

■ NOT HOME-GROWN

Sometimes by preference and sometimes by necessity, winemakers don't grow all the grapes they need. Small wineries with only a few acres of grapes are limited in the varietals and quantities they can grow. (The smallest producers don't even have their own wineries, so they pay to use the equipment and storage space at a custom crush facility.) Mid-size wineries may aim to get bigger. If it doesn't buy more acreage, a winery that wants to diversify or expand production has to buy grapes from an independent grower.

Many winemakers—perhaps half of those in Napa, for instance—purchase at least some of their grapes. Some wineries have negotiated long-term contracts with top growers, buying grapes from the same supplier year after year. This way, the

(following pages) Working the rows at Artesa Winery's vineyards.

winemaker can control the consistency and quality of the fruit just as if it came from the winery's own vineyard. Other wineries buy from several growers, and many growers sell to more than one winery.

Winemakers who buy from growers face a paradoxical problem: it's possible to make a wine that's too good and too popular. As the demand for a wine—and its price—rises, so will the price of the grapes used to make it. Other wineries sometimes bid up the price of the grapes, with the result that a winemaker can no longer afford the grapes that made a wine famous. This competitiveness among winemakers for specific batches of grapes underscores the importance of terroir as well as of growers. Where grape quality is concerned, growers may have the edge over many wineries, because they must stay on the forefront of viticultural innovation in order to please demanding winemakers. Without producing a single bottle of wine, large growers are pivotal to the success of California's wine industry.

■ WHAT'S IN A VINTAGE?
Oenophiles make much of wine's vintage—the year in which it was harvested—because the climate in the vineyard does have a big impact on a wine's character. From one year to the next, depending on the weather, a single vine can yield very different wines. It's impossible to generalize about vintages for California as a whole, because growing conditions vary so much from region to region. Sorting out the many elements that define a wine can be as confusing as untangling a string of last year's Christmas lights. Even within regions, conditions can vary greatly across numerous microclimates. Vines that grow just around a bend from each other can have a completely different weather year. Knowing the grower and winemaker and knowing about local conditions is far more important than knowing a wine's vintage.

In the most general terms, grapes grown in cool, wet regions tend to do better in relatively warmer years, while hotter regions tend to get better results in cooler years. A cool growing season can suppress crop yield, and lower crop yield boosts quality. Grapes ripen more slowly in cool years, gaining more intense flavors and higher acid; the potential of wines meant for aging improves. Cold spring weather, however, can prevent fruit from forming in the first place. Rain can have the same effect. Too much rain any time during the growing season, or any rain at all in late summer worries growers because it can bring mildew, bunch rot, and off-flavors. Grapes like a reasonably wet winter and a dry summer. Sometimes a warm fall and summer can help make up for a cool or wet spring.

Working with the raw material.

All of this comes with caveats. Weather affects different varietals differently: for example, cabernet sauvignon does well in most conditions, but zinfandel and chenin blanc are especially susceptible to bunch rot from late-season rain. The notoriously finicky pinot noir grape suffers in hot weather and can get sunburned, but it is also sensitive to a too-cool growing season. From region to region, a given varietal might respond to similar conditions differently. Frequent fog, for instance, to some extent hardens Central Coast grapes against mildew, while a drizzly day at the wrong time of year can spell doom for a Sierra Nevada crop. Better soil somewhat protects vines from vagaries in the weather—think what rain can do to a vineyard with poor drainage, compared to one with the rocky soil that drains more easily.

Federal law requires that at least 95 percent of the wine in a bottle labeled with a vintage year must be grown that year. If you see no vintage on the bottle, as is common with jug wines, what's inside is probably a blend of wines (of lesser quality) from different years. If you do know the vintage, however, you can glean some information about the wine by looking at the conditions when and where it was grown. Knowing the age of the wine can also help you decide when to open it.

The portion of wine that evaporates during barrel aging is called the "angel's share."

GRAPE VARIETIES

Below are short profiles on California's most widely planted whites and reds, in alphabetical order.

■ WHITE

CHARDONNAY
One of the most commonly planted grapes. When grown in austere soils of cool vineyards, this grape from Burgundy can be made into great California wine, but winemakers sometimes overwhelm the grape with the buttery vanilla flavors imparted by oak. Many premium vintners have started moving toward a subtler style, some even trying unoaked versions, but because of warmer, longer growing seasons California chardonnay will always be bolder than Burgundian.

CHENIN BLANC
Although a lot of it goes into mediocre mass-market wines, this Loire Valley native can produce a smooth, pleasingly acidic California wine. It gets short shrift with many critics because of its relative simplicity and light body, but many drinkers appreciate the style.

GEWÜRZTRAMINER
A German-Alsatian grape variety that makes aromatic, almost spicy white wine. Though most California Gewürz is fairly sweet, some vintners make it in the dry or off-dry style.

MARSANNE
A white wine grape of France's northern Rhône Valley that can produce a full-bodied, overly heavy wine unless handled with care. Becoming more popular in California in these Rhône-blend-crazy times.

PINOT BLANC
When cultivated in well-drained soils of cool vineyards, as it is in France's Alsace region, this grape can create a firm, medium-bodied California wine.

PINOT GRIS
The same grape as Italy's pinot grigio, this varietal yields a more deeply colored wine in California. It's not highly acidic, and has a medium to full body.

RIESLING
This cool-climate German grape has a sweet reputation in America. When made in a dry style, though, as it more and more often is, it can be crisply refreshing, with lush aromas.

ROUSSANNE
This grape from the Rhône Valley makes an especially fragrant California wine that can achieve a lovely balance of fruitiness and acidity.

Sauvignon Blanc

Hailing from Bordeaux and France's Loire Valley, this white grape does very well almost anywhere in California. Crisper and lighter-bodied than chardonnay, it often makes more interesting wine. From region to region, vintage to vintage, and vintner to vintner the grape displays a wide range of personalities.

Sémillon

A white Bordeaux grape that, blended with sauvignon blanc, has made some of the best sweet wines in the world. Like the riesling grape, it can benefit from botrytis, also known as the noble rot, which intensifies its flavors and aromas.

Viognier

This white grape from France's Rhône Valley, when grown in California, makes complex, flavorful wines with a fruity bouquet. The state's Rhône revolution has helped make viognier very popular.

■ Red

Barbera

Prevalent in California thanks to 19th-century Italian immigrants, barbera yields easy-drinking, low-tannin wine that's got big fruit and high acid.

Cabernet Franc

Most often used in blends, often to add complexity to cabernet sauvignon, this French grape can produce aromatic, soft, and subtle wine. The often earthy, or even stinky, aroma that can turn some drinkers off wins avid fans among others.

Cabernet Sauvignon

The king of California reds, this Bordeaux grape grows best in austere, well-drained soils. At its best, the California version is dark, bold, and tannic, with black currant notes. On its own, it can need a long aging period to become enjoyable, so it's often blended with cabernet franc, merlot, and other red varieties to soften the resulting wine and make it ready for earlier drinking.

Gamay

Also called Gamay Beaujolais, this vigorous French grape variety is widely planted in California. It produces pleasant reds and rosés that should be drunk young.

Grenache

This Spanish grape, which makes some of the southern Rhône Valley's most distinguished wine, ripens best in hot, dry conditions. Done right, grenache is dark and concentrated, improved with age. Although it has limited plantings in California, it has gotten more popular along with other Rhône-style California wines.

Merlot

This blue-black Bordeaux variety makes soft, full-bodied wine when grown in California. It is often fruity, and can be quite complex even when young. The easy quaffer was well on its way to conquering cabernet sauvignon as the

most popular red until anti-merlot jokes (popularized in the hit movie *Sideways*) slowed the trend.

Mourvèdre

This red wine grape makes wine that is deeply colored, very dense, high in alcohol, and at first harsh, but it mellows with several years of aging. It is a native of France's Rhône Valley and is increasingly popular in California.

Nebbiolo

The great red wine grape of Italy's Piedmont region is now widely planted in California. It produces full-bodied, sturdy wines that are fairly high in alcohol and age splendidly.

Petite Sirah

This may be a hybrid created in the mid-19th-century California vineyard—no one is sure—and is unrelated to the Rhône grape Syrah. It produces a hearty wine that is often used in blends.

Pinot Noir

In cooler parts of California this finicky grape is being turned into great wine, sometimes on the earthy side and sometimes fruitier, and not as inky as some other California reds. It's known as a hard-to-grow "heartbreak grape" and is a favorite among serious wine lovers.

Sangiovese

The main red grape of Italy's Chianti district and of much of central Italy. Depending on how it is grown and vinified, it can be made into vibrant, light- to medium-bodied wines, as well as into long-lived, very complex reds. Increasingly planted in California.

Syrah

Another big California red, this grape comes from the Rhône Valley. With good tannins it can become a full-bodied, almost smoky beauty, but without them it can be flabby and forgettable. Once very limited in California, syrah plantings increased rapidly after the mid-1990s, thanks in part to the soaring popularity of Rhône-style wines in general, and in part to the popularity of syrah from Australia, where it is called shiraz.

Zinfandel

Celebrated as California's own (though it has distant, hazy Old World origins), zinfandel is a rich and spicy wine. Its tannins can make it complex, well-suited for aging, but too often it is made in an overly jammy, almost syrupy, style. Typically grown to extreme ripeness, the sugary grape can produce high alcohol levels in wine.

Wild mustard blooms in late winter between the vines at Opus One.

SOUTHERN NAPA VALLEY

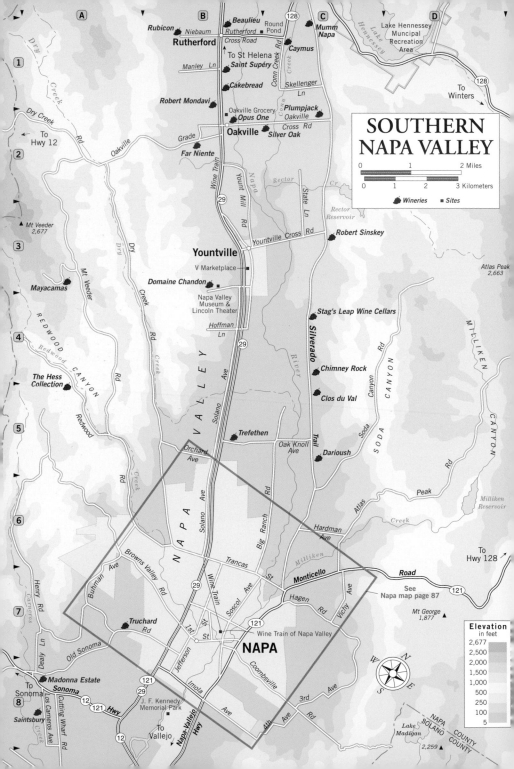

SOUTHERN NAPA VALLEY

0   1   2 Miles
0   1   2   3 Kilometers

🍇 Wineries ■ Sites

A B C D

1 2 3 4 5 6 7 8

Rubicon
Niebaum
Beaulieu
Rutherford
Round Pond
128
Mumm Napa
Lake Hennessey
Lake Hennessey Muncipal Recreation Area

Rutherford
Cross Road
Caymus
To St Helena
Manley Ln
Saint Supéry
Conn Creek Rd
Skellenger Ln
To Winters
128

Cakebread
Robert Mondavi
Opus One
Oakville Grocery
Plumpjack
Oakville
Cross Rd

Oakville
Silver Oak
Grade
Far Niente

29
Oakville
Wine Train
Yount Mill Rd
Napa
State Ln
Rector
Cr
Rector Reservoir

Mt Veeder 2,677

Yountville Cross Rd
Robert Sinskey
Atlas Peak 2,663

Mayacamas
Mt Veeder
Yountville
V Marketplace
Domaine Chandon
Napa Valley Museum & Lincoln Theater
Stag's Leap Wine Cellars

REDWOOD CANYON
Redwood Canyon
Hoffman Ln
29
Silverado Trail
Chimney Rock
MT MILLIKEN CANYON

The Hess Collection
Redwood Rd
Solano Ave
Napa River
Clos du Val
Canyon Rd
Soda Canyon
SODA CANYON

Trefethen
Oak Knoll Ave
Darioush
Soda Canyon Rd
Peak
Milliken Reservoir

Orchard Ave
Solano Ave
Big Ranch Rd
Atlas
Creek

Browns Valley Rd
Trancas
St
Hardman Ave
To Hwy 128

NAPA VALLEY
Buhman Ave
29
Wine Train
Soscol Ave
Monticello
Milliken
Hagen Rd
Vichy Ave
Road
See Napa map page 87
121
Mt George 1,877

Henry Rd
Carneros
Truchard Rd
1st St
St
121
Wine Train of Napa Valley
Coombsville

Old Sonoma
Jefferson
NAPA
Ave

Deely Ln
Madonna Estate
Sonoma
121
29
Imola Ave
3rd Rd
4th Ave

To Sonoma
12
121
Hwy
J. F. Kennedy Memorial Park
Napa-Vallejo Hwy
NAPA COUNTY
SOLANO COUNTY

Saintsbury
Cutting Wharf Rd
Los Carneros Ave
12
To Vallejo
Lake Madigan

2,259

W N E S

Elevation
in feet
2,677
2,500
2,000
1,500
1,000
500
250
100
5

To Hwy 12
Dry Creek Rd
Dry Creek

■ OVERVIEW OF THE NAPA VALLEY

The Napa Valley, a long, narrow trough between mountain chains, is America's wine-making mecca. You'll find more splashy wineries and big-name vintners here—Robert Mondavi, Charles Krug, Beringer, and Stag's Leap Wine Cellars, to name only a very few—than anywhere else in California.

Interspersed with all the nouveau Tuscan villas and restored 19th-century Victorians, you'll also find some low-frills wineries, warmly welcoming you into their modest tasting rooms with glasses of wine that are just as exciting as those made by the household names. On the other end of the spectrum are Napa's "cult" cabernet producers—Screaming Eagle, Harlan Estate, Dalla Valle, and Dominus Estate among them—whose doors are closed tight to visitors.

Because the Napa Valley attracts everyone from hardcore wine collectors to bachelorette partiers, the Napa Valley is not necessarily the best place to get away from it all. But there's a reason it's the number-one Wine Country destination. In addition to the wealth of wineries, the up-and-coming town of Napa lures people with its cultural attractions and reasonably priced accommodations (reasonably priced for the Wine Country, that is). A few miles farther north, tiny Yountville is Napa's culinary hotspot, densely packed with top-notch restaurants. Continuing north, St. Helena teems with elegant boutiques and restaurants, while mellow Calistoga is chock full of spas and hot springs where you can be soaked, kneaded, and dipped in mud until you've been reduced to a limp noodle.

■ NAPA'S APPELLATIONS

In terms of appellations, Napa's a hodgepodge. Almost the entire county, east to Lake Berryessa, is known as the Napa Valley AVA, but several areas within that appellation have themselves been designated as subappellations. Four of these, Oak Knoll, Oakville, Rutherford, and St. Helena, stretch clear across the valley floor. Stags Leap is a small district on the east side of the valley, and Mount Veeder, Spring Mountain, and Howell Mountain each encompass parts—but not all—of the mountains from which they take their names. Napa's newest AVA, Calistoga, is centered around the town of the same name, at the north end of the valley. East of Howell Mountain, a narrow slice in the Vaca Mountains is home to the tiny Chiles Valley AVA. The Atlas Peak AVA lies east of Stags Leap, and the Wild Horse Valley appellation is a small area south of Atlas Peak. Los Carneros overlaps both the Napa Valley and Sonoma Valley appellations.

As you drive the 35 miles from San Pablo Bay to the foothills of Mount St.

Helena, passing through seven or so of these AVAs, you'll also pass through several different climate zones. The great variety in the climate as well as the soils explains why valley vintners can make so many different wines, and make them so well. Most of the wineries grow grapes in several of the regions or buy them from growers in other appellations. Mumm Napa, for example, gets the grapes for its sparkling wines from the cool Carneros region, while the grapes in the vineyards surrounding the winery are sold to other wineries.

■ NAVIGATING NAPA

Highway 29, the Napa Valley Highway, heads north from Vallejo first as a busy four-lane highway with traffic lights, then as a freeway, and finally as a two-lane highway. At one point the state of California had plans to convert Highway 29 into a freeway all the way to Calistoga. Local winemakers stopped that plan by turning the Napa Valley into an agricultural preserve. And so, Highway 29 is a freeway only until Yountville. Beyond that it is a two-lane road, congested with visitors eager to see the Napa Valley and taste its fabled wines. You'll probably find slightly less traffic on the Silverado Trail, which roughly parallels Highway 29 all the way from the town of Napa to Calistoga. Cross streets connect the two like rungs on a ladder every few miles, making it easy to cross over from one to the other.

■ ENTERING THE NAPA VALLEY

Because Highway 29 passes through unpleasant urban sprawl as it leaves the town of Napa, many visitors rush north to Yountville, where some feel the real valley starts. But it would be a shame not to slow down and check out a few of the wineries here, in the Oak Knoll and Yountville AVAs, two of the most southern. The Oak Knoll appellation, formally recognized in 2004, is one of the coolest in Napa, as coastal fog creeps up it from San Pablo Bay. You'll find more than a dozen grape varieties grown here on the broad, flat valley floor, from delicate chardonnay grapes to Bordeaux varietals. The similar climate in Yountville works well with chardonnay, pinot noir, and merlot, among other varietals, which are grown in volcanic soil to the east and primarily alluvial soil to the west.

A horse-drawn cart delivers grapes to the Eshcol Winery for crushing.

Trefethen Vineyards   *map page 78, B-5*

The big terracotta-colored building here is the old Eshcol Winery, built in 1886. This huge three-story gravity-flow winery is built from wood rather than stone, making it somewhat of a rarity, since most wooden wineries haven't weathered the last century so well. Gene Trefethen and his wife, Catherine, bought the property in 1968 as a retirement home. Like so many folks "retiring" to the Napa Valley, they began replanting the vineyards and restoring the winery, and they started making wine sometime around 1973.

The Trefethen winery gained recognition for its excellent wines almost right out of the gate: a 1976 chardonnay placed first in a 1979 tasting held in Paris by Gault Millau. Trefethen continues to make superb chardonnay, cabernet sauvignon, and merlot, as well as an excellent dry riesling. For an additional fee, the very welcoming staff will pour some of their library wines in the tasting room, so you can taste for yourself how well their wines age. There's a cork tree planted in the garden outside the tasting room—so *that's* what the stuff looks like before it ends up on the sharp end of your corkscrew. The tasting room is open daily, but tours of the winery are by appointment only. *1160 Oak Knoll Avenue; 707-255-7700.*

★ **Domaine Chandon**   *map page 78, B-3/4*

Just to the west of Yountville's only freeway underpass sprawls the expansive sparkling-wine complex of Domaine Chandon. The winery here is built into a hillside, surrounded by ancient oaks, blending into the landscape like no other. You can hardly see it from the highway even though it's just off the road, but its south side of windowed arches is dramatic.

Sparklers here are made only by the labor-intensive—and costly—*méthode champenoise,* meaning the wine is fermented individually in the bottle and individually disgorged (see the "Champagne and Sparking Wines" box in the Northern Napa Valley chapter for more about disgorging). Most of the wines are *cuvées* (blends); the top of the line Etoile Tête de Cuvée is a cuvée of older vintages. It is a splendid accompaniment for the exquisite dishes served at Domaine Chandon's restaurant—a Wine Country first that was an instant hit when it opened in 1977. Although the tasting room is lovely, with views of the hillside through the windows, the grounds are even more spectacular. Save some time to wander around and see the fountains shooting out of the spring-fed ponds. You'll also find the occasional whimsical artwork, like a field of sculpted stone mushrooms sprouting out of the lawn. *1 California Drive; 707-944-8844.*

■ **TOWN OF NAPA**   *map page 78 A/B-6F7, and page 87*

After many years as a blue-collar town with its back to the whole Wine-Country scene, Napa feels like it's just on the verge of becoming a popular—perhaps even hip—destination. In recent years, in part because of the recent expansion of the nearby Carneros vineyards, Napa has been busily sprucing up its historic downtown area. Many of the once-empty storefronts have morphed into wine bars, bookstores, and Internet cafés. The Napa River, neglected for more than a century, has been cleared of weeds, and exciting new restaurants are popping up along the riverbanks, especially in the **Historic Napa Mill,** a complex of late-19th-century brick buildings. A riverfront promenade that opened in 2008 leads from the mill buildings, past new residences and retail spaces, through the small Veterans Memorial Park, toward First Street. All the more reason not to speed through on Highway 29.

(previous pages) Harvesting grapes for Chandon's sparkling wines. (opposite) Domaine Chandon's dining room has been a Napa Valley star for more than a quarter century.

Napa, the oldest town in the Napa Valley, was founded in 1848 in a strategic location on the Napa River, where the Sonoma-Benicia Road (Highways 12 and 29) crossed at a ford. The first wood-frame building was built that year—surprise, a saloon. Before then, a few Mexican adobes were the only houses in the region. One of these, built in the 1840s, survives at the corner of Soscol Avenue and the Silverado Trail.

The first commercial Napa Valley wine was made by an Englishman named Patchett in the 1850s. Patchett also built the first stone cellar in the Napa Valley and shipped wine regularly from 1857 on. By the late 1800s, large wineries lined the river. These dominated the trade until Prohibition hit; unlike the small family-owned wineries up-valley, they never recovered.

Downtown still preserves an old river-town atmosphere. Many Victorian homes survive from the early residential areas, and in the original business district a few historic buildings have been preserved, including the turn-of-the-20th-century courthouse and several riverfront warehouses. After years of renovation, the 1879 Italianate Victorian **Napa Valley Opera House** (1030 Main Street; 707-226-7372) reopened in 2003. Now the intimate venue is the best spot in the valley for all sorts of musical performances.

Near the opera house are several stores worth checking out. Just around the corner, **Bounty Hunter Rare Wine and Provisions** (975 First Street; 707-255-0622) stocks Napa cult cabernets and other hard-to-find wines. The store shares space with a charming wine bar, where the brick walls and stamped tin ceiling set a turn-of-the-century mood. Inside the Napa Town Center (bounded by First, Pearl, Main, and Franklin streets), a pedestrian-friendly complex of shops connected by brick-lined walkways, **Wineries of Napa Valley** (1285 Napa Town Center; 707-253-9450), is one of several downtown tasting rooms. The friendly staffers pour samples from five different small wineries, such as Goosecross Cellars and Burgess Cellars. **Shackford's Kitchen Store** (1350 Main Street; 707-226-2132) looks something like a hardware store, with its bare-bones concrete floors, but there's no better place in town for all your cooking needs, whether it's ceramic serving pieces or a chef's jacket. If you're lucky enough to be in town on a Tuesday or Saturday morning from May to November, stop by the **farmers' market** in the Wine Train parking lot at 1275 McKinstry Street to browse through beautiful, unusual produce, baked goods, and locally made beef jerky.

Food lovers who miss the farmers' market can visit the **Oxbow Public Market**

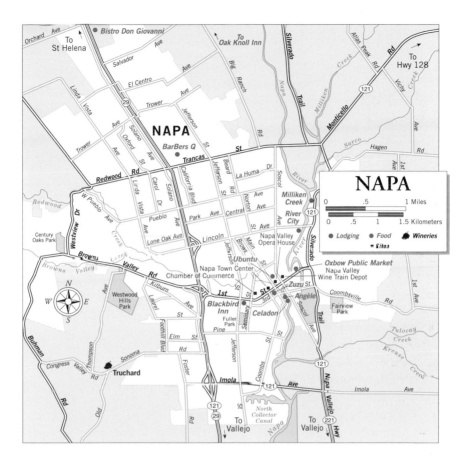

and its wealth of food and wine from Napa Valley. At this collection of about 20 small shops, wine bars, and artisanal food producers, you can swoon over the decadent charcuterie at the Fatted Calf, slurp oysters on the half shell at Hog Island Oyster Company, sample local olive oils at The Olive Press, or get a whiff of the hard-to-find seasonings at the Whole Spice Company before sitting down to a glass of wine at one of the two wine bars, such as Folio Enoteca & Winery. In addition to serving salads, pasta, and pizzas, Folio, which is owned by Michael Mondavi, is actually a tiny "microwinery," and a couple of wines are made on site. A branch of the retro fast-food joint Taylor's Automatic Refresher tempts

The produce bins runneth over at the Oxbow Market.

those who prefer hamburgers to duck-liver mousse. *610 and 644 First Street; no phone.*

Just down the street from Copia, vintage Pullman rail cars depart daily to chug slowly up to St. Helena and back. These **Napa Valley Wine Train** (1275 McKinstry Street; 707-253-2111) trips follow part of an 1847 rail route. Trips vary in price and poshness, but the most lavish is a romantic late-evening dinner in the circa-1950 railcar with a glass dome that lets in the moonlight.

■ YOUNTVILLE   *map page 78, B-3*

Come hungry! Small-town Yountville, on the eastern edge of the Mayacamas Mountains, lacks the bustle of Napa, the chichi boutiques of St. Helena, or the beautiful town plaza of up-and-coming Healdsburg—but what it does have is food, glorious food. With several of valley's best restaurants, including the French Laundry, Bottega, and Bouchon, Yountville has earned the unofficial title of Napa Valley's Culinary Capital. And, considering the generally high quality of food throughout California's Wine Country, this is really saying something.

In the wake of such outstanding restaurants, a number of luxurious inns and hotels have sprung up, so you can toddle a short way home after a decadent dinner. And though nightlife in Yountville is generally limited to an after-dinner snifter of cognac, the 2005 opening of the **Lincoln Theater** (100 California Drive; 707-944-1300), on the grounds of the Veterans Home of California, means you can attend concerts by the Napa Valley Symphony and other cultural events.

Yountville became a wine-growing center back in 1870, when wealthy San Francisco immigrant Gottlieb Groezinger built a large winery here. The brick winery building still stands, but it has been turned into a shopping complex called **V Marketplace** (6525 Washington Street; 707-944-2451), where a handful of clothing boutiques, art galleries, and gift shops are worth a quick look. Napa Style, a large store, deli, and wine bar, sells cookbooks, luxury food items, kitchenwares, and prepared foods. The town was founded a few decades earlier by George Calvert Yount, a mountain man from North Carolina.

Though many people use Yountville as a home base, touring wineries by day and returning to town for dinner, you could easily spend a few hours shopping and visiting local attractions. While strolling through town, you might want to visit the

Pioneer Cemetery and Indian Burial Ground, off Jackson Street, which were established in 1848. George Yount is buried here. For lunch you might pick up a baguette sandwich and one of the ethereal macaroons at **Bouchon Bakery** (6528 Washington Street; 707-944-2253) and head to **Yountville Park** on Washington Street at the north end of town, where you'll find tables, barbecue grills, and public restrooms.

The Veterans Home, just across Highway 29 from downtown Yountville, was established in 1881 for disabled veterans of the Mexican War and the Grand Army of the Republic. The modest **Napa Valley Museum** has been built on Veterans Home property. Downstairs its permanent exhibit, "The Land and People of Napa Valley," focuses on the geology and the history of the area, from the Native Americans who once lived here through the pioneer period to the modern winemakers who made it famous. The rotating fine-arts shows upstairs feature the work of Napa Valley artists. *55 Presidents Circle; 707-944-0500.*

■ OAKVILLE APPELLATION

The Oakville appellation, just north of the town of Yountville, is an intriguing blend of the old and the new. Big-name wineries like Far Niente, Robert Mondavi, and Opus One have been producing well-regarded wines—mostly notably cabernet sauvignon—for decades. But upstarts such as Plumpjack and Darioush are getting just as much press recently. Tiny **Screaming Eagle Winery** (closed to the public) is hotter than hot these days. The winery makes only about 600 cases annually of their "cult" cabernet. (Think hundreds of dollars per bottle . . . *if* you're lucky enough to get your hands on one.)

Slightly warmer than Yountville and Carneros to the south, but a few degrees cooler than Rutherford and St. Helena to the north, Oakville benefits from gravelly, well-drained soil in most locations. This allows roots to go deep—sometimes more than 100 feet deep—so that the vines produce intensely flavored grapes.

The ultimate picnic-packers stop in Oakville at the always-crowded **Oakville Grocery** (7856 Highway 29; 707-944-8802), just north of Oakville Cross Road. A great selection of local bread, cheese, olive oils, and wines, as well as sandwiches and baked goods, is sold from a building that has been in continuous operation as a grocery and general store since 1881.

Ripe tomatoes ready for preparation at the French Laundry.

The design of the Opus One winery combines space-age and Mayan elements.

★ Far Niente   *map page 78, B-2*

Although serious wine collectors have enjoyed Far Niente's highly touted chardonnay and cabernet sauvignon for decades, the winery itself has only been open to the public since 2004. Although the tour and tasting require an appointment and a heftier fee than most other winery tours, it's worth the expense. Tours begin with a walk through the stunning 1885 tri-level stone winery, one of the Napa Valley's first gravity-flow wineries, and continue through a small portion of the caves. The tour finishes up in the Carriage House, where you can ogle a collection of classic race cars, including a 1951 Ferrari. Finally, you get to taste the current release of the cabernet, which tends to combine a rich berry flavor with an earthy or toasty aroma, and the chardonnay, with bright citrus and herbal aromas and a lingering finish. These treats come with paired cheeses and a dessert wine by Far Niente's sister winery, Dolce. *1350 Acacia Drive; 707-944-2861.*

Silver Oak Cellars   *map page 78, B/C-2*

The cab and nothing but the cabernet sauvignon. Although there are only two wines here (both pricey) and the tasting fee buys only two pours, Silver Oak is

worth a stop for serious cabernet collectors interested in wines that can stand up to 20 years of cellaring. If you reserve ahead for their daily tour, the guide will pour you a taste of wine before leading you out into the vineyard. The Alexander Valley cab pulls together smooth tannins and big berry flavor with a subtle suggestion of chocolate in the finish, while the more expensive Oakville wine is similar but more intense, with firmer tannins and a longer finish. *915 Oakville Cross Road; 707-942-7022.*

Opus One   *map page 78, B-2*
The namesake wine here is virtually shorthand for "out to impress." Built into a hillside amid vineyards just off Highway 29, the winery is a joint venture of the Napa Valley's Robert Mondavi and France's Baron Philippe Rothschild. Its modern design mixes in classical references, such as a pale limestone colonnade. Though the architects designed it as a semi-subterranean facility, so that the cool earth would keep the aging cellars at a constant temperature, a natural hot spring foiled that plan. The cellars are thus cooled by mechanical rather than natural air-conditioning. The winery has been producing only one wine annually since 1979, a big, inky Bordeaux blend that was the first of Napa's ultra-premium wines, fetching

The late Robert Mondavi (foreground) with friends at a fund-raising event in his vineyards.

unheard-of prices before it was overtaken by cult wines like Screaming Eagle. Tours, offered once daily, are $35, while tasting alone costs $30. Call ahead for a reservation in either case, although walk-ins can occasionally be accommodated in the tasting room (check in at the concierge desk and you'll be admitted "as space is available"). Head up to the roof terrace to drink in the view of the orderly vines below. *7900 St. Helena Highway; 707-944-9442.*

★ Robert Mondavi Winery   *map page 78, B-1/2*

A short distance north of Oakville Cross Road, on the west side of the highway, rise the tower and large entrance gate of the Napa Valley's best-known winery. Earlier in the 20th century, the huge To-Kalon Winery dominated this part of the Napa Valley, both with the quantity and the quality of its wines. Today, its place—and some of its vineyards—has been taken over by Robert Mondavi Winery. No other winery has done more to promote the excellence of Napa Valley wines throughout the world (even though Mondavi wines were absent from the 1976 Paris tasting that brought the Napa Valley such fame).

Robert Mondavi forever changed the nature of the wine known as California

Since its inception in the 1960s, the Robert Mondavi Winery has been one of the Napa Valley's greatest promoters.

sauterne by taking sauvignon blanc grapes, leaving them on the skins after the crush, fermenting the juice in stainless steel, and aging it in French oak barrels. He called his creation fumé blanc (a play on blanc fumé, the steely-crisp wine made from sauvignon blanc in France's Loire Valley, and on Pouilly-Fumé, a dry white from the same area). Both the style and the name caught on: dozens of wineries in both Napa and Sonoma counties now make fumé blanc.

If your only experience of Mondavi wines is the $10 or $15 stuff you've seen in the grocery store, you might be surprised to learn that Mondavi's top wines are revered. Wines like their pinot noir, merlot, and chardonnay grown in the Carneros District consistently garner high marks, but it is the reserve cabernet sauvignon that cemented the winery's reputation. Aged in new oak, this deep, inky blend has enough tannins to stand up to long bottle aging. If you've never been on a winery tour before, the one here provides a good introduction to the wine-making process, including past methods and the many Mondavi innovations. *7801 St. Helena Highway; 888-766-6328.*

tributes to the loamy, claylike soil. Cabernet sauvignon and merlot are by far the favored grapes here. Cool evening breezes blowing up from the San Pablo Bay encourage a long growing season and intensely flavored grapes. Some describe the resulting wines as "rock soft" or an "iron fist in a velvet glove"— bold and power-ful, but still somehow soft.

The Stags Leap District (no apostrophe) is close to Yountville, connected by Yountville Cross Road. It is home to two wineries whose names may pose some confusion. Because of a trademark battle, the Stag's Leap Winery moved its apos-trophe one space to the right to become the Stags' Leap Winery, while the winery down-valley is called Stag's Leap Wine Cellars. Seem a trifle picky? Remember, these distinctions were decided on by winemakers, who spend their lives judging nuances. Stags' Leap Winery produces an intense, well-rounded estate-grown petite sirah that is on a par with the best of France's Rhône wines, as well as a lean, complex cabernet sauvignon. Unfortunately for us, the winery is only open on a very limited basis.

Robert Sinskey Vineyards *map page 78, C-3*

The northernmost Stags Leap winery on the Silverado Trail is Robert Sinskey Vineyards, which from the road appears as austere as the landscape. The build-ing looks like an oversized horse barn, which is fitting because the grapes here grow on old pasture land. The quality of Robert Sinskey wines is amazingly high, but take note that most of the grapes used are grown in the Carneros District. Thereby hangs a tale.

As Rob Sinskey tells it, his father, Robert Sinskey, M.D., got together with two friends, Mike Richmond and Jerry Goldstein, and became limited partners in Acacia Winery. Robert Sr. became seriously bitten by the wine bug, so in 1982 he bought 32 acres along Las Amigas Road in the Carneros. In 1985, by the time the vines in the Carneros were ready to bear fruit, the partners had decided to sell Acacia. Sinskey had his vineyard—all he needed was a winery to put his grapes to use. He bought land in Stags Leap and construction began. The first crush in this winery occurred in 1988. Sinskey's son, Rob, took some time off to help in the winery. "I think a week had passed," he says, "when I discovered that my father's avocation had become my obsession." Rob is now the winery's vintner.

At first sniff and sip, you will know you are onto something good in Sinskey's pinot noir. The merlot is even better. Rob Sinskey explains that the Carneros is cool by California standards but still warmer than some of the world's other growing

A blessing-of-the-grapes ceremony at Stag's Leap Wine Cellars.

regions such as St. Emilion and Pomerol, where some of the greatest merlots are produced. An open kitchen in the tasting room shows the influence of Maria Helm Sinskey, a chef and cookbook author. Call ahead if you're interested in taking a culinary tour through their garden and tasting wines paired with cheese and charcuterie. *6320 Silverado Trail; 707-944-9090.*

★ **Stag's Leap Wine Cellars**   *map page 78, C-3/4*
Though the plain, low, earth-colored buildings are quite modest, this is a truly eminent spot. Warren and Barbara Winiarski's winery is the home of the 1973 cabernet that won the red wine section of the famous 1976 Paris tasting; it is also the home of the famed "Cask 23" cabernet sauvignon. Because of this, the place tends to attract serious oenophiles. Taste the wines: not just the cab, but also whatever else they're pouring. The riesling has enough crisp acidity to be an excellent food wine. The sauvignon blancs tend to have a flinty, mineral quality that is more common in French whites than Californians. Their famed cabernet, of course, is intense and complex and should be even better 10 years down the road.

Newlyweds, their cow, and a friend pose at Stag's Leap Vineyard in 1888.

It's no exaggeration to say the Winiarskis had a big hand in shaping the world's perception of California wines. In the 1960s, Warren worked with some of the greats: Lee Stewart of the original Souverain Winery and André Tchelistcheff of Beaulieu Vineyards, plus a stint as assistant winemaker at the newly established Robert Mondavi Winery. By 1972, the Winiarskis had their vineyard and winery. Just four years later, they catapulted to international fame when their 1973 cabernet sauvignon bested four top-ranked Bordeaux entries, including first-growths Château Mouton-Rothschild and Château Haut-Brion. Not bad for the first wine produced at their winery! In the 2006 Paris tasting rematch, that legendary vintage held its own by nabbing second place. *5766 Silverado Trail; 707-265-2441.*

Bernard Portet (left) in the Clos du Val vineyards.

Chimney Rock Winery   *map page 78, C-4/5*

This winery's low white building is usually easily spotted from the road—unless the poplar trees surrounding it are in full leaf, hiding it from view. In the somewhat ornate Cape (as in Cape of Good Hope) Dutch style of the 17th century, it seems a bit out of place amid the austere Stags Leap landscape. But you have to love a winery that gradually took over a golf course, putting the land to a much nobler use. The cabernet tends to be softer and more supple than other cabernets hereabouts, and there's also a very fine sauvignon blanc and dry rosé of cabernet franc. The comfortable tasting room mirrors the Cape Dutch style of the exterior, with high, wood-beamed ceilings and a fireplace that warms it in winter. *5350 Silverado Trail; 707-257-2641.*

Clos du Val   *map page 78, C-5*

Although this austere winery doesn't seduce you with dramatic architecture or lush grounds, it doesn't have to: the wines, crafted by winemaker John Clews, have a wide following, especially among the cabernet cognoscenti who are patient enough to cellar their collections. Co-founded by American businessman John Goelet, descended from a family of Bordeaux wine merchants, and Bernard Portet, a French winemaker, Clos du Val specializes in wines that are French in character and structure, not revealing their complexity until after they have been aged for several years. Although Stags Leap District cab is their claim to fame, Clew's team also makes great pinot noir and chardonnay, grown in the nearby Carneros region. The few picnic tables in their olive grove fill early on summer weekends, and anyone is welcome to try a hand at the boccie-style game of *pétanque. 5330 Silverado Trail; 707-259-2200.*

■ MOUNT VEEDER APPELLATION

South of the Oakville Grade, the Mayacamas Range is deeply cut by several creeks that flow from northwest to southeast. Farther south, the mountains break up into a series of hillocks, ridges, and mountain glades. Unlike on the valley floor, where wineries stand cheek by jowl along Highway 29 and the Silverado Trail, here wineries are fewer and farther between, hidden among the stands of oak, madrone, and redwood trees. Growing grapes in the Mount Veeder AVA takes a certain temerity—or foolhardiness, depending on your point of view.

Even though this region gets more rain than the Napa Valley (as witnessed by those redwoods), soils are poor and rocky and the water runs off quickly, forcing any grapevines planted here to grow deep roots. Vines thus stressed produce grapes with a high ratio of grape surface to liquid volume, resulting in intensely flavored wines. But it's not easy to harvest these grapes. The vines on the steep slopes of the 2,677-foot volcanic peak of Mount Veeder must be picked by hand—in fact, most vineyard machinery is useless here. In addition to all that rain, the temperatures are generally cooler than on the valley floor. Merlot and syrah thrive in these conditions, but the big winner is cabernet. Mount Veeder cabernets tend to be muscular and earthy, with firm tannins.

★ The Hess Collection   *map page 78, A-4/5*

Not all the wines made by the Hess Collection are austere, because grapes from other growing regions are used as well. Still, when the Swiss brewer and soda merchant Donald Hess arrived in 1986, he planted vineyards on ridges and mountaintops. Some of these sites are so steep the grapes have to be picked by hand. This literally hands-on care definitely shows in the quality of the estate wines. The drive up may be convoluted, but there's an extra lure here besides a close-up look at these typically Veeder slopes: a trove of modern art.

The Hess Collection offers free self-guided tours of its world-class modern art collection, but it charges a fee for tasting its wines. Although the wines are worth paying for, you'll probably remember the art more than the cabernets or chardonnay. It is hard to forget Leopoldo Maler's striking *Hommage*, a flaming typewriter created as a protest piece against the repression of artistic freedom by totalitarian regimes. There are some spectacular views from the terrace here into the heart of the Mayacamas Range, with hills as tortured as those in a Chinese landscape painting. And yes, those green patches on the mountaintops are vineyards. *4411 Redwood Road; 707-255-1144.*

Mayacamas Vineyards   *map page 78, A-3/4*
The drive up Mount Veeder Road to Mayacamas Vineyards has been known to try the faint of heart. The stone winery, built in 1889, was resurrected in 1941 by Jack and Mary Taylor, pioneers of the Napa Valley wine renaissance who demonstrated that great wines can be made from cabernet sauvignon and chardon-

Johanna II, *by artist Franz Gertsch, is part of the Hess Collection.*

A GREAT DRIVE IN SOUTHERN NAPA

If you're most interested in efficiency, stick to the wineries just off Highway 29 or the Silverado Trail. But if you're after a leisurely drive on beautiful, winding mountain roads—and aren't prone to carsickness—try this less-traveled alternative.

From Napa, drive north on Highway 29 to the Trancas Street/Redwood Road exit. Take the shady Redwood Road (to the left) and when it narrows down from four lanes to two, stay to your left. (Otherwise, you'll end up going right onto Dry Creek Road.) Just after a sharp curve, look for the Hess Winery sign. When you see it, turn sharply left to stay on Redwood Road and you'll see the entrance to the winery almost immediately. (The trip from Napa to Hess should take about 15 minutes.)

After your visit, turn right out of the winery back onto Redwood Road. At the next T, turn left onto Mt. Veeder Road. Next, turn right on Oakville Grade, and you'll be twisting and turning your way downhill. If you've made reservations at Far Niente for a tour and tasting, look for the sign for the Diamond Oaks Winery. Shortly after you pass it, look for two tall pine trees on either side of a driveway on the right side of the road; a wooden sign reads 1350/1360 Acacia Drive. This is where you turn in for Far Niente. Otherwise, head for Robert Mondavi, where their introductory tours are particularly good for wine newbies. Continue past the Far Niente driveway about a mile to Highway 29 and turn left. You'll see the Mondavi driveway almost immediately on your left. To return to Napa, simply turn right on Highway 29 for the quick drive back to town.

nay grapes grown at high elevations. The winery, owned by Bob Travers since 1968, now makes sauvignon blanc as well. The wines are big, flavorful, and concentrated. Call ahead for an appointment before you visit. They're open on weekdays only. *1155 Lokoya Road; 707-224-4030.*

A vineyard at Schramsberg.

NORTHERN NAPA VALLEY

Nowhere else in California will you find wineries as densely clustered as in the northern Napa Valley, or "up valley" to the locals. It seems you can't drive more than a few feet along Highway 29, which narrows to one lane north of Yountville, without seeing another sign touting a tasting room. Along the Silverado Trail, roughly parallel to Highway 29 on the other side of the valley floor, traffic is a bit lighter and the tasting rooms fewer—but not by much. Many of the biggest names in wine, such as Grgich Cellars, Rubicon Estate (formerly Niebaum Coppola), Beringer, Louis M. Martini, Beaulieu, and Mumm Napa, are rooted here, drawing wine pilgrims from all around the world.

Guenoc Valley

Calistoga AVA
Calistoga
Napa Valley AVA
Diamond Mountain
Howell Mountain
Spring Mountain
St. Helena
Chiles Valley
Rutherford
Oakville

All the wineries in this chapter are in the Napa Valley AVA, but within this appellation are smaller subappellations such as Rutherford, St. Helena, Spring Mountain, and Calistoga. Soil conditions, elevation, and weather patterns vary greatly from one part of northern Napa to another, but in general this area is hotter than southern Napa and most of Sonoma County, so consider visiting in spring or autumn. Another incentive to come outside of the summer and early autumn peak tourist season: avoiding crowds. St. Helena, for instance, gets packed with glossy weekenders reeled in by the town's fancy boutiques and restaurants. Calistoga, a larger town a bit farther north, feels more relaxed—maybe it's the result of all those mud baths and massages everyone's indulging in.

■ RUTHERFORD APPELLATION

You could easily drive through the tiny community of Rutherford, at the intersection of Highway 29 and Rutherford Cross Road, in the blink of an eye, but this may well be one of the most important wine-related intersections in the United States. For here, on either side of the highway, stand the ivy-clad wineries of Rubicon Estate and Beaulieu. The former was founded in 1879 by Gustave Niebaum, a Finnish sea captain; the latter by the French vintner Georges de Latour in 1900.

Though Rutherford has been designated an AVA only since 1993, it is generally regarded as one of the best locations for cabernet sauvignon in California, if not

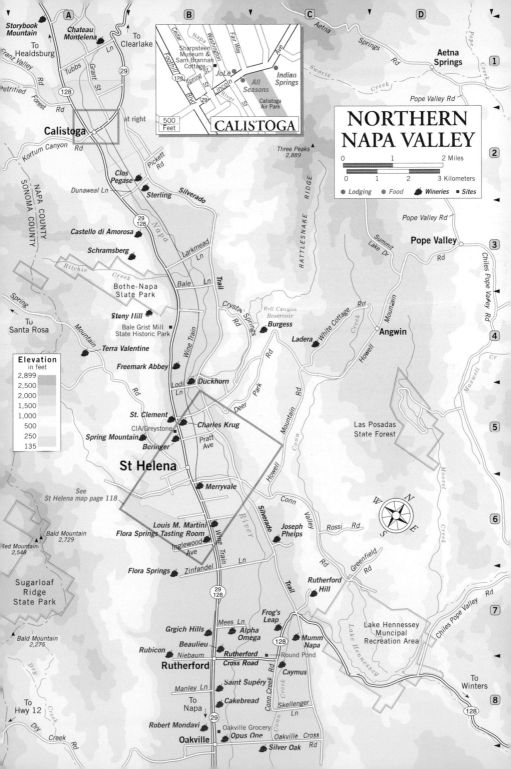

the world, and most of the superstar cabernets are produced here. Legendary wine-maker André Tchelistcheff's claim that "it takes Rutherford dust to grow great cabernet" is now quoted by every winery in the area that produces the stuff.

That "Rutherford dust" varies from one part of the region to another, but the soils here are primarily gravel, sand, and loam, a well-drained home for cabernet grapes that don't like to get their feet wet. And because Rutherford is poised at Napa Valley's widest point, it gets more sun than most valley locations. Warm daytime temperatures lead the grapes to develop both intense flavor and well-developed tannins, perfect for making a bold, structured cabernet that will need years in the bottle to soften and reach their peak. About 70 percent of Rutherford vineyards are planted with cabernet; merlot, sauvignon blanc, and chardonnay lag well behind.

You might want to switch your taste buds to olive oil for an hour or two. Olive-oil tasters quaff the stuff almost as you would wine, analyzing it for various characteristics and determining how different varieties might be blended together. At **Round Pond** (887 Rutherford Road; 888-302-2575), an excellent tour of the olive groves and the mill ends with an opportunity to taste their fresh oils and red wine vinegars. Call ahead for a reservation.

Cakebread Cellars   *map page 107, B-8*

This great winery is run by one of the nicest and most creative families in the business. Jack Cakebread, who founded the winery in 1973 with his wife, Dolores, is also a renowned photographer, and some of his work can be seen hanging on the winery's walls. Dolores is a superb cook who has played a major role in making the Napa Valley a food as well as a wine region. Her kitchen garden occupies a prominent (and perhaps symbolic) spot between the winery and the vineyards. Their two sons, Bruce and Dennis, are also involved in the business. Under winemaker Julianne Laks, they produce a sauvignon blanc of great character and depth, a beautifully complex cabernet sauvignon, and a luscious chardonnay. The winery is truly beautiful, with an unmatched attention to detail in the woodwork and brickwork. Tastings and tours are by appointment only. *8300 St. Helena Highway; 707-963-5221.*

Saint Supéry Vineyards & Winery   *map page 107, B-8*

Set well back from the road, Saint Supéry is a study in contrast. The first building you see after you park your car is the beautifully restored Queen Anne Victorian. The next building, however, looks like it belongs in a suburban office park. Ignore the ugly exterior. Inside, you'll find one of the most thoughtfully

Gustave Niebaum in 1880, the year after the Finnish sea captain completed his purchase of the Inglenook farm.

appointed visitors centers in the Wine Country. Besides a relief map of the Napa Valley and other displays, you'll appreciate the sniffing station, an ingenious contraption that lets you smell some of the elements that determine the character of red and white wines—the cherry, black pepper, bell pepper, and cedar aromas of reds, and the wildflower, new-mown hay, green olive, and grapefruit of white wines. You can go on a self-guided tour or take the formal tour, which includes the 1881 farmhouse.

Primarily a "red wine house," Saint Supéry makes very good cabernet sauvignon and sauvignon blanc from grapes grown on its Dollarhide Ranch, in Pope Valley. A 35-acre vineyard next to the winery is planted with cabernet sauvignon, merlot, and petit verdot, which thrive in the Rutherford soil. (To taste these limited production estate wines, plan to visit on the weekend, when the "Divine Wine Room" is open for an additional fee.) There's also a well-structured barrel-fermented chardonnay and an oak-free chardonnay, as well as an excellent sauvignon blanc and a crisp moscato. *8440 St. Helena Highway; 707-963-4507.*

★ **Rubicon Estate**   *map page 107, B-7/8*
What started in the 1970s as a family getaway for famed movie director Francis Ford Coppola has grown into a tremendous wine business. In 2006, Coppola opened a second winery in Geyserville (see the Northern Sonoma County chapter), as a more casual visitors center highlighting his less-expensive wines. This, his first property, formerly called Niebaum-Coppola Estate Winery, now showcases the finest estate wines. The high-ceilinged, stone-walled tasting room, with several highly polished wine bars, recalls the property's late-19th-century origins.

Japanese plum trees bloom along the road leading to the Rubicon Estate.

For $15 you can sample the modest Sofia wines; the $25 tasting gives you a good sense of the diversity of the excellent wines made here. The five pours might include a bright, floral chardonnay, the Captain's Reserve Pinot Noir, a zinfandel produced from estate-grown grapes, an inky cabernet franc, and the current vintage of their flagship Rubicon, a deep-red Bordeaux blend. For $50 you can experience a seated tasting of several top wines.

The latter two tastings include a spot on the Legacy Tour, which focuses on the history of the estate. You'll learn about Gustave Niebaum, who made his money in the Alaska fur trade, then set out to make California wines that would rival the best in Europe. In 1880 he purchased two farms, one of which had been named Inglenook by its former owner. By 1887, construction on the state-of-the-art Niebaum winery had been completed, and by 1889, he was producing wines of such excellent quality that they won prizes at an exposition in Paris.

Prohibition brought a dry spell, though, and for decades afterwards various owners turned out mediocre wine. In 1975, Coppola arrived on the scene, buying up Niebaum's mansion and part of the Inglenook land. With Rubicon, he established his chops as a winemaker. In 1995, Coppola restored the Inglenook

The late and much respected André Tchelistcheff, the doyen of the California wine industry.

estate by buying the rest of the original acreage and the historic Inglenook château.

The tour also provides a great opportunity to appreciate some of the architectural details of the Inglenook château, such as a grand staircase that took four master woodworkers more than a year to create. Although the Coppola film memorabilia that was once housed at the winery has been moved to Geyserville, at the bottom of the staircase you can still see a few exhibits about Coppola's filmmaking career and his family history alongside several displays about Niebaum and the history of the historic château. *1991 St. Helena Highway; 707-968-1100.*

Beaulieu Vineyard   *map page 107, B-7/8*
The ivy-covered edifice of Beaulieu Vineyard sits prominently in the center of Rutherford. The winery was founded in 1900 by Georges de Latour, but his wife, Fernande, had much to do with the winery's success. A Californian of French parentage, she introduced de Latour to the San Francisco social circles in which his wine became fashionable. The winery stayed open during Prohibition, making "wines for sacramental and governmental purposes" (throughout Prohibition the government served wine at functions at which foreign dignitaries were present).

The late André Tchelistcheff, Beaulieu's winemaker from 1938 to 1973, placed Beaulieu among the world's great wineries and may well have been the most influential American winemaker ever. Not only did he set an example by making great wine, he also advised winemakers from California to the Pacific Northwest. Look at the historical records of the West Coast's most successful wineries, and Tchelistcheff's name is sure to pop up.

Beaulieu continues to make a wide variety of top-quality wines, from some reasonably priced chardonnays, merlots, and zinfandels to the higher-end reserve pinot noir and Dulcet Reserve, a cabernet and syrah blend. It's worth the few extra dollars to taste wines in the reserve tasting room—more intimate and usually less crowded than their main tasting room—in order to taste their flagship wine, the outstanding Georges de Latour Private Reserve Cabernet Sauvignon, which Beaulieu has been making since 1936. *1960 St. Helena Highway; 707-963-2411.*

Grgich Hills Estate *map page 107, B-7*
Just north of Rutherford center, look for Grgich Hills, a small ivy-covered winery on the west side of the highway. In 1976, Miljenko (Mike) Grgich's Chateau Montelena chardonnay bested several top French white Burgundies at the famous 1976 "Paris Tasting," immediately earning him a reputation as one of the best winemakers in the world. That chardonnay helped serve notice that California wines were a force to be reckoned with. Now in his late eighties, Grgich, something of a Napa Valley celebrity, is still involved with the winery operations.

It's almost too bad that Grgich won early fame with chardonnay, a grape that has almost been turned into a Napa Valley cliché, because in the public eye it often overshadows the excellent estate-grown cabernet sauvignon, fumé blanc, merlot, and zinfandel. Tastings are offered daily, but the twice-daily tours are by appointment only. If you can arrange to visit on a Friday between 2 and 4 P.M. (except during harvest), you'll be treated to a barrel tasting that will give you a sneak preview of a soon-to-be-released wine. You might want to lay away a few bottles, as Grgich wines are aging well. *1829 St. Helena Highway; 707-963-2784.*

Alpha Omega *map page 107, B-7*
In addition to growing grapes on seven on-site acres, Alpha Omega obtains fruit from all over the Napa Valley, from chardonnay grown in the cool Carneros District to cabernet cultivated on the sunny slopes of Atlas Peak. Although there

are few bargains on their list, fans of rich, velvety chardonnays may enjoy the one made here, and the Proprietary Red Wine promises to age well. There's an additional fee to taste their flagship Era, a Bordeaux blend that has impressed the critics from its first vintage. A picnic area overlooking a dramatic fountain makes it a particularly nice place to linger. *1155 Mee Lane; 707-963-9999.*

Caymus Vineyards *map page 107, C-8*
Tastings here are especially intimate and informative—and the family's Napa holdings go way back. The Wagner family began farming in the Napa Valley in 1906, when it grew prunes as well as grapes. In 1972, Charlie Wagner converted an old barn into a winery and started making wine. After he hired Randy Dunn as winemaker, Caymus cabernet sauvignon gained national stature. Dunn left in 1984 to run his own winery on Howell Mountain, and Charlie's son, Chuck, took over the winemaking. The Caymus reds—the concentration here is solely on cabernet sauvignon these days—are as good as ever. Their flagship Special Selection Cabernet maintains a consistently luscious quality year after year, with a deep aroma of black currants, blackberries, and dark coffee, backed by firm tannins that stand up to cellaring. Tastings, limited to 10 visitors, are by appointment only. Although no tours are given, you can see historical photos of the property on the walls of the tasting room. *8700 Conn Creek Road; 707-967-3010.*

★ Mumm Napa *map page 107, C-7*
Built in 1986, long after other French winemakers had become entrenched in the Napa Valley, Mumm had some catching up to do. It did so with the winery's intelligent layout, intriguing art exhibits, and with the quality of its sparkling wines. The sparklers, served by the glass or flight in a glass-enclosed tasting salon or on a terrace, both with a view of the vineyards, vary greatly in style. Reserve ahead to indulge in a two-hour tasting of library wines seated under the trees on the Oak Terrace. The Brut Prestige, for instance, snaps with crisp acidity, while the somewhat sweet Cuvée M emphasizes fruit flavors. Once you've found the one you like, take your glass and wander next door to the art gallery, where 30 Ansel Adams photographs—including iconic images like Yosemite's Half Dome—form a permanent exhibit. Hung along the dramatic long corridors you'll find additional photos belonging to the rotating photography exhibit. Frequent daily tours sketch out the traditional *méthode champenoise* and give you a look at a demonstration vineyard. *8445 Silverado Trail; 707-967-7700.*

★ **Frog's Leap**   *map page 107, C-7*
This Rutherford appellation winery should be on your must-see list. The wines
are great—especially the zinfandel, sauvignon blanc, and cabernet sauvignon—
and the friendly, sometimes goofy staff are determined not to take themselves, or
their wines, too seriously. What else would you expect from a place that names one
of its wines Frögenbeerenauslese (after the German wine Trockenbeerenauslese)?

In 1994, after splitting up with partner Larry Turley, owner John Williams took
his leaping-frog label from the old frog farm north of St. Helena, where it was
founded in 1981, to this Rutherford location. Williams has restored the big red
barn, the oldest board-and-batten building in the Napa Valley, and turned it into a
winery. Gardens, olive trees, a chicken coop and, of course, a frog pond with lily
pads surround the winery.

On the tour you'll walk to the edge of the vineyard, where you'll learn about their
organic growing techniques and see some of the solar panels that power the facilities.
Frog's Leap was the first Napa Valley vineyard to be certified organic, in 1987, and
their commitment to the environment is evident everywhere, from the 5 acres of
organic gardens, to the guides' enthusiasm for the beneficial insects. During a tasting
in the new eco-conscious visitors center, guides are as likely to wax poetic about the
building's use of recycled building materials as they are about Frog's Leap's latest
petite sirah. If you've forgotten to call ahead for the free tour, you can also drop by for
a seated tasting ($15) on the lovely porch. *8815 Conn Creek Road; 707-963-4704.*

Rutherford Hill Winery   *map page 107, C-7*
A rare Rutherford winery that's not dominated by cabernet sauvignon. In fact,
it's known for that less-glam grape, merlot—and it does a great job with it.
When the founders of Rutherford Hill were deciding what grapes to plant, they discovered that the climate and soil conditions of their vineyards resembled those of
Pomerol, a region of Bordeaux where merlot is king. Today this winery produces
merlots notable for both quantity (about 10 percent of all Napa Valley merlots) and
quality. Its reserve merlot, for instance, is likely to stand up for another decade or so.

The wine caves here are some of the most extensive of any California winery—
nearly a mile of tunnels and passageways. You can get a glimpse of the tunnels and
the 8,000 barrels inside on the tours, which are given three to five times a day.
There are also picnic areas in oak and olive groves. *200 Rutherford Hill Road; 707-
963-1871.*

(opposite) Frog's Leap shows the upside of being green—that is, organic.

■ St. Helena Appellation

North of the Rutherford AVA lies the St. Helena AVA, which encompasses the town of St. Helena. Here the valley floor narrows between the Mayacamas and Vaca mountains. These slopes reflect heat onto the 9,000 or so acres below, and since there's less fog and wind, things get pretty toasty. In fact, this AVA is one of the hottest places in Napa Valley, with mid-summer temperatures often reaching the mid-90s. Bordeaux varietals are the most popular grapes grown here—especially cabernet sauvignon but also merlot. You'll also find chardonnay, petite sirah, and pinot noir in the vineyards.

Town of St. Helena   *map page 107, B-5/6, and page 118*

Tree-shaded sidewalks lead from one sun-mellowed redbrick building to another; chic-looking visitors flit between boutiques and storefront tasting rooms. Rough life, isn't it? Genteel St. Helena pulls in rafts of Wine Country tourists during the day, though like most Wine Country towns it fairly rolls up the sidewalks after dark.

Main Street and its side streets have plenty of places to flex your credit card. St. Helena diners are spoiled for choice, with The Restaurant at Meadowood, Terra, and Martini House acclaimed as three of the better restaurants in all of Napa Valley. More casual spots like Market and Tra Vigne Pizzeria draw the younger crowds. There's particularly good shopping, too, especially for women's clothing and upscale housewares. **Footcandy** (1239 Main Street; 707-963-2040) lines up precarious stilettos and high-heeled boots, and **Jan de Luz** (1219 Main Street; 707-963-1550) stocks fine French table linens and other high-quality housewares. **Woodhouse Chocolate** (1367 Main Street; 707-963-8413) sells elaborate hand-made confections in a lovely shop that resembles an 18th-century Parisian salon.

Many visitors never get away from Main Street magnets, but you should explore a bit farther, to stroll through quiet residential neighborhoods. A few blocks west of Main Street you'll be surrounded by vineyards, merging into the ragged wilderness edge of the Mayacamas Mountains. Several blocks east of Main Street, off Pope Street, is the Napa River, which separates St. Helena from the Silverado Trail and Howell Mountain. You might see deer at the edge of the road, or a heron rising from a riparian pool.

Unlike many other parts of Napa Valley, where milling grain was the primary industry until the late 1800s, St. Helena took to vines almost instantly. The town

(left) Robert Louis Stevenson, who visited Jacob Schram's winery north of St. Helena in 1880. (right) Ambrose Bierce, who lived in St. Helena for a time at the end of the 19th century.

got its start in 1854 when Henry Still built a store. Still wanted company and donated lots on his town site to anyone who wanted to erect a business here. Soon his store was joined by a wagon shop, a shoe shop, hotels, and churches. Dr. George Crane planted a vineyard in 1858 and was the first to produce wine in commercially viable quantities. A German winemaker named Charles Krug followed suit a couple of years later, and other wineries soon followed.

In the late 1800s, phylloxera had begun to destroy France's vineyards and Napa Valley wines caught the world's attention. The increased demand for Napa wines spawned a building frenzy in St. Helena. Many of the mansions still gracing the town's residential neighborhoods were built around this time. Also in the late 1800s, some entrepreneurs attempted to turn St. Helena into an industrial center to supply specialized machinery to local viticulturists. Several stone warehouses were built near the railroad tracks downtown. Other weathered stone buildings on Main Street, mostly between Adams and Spring streets, and along Railroad Avenue, date from the same era. Modern façades sometimes camouflage these old-timers, but you can study the old structures by strolling the back alleys.

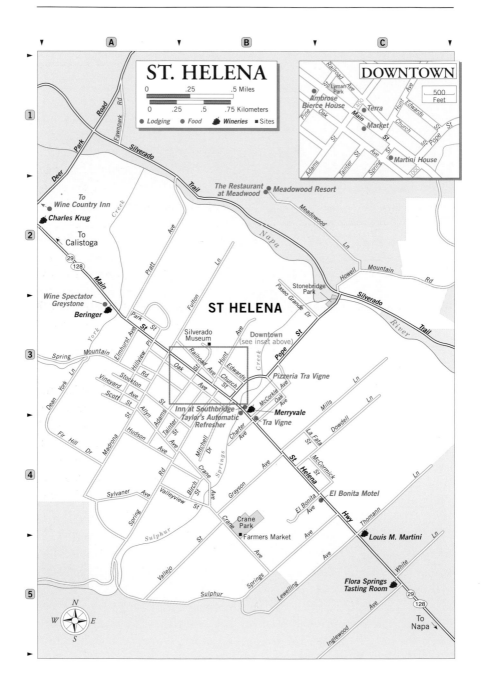

ST. HELENA

0   .25   .5 Miles

0   .25   .5   .75 Kilometers

● Lodging   ● Food   🐝 Wineries   ■ Sites

DOWNTOWN

500 Feet

Railroad Ave
Lyman Park
Ambrose Bierce House
Pine
Oak
Main
Terra
Market
Church St
Pope St
Adams
Tainter St
Spring
Martini House

Road
Fawnpark Rd
Park
Deer
Silverado

Trail

The Restaurant at Meadowood
Meadowood Resort
Meadowood

To Wine Country Inn
🐝 Charles Krug
Creek
Ave
Napa
Ln

To Calistoga
29 128
Main
Pratt
Ln
Stonebridge Park
Paseo Grande Dr
Howell
Mountain
Rd
Silverado

Wine Spectator Greystone
🐝 Beringer
York
Park St
St
Elmhurst Ave
Hillview Pl
Fulton
Silverado Museum ■
Ave
Railroad Ave
Hunt
Edwards
ST HELENA
Downtown (see inset above)
Pope St
River
Trail

Spring
Mountain
York Ln
Rd
Oak St
Church St
Creek
Pizzeria Tra Vigne
Ln

Vinevard Ave
Stockton
Scott St
Ave
Allyn
Adams St
Tainter St
Ave
McCorkle
Oak Ave
Mills
Ln

Dean
Fir Hill Dr
Madrona
Hudson Ave
Mitchell Dr
Inn at Southbridge 🐝
Taylor's Automatic Refresher
Charter Ave
Tra Vigne
Merryvale
La Fata St
Dowdell
St. Helena Hwy

Sylvaner Ave
Valleyview St
Birch St
Crane Ave
Springs
Grayson Ave
Ave
El Bonita Ave
El Bonita Motel
McCormick Ln

Spring
Sulphur St
Crane St
Crane Park
■ Farmers Market
Ave
Hwy
Thomann
Louis M. Martini
Ln

Vallejo
Sulphur
Springs
Lewelling
Ave
Flora Springs Tasting Room
29 128
White
To Napa

N
W   E
S

Inglewood

The 1872 **Ambrose Bierce House** (1515 Main Street) has been restored and now serves as an inn. Inside is a small collection of memorabilia of the cantankerous writer of *The Devil's Dictionary* and other works, who lived here before vanishing in Mexico in 1913. He made his drinking preferences clear in his famous quote, "Wine, madam, is God's next best gift to man."

The small **Silverado Museum,** east of downtown at the public library on Library Lane, has one of the best collections of Robert Louis Stevenson memorabilia in the world. Early editions of his books line the walls in barrister bookcases and paintings and photographs cover the walls, making the room look something like a private library. Display cases exhibit everything from manuscripts to a lock of his hair. *1490 Library Lane; 707-963-3757.*

The water-powered mill at the **Bale Grist Mill State Historic Park** (3 miles north of St. Helena off Highway 29; 707-942-4575) was built in 1846 and partially restored in 1925. Take the short trail from the parking lot, over a creek and to the mill and granary, where exhibits explain the milling process. At this writing, the park is open weekends only, when a docent offers milling demonstrations. A trail leads from the park to Bothe–Napa Valley State Park, where you can pick up a number of hiking trails or linger for a picnic.

Flora Springs Winery and Vineyards   *map page 107, B-6/7 and B-6*
This 1880s stone winery served as home for Louis M. Martini, a Wine Country pioneer, from 1930 to 1976 and was purchased in 1977 by Jerry and Flora Komes as a retirement getaway. In recent years, Flora Springs has made a splash with its reds, especially its red meritage called Trilogy because it was originally blended from three traditional Bordeaux grape varietals—cabernet sauvignon, cabernet franc, and merlot—though more recent vintages might also contain malbec and petit verdot. There's a good reason for the quality of the wines: they own 650 acres of prime organically farmed vineyards not only in the Rutherford AVA, but also in the Carneros, Oakville, St. Helena, and Pope Valley areas. If you'd like to visit, you must call ahead to book a "VIP Tour and Tasting," which includes a barrel tasting. Or, to simply taste their wines, drop into their thoroughly modern tasting room in St. Helena, next to Dean and Deluca. *Winery: 1978 West Zinfandel Lane; 707-963-5711. Tasting Room: 677 South St. Helena Highway; 707-967-8032.*

Louis M. Martini *map page 107, B-6*

The Martini name certainly has Wine Country cred, although it may not always get the recognition it deserves. Louis M. Martini built this winery in 1933 and was one of the first vintners to identify and propagate vinifera clones and to release vintage-dated varietal wines. Martini's was also the first large winery to invest in Carneros and Mayacamas vineyards. But it has always kept a relatively low profile, both in its physical plant and in its public image. In 2002, it was sold to mega-company E. & J. Gallo, but Martini's grandchildren still make the wine, which has maintained its high quality. The winery's best wines are its reds, especially the cabernet sauvignons, grown in Napa, Sonoma, and Alexander valleys, and the zinfandel, produced from vines more than 100 years old. Both profit from bottle aging. *254 St. Helena Highway South; 707-963-2736.*

Merryvale Vineyards *map page 107, B-5/6*

Just north of the ivy-covered fieldstone buildings of the restaurant Tra Vigne in St. Helena sits Merryvale Vineyards, founded in 1983. This is a good place to save for the end of a day, since the winery stays open until 6 or 6:30 P.M.

(above) The late Louis P. Martini inspects grapes in one of his vineyards. (opposite) Napa's Ubuntu is a "vegetable restaurant" with its own biodynamic gardens.

Chardonnay and cabernet are their claims to fame. Their Bourdeaux blend called Profile is their top-of-the-line wine; though it's not typically poured in the tasting room, it's worth asking if there's an open bottle around so you can taste it. For the full Merryvale experience, though, reserve ahead for a spot in one of their weekend Wine Component Tasting seminars. A tour of the winery winds up in the enchanting Cask Room, where the guides focus on wine's essential components—sugar, alcohol, acid, and tannins—and discuss how these elements are balanced by the vintner. *1000 Main Street; 707-963-2225.*

Joseph Phelps Vineyards   *map page 107, C-6*

Joseph Phelps originally came to Wine Country to build wineries for Pillsbury, but he soon split off to make his own way. He opened his winery in 1972, with Walter Schug as his first winemaker. It was a strong start; in Schug's decade with Phelps, the two got a lot of attention for rieslings. Today, Phelps is known for reds, including the cabernet sauvignon, and several Rhône-style blends. The 2002 vintage of their superb Bordeaux blend called Insignia was selected as *Wine Spectator's* wine of the year, immediately pushing up prices and demand. You'll need to make a reservation for a tasting, which, weather permitting, takes place on a terrace with stunning views down the slopes. While you're at it, ask about booking a spot in one of their informative seminars, in which you can test your ability to identify different aromas or compare your wine-blending skills with those of the experts. *200 Taplin Road; 707-963-2745.*

★ Beringer Vineyards   *map page 107, B-5*

North of St. Helena, on the west side of Highway 29 just before a tunnel of elm trees, is the entrance gate to Beringer Vineyards, the Napa Valley's oldest winery in continuous operation. The big, beautifully landscaped grounds, historic buildings, and selection of tours make this one of the most-visited wineries in Napa. If you're seeking an intimate experience, you may be tempted to drive right past, but if you're a newbie who's interested in learning more about the history of the Napa Valley, Beringer makes a great first stop.

Founded in 1876 by Rhine Valley emigrants Jacob and Frederick Beringer, the winery made sacramental wines as well as a little brandy for "health purposes" during Prohibition. Beringer had fallen on hard times when it was rescued by the Swiss Nestlé corporation in 1971. The company hired the legendary Myron

A huge redwood gate marks the entrance to Joseph Phelps Vineyards.

Nightingale as winemaker and supplied him with everything he needed to produce first-rate wine. It also renovated the old Beringer mansion, updated the winery and wine-making equipment, restored the caves, and invested in excellent vineyards.

Nestlé sold its wine interests in late 1995 to American investors, and Beringer is now owned by Foster's Wine Estates. The Napa Valley cabernets and chardonnays—especially the reserve wines—put Beringer in the ranks of California's top wineries; the Knights Valley cabernet and sauvignon blanc, made from grapes grown in alluvial soil in Sonoma Valley, are also highly regarded.

A variety of tours caters to different interests, such as the historic property or the wine-making process. The introductory tour, "Taste of Beringer," should not be missed, especially the stone tunnels dug by Chinese laborers in the 19th century, which now serve as storage cellars for the reserve cabernets. The old winery, built from squared stones, is much too small for current operations, but a state-of-the-art winery, not open to the public, is located across the street.

The winery's grounds are beautifully landscaped, and its two mansions have been meticulously restored. The Rhine House, built in the 1880s to resemble the Beringers' ancestral home, was Frederick's residence and now contains the reserve

(above) Frederick Beringer (fifth from right) poses in front of his winery.
(opposite) A candlelit banquet in the cask room of Merryvale Vineyards.

The Beringer estate and winery is probably the biggest tourist attraction in the Napa Valley.

tasting room. Jacob and his family lived north of the redwood grove in the Hudson House, built in 1848 by the property's first settler. The building now serves as home to Beringer's Culinary Arts Center (open only for special events). *2000 Main Street; 707-963-4812.*

Charles Krug Winery   *map page 107, B-5*
Napa Valley's oldest surviving winery has had quite a rollercoaster reputation. Founded by the namesake Charles in 1861, it met early success, then closed during Prohibition. Cesare Mondavi and his sons, Robert and Peter, rescued it in 1943 (yes, *those* Mondavis) and got it back into the limelight. But when Robert Mondavi left in the 1960s, Krug lost its luster. Now under Peter Mondavi and his two sons, the winery continues to make very good wines. The red Bordeaux-style blends are especially lush, and there is also a New Zealand–style sauvignon blanc with the zingy citrus and tropical notes common in whites produced down under. Those with a sweet tooth can finish up their tasting with a chocolate and port pairing. Though wine tasting is offered daily, tours have been suspended indefinitely while renovations take place. *2800 Main Street; 707-967-2229.*

CULINARY INSTITUTE OF AMERICA

Just north of downtown St. Helena is a huge stone building known as Greystone. Built in 1889, Greystone was intended as a cooperative winery for Napa growers, but was never used as such and was not even equipped as a winery until Christian Brothers bought it in 1950. In 1995 it became the West Coast campus of the Culinary Institute of America (CIA), where aspiring chefs study food and wine. The CIA restored the stone edifice, installed teaching kitchens, planted herb and vegetable gardens, and opened a quirky museum of corkscrews and a 125-seat restaurant serving solid Mediterranean food. A well-stocked culinary store next to a small café attracts both serious chefs and home cooks with its gleaming displays of stand mixers and copper mixing bowls. Frequent one-hour cooking demonstrations allow visitors a small taste of the education that students here get. Late on a warm afternoon, the restaurant's terrace is a fine place to enjoy a glass of wine. *2555 St. Helena Highway; 707-967-1100.*

Greystone being built in 1889. The massive structure became Christian Brothers Winery in 1950 and now accommodates the Culinary Institute of America's West Coast campus.

Cesare Mondavi and his sons rescued the Charles Krug Winery in 1943.

Duckhorn Vineyards   *map page 107, B-4/5*
Co-founded in 1976 by Dan and Margaret Duckhorn, this winery struggled for the first few years, but its wisely planted vineyards assured a reliable supply of great grapes, and the wines soon gained widespread attention. Although the reputation of merlot took a hit after the release of the 2004 movie *Sideways*, both its critics and fans agree that Duckhorn's merlots are some of the finest made anywhere, typically full of juicy berry and plum flavors balanced with spice. In fact, Duckhorn fans tend to be such rabid merlot fans that they sometimes forget that Duckhorn produces some very fine cabernet sauvignon and sauvignon blanc as well.

The airy, high-ceilinged tasting room in the modern Arts and Crafts–style building looks more like a sleek restaurant than your typical tasting room. It feels like a restaurant, too; you'll be seated at tables and served by staffers who make the rounds to pour. It makes for a relaxed tasting experience, although it's a bit more difficult to get into a full conversation with the knowledgeable tasting room employees. Reservations are required for tours and tastings, although they can often accommodate walk-ins for both on weekdays. *1000 Lodi Lane; 707-963-7108.*

Freemark Abbey   *map page 107, B-4*
The stone winery here was begun in 1886 by Josephine Tychson after her husband, John, died. Taking over the project the couple had planned together, Josephine became the first woman to oversee the building of a winery in California. Since Josephine sold the winery in 1894, it has passed through many different hands (since 2006 it has been owned by Kendall-Jackson), but Freemark Abbey has been making great wines—especially cabernet sauvignon—since the late 1960s.

Although they produce several varietals, they're known for their single-vineyard cabernets from the Sycamore and Bosché vineyards, both on the Rutherford Bench, a strip of land stretching between Oakville and Rutherford to the west of Highway 29. Wines made from the highly coveted grapes grown in that gravelly soil generally have firm tannins and are thought to have a unique but ineffable spicy berry flavor sometimes compared to allspice. The winery has also gained notice for its late-harvest riesling named Edelwein Gold, produced only in years when the climate and harvest conditions are right. Its cozy visitors center is open daily. *3022 St. Helena Highway North; 707-963-9694.*

■ SPRING MOUNTAIN APPELLATION

Rising sharply west and north of the St. Helena appellation is the Spring Mountain AVA, which spreads out along the eastern and northern slopes of the Mayacamas range. Viticulture is no piece of cake here. Because of the steep slopes, these small and even smaller vineyards must usually be tilled and harvested by hand. The hills rise to about 2,500 feet above sea level, above the fog that filters into the valley below, and cooled by an afternoon breeze. Though Spring Mountain was originally known for its white wines such as chardonnay and riesling, which thrive in the region's cool weather but bright sun, in the past decade or so the cabernet sauvignons have monopolized attention. They're dark and full-flavored, made from intensely flavored grapes that grow in the lean, shallow soil. (Another example of stress being a good thing.)

★ Spring Mountain Vineyard   *map page 107, A/B-5*
Hidden off a winding road behind a security gate, Spring Mountain has the feeling of a private country estate, even though it's only a few miles from down-

town St. Helena. Although it's not well known to the general public, oenophiles know that the winery made its first big splash in 1976, when its chardonnay beat out three renowned white Burgundies at the Judgment of Paris. These days, however, it's all about cabernet—big, chewy wines that demand some aging but promise great things. A small amount of excellent sauvignon blancs, syrahs, and pinot noirs round out their offerings.

To visit, call to arrange a spot on a tour that concludes with a tasting. Tours meander through the beautiful property, from the cellars, a portion of which were dug by Chinese immigrants in the 1880s, to a 120-year-old barn, to the beautifully preserved 1885 mansion. If you're interested in finding out what their wines taste like after years in the bottle, set aside at least an hour and a half for your visit, and spring for the reserve tasting, when they'll pour wines of various vintages while you're seated in the mansion's dining room. Otherwise, tastings take place in their cellars. *2805 Spring Mountain Road; 707-967-4188.*

Terra Valentine   *map page 107, A-4*
A second lease on life here is showing delicious results. In 1999, Angus and Margaret Wurtele bought this abandoned 1970 winery 2,100 feet above the valley floor. They've carefully restored the native stone-and-concrete winery building; check out the cast-iron staircases, elaborate copper-plated doors, and ubiquitous wine-themed stained-glass windows. The cabernet sauvignon plantings were augmented with smaller plantings of traditional Bordeaux blending grapes (merlot, cabernet franc, and petit verdot), and the result so far has been several superb cabernet sauvignons as well as some fine pinot noir and viognier, made from grapes grown in the Russian River Valley. *3787 Spring Mountain Road; 707-967-8340.*

St. Clement Vineyards   *map page 107, B-5*
Just north of the CIA on the same side of the road is St. Clement Vineyards, where the Rosenbaum House, a beautifully restored 1878 home, houses a tiny tasting room. Originally built as a family home, the Victorian mansion is now notable for its splendid views from the swing and café tables on the front porch. Tours of the property reveal details about the mansion's history, as well as the

(top) The Freemark Abbey stone winery dates back to 1886.
(bottom) Drying trays at Stony Hill Vineyard.

workings of the winery in back. Only about 10 percent of the fruit for their wines is grown on the estate; instead, they purchase wine from about a dozen different vineyards all up and down the valley to produce their sauvignon blanc, chardonnay, merlot, and cabernet sauvignon. Their most impressive offering is a full-bodied Bordeaux-style blend called Oroppas, a holdover from the days when the winery was owned by Sapporo (read it backwards). *2867 St. Helena Highway; 707-963-7221.*

★ **Stony Hill Vineyard** *map page 107, A/B-4*

A narrow unmarked road winds up Spring Mountain to Stony Hill Vineyard, a wine-making legend that preceded others by some 30 years. This is another Napa Valley winery that started out as a weekend retreat. Eleanor and Fred McCrea fell in love with a goat farm on Spring Mountain and bought it as a summer home in 1943. They planted chardonnay vines in 1947, when that grape was virtually unknown in the Wine Country, and sold their first wines in 1954. Now run by the McCrea's descendants, Stony Hill is best known for its excellent chardonnay, which emphasizes the pure flavor of the chardonnay grapes (no malolactic fermentation here). It also produces a small quantity of riesling, dry gewürztraminer, and a sweet semillon, which are also top-notch.

You must call ahead for a tour and tasting. The tour is about as low-key as they come, and the guide is likely to simply lead visitors to the barrel room and through the vineyard, answering questions rather than launching into an exhaustive description of the wine-making process. The tour ends up on the terrace of the McCrea's home (or in their great room in bad weather), reinforcing the welcoming, rustic feel of the property. Best of all, the tour provides an opportunity to wander through one of the loveliest properties in Napa Valley. Well off Highway 29, the secluded vineyards are interspersed with stands of sycamore, cypress, and oak trees, and the views of the rolling hills make it clear why the McCreas set up house here in the first place. *3331 St. Helena Highway North; 707-963-2636.*

■ CALISTOGA APPELLATION

After six years spent locking horns with the Alcohol Tax and Trade Bureau, many winemakers in the northern Napa got their wish granted in 2009, when the application to have the Calistoga deemed its own AVA was finally approved. Instead of labeling its wines with the less-specific "Napa Valley," wineries like Chateau Montelena can now tell consumers exactly where the grapes in their wine were grown: the Calistoga AVA, the 15th (and newest) subappellation in Napa Valley. This area is the farthest in Napa from the San Pablo Bay, and thus least subject to its moderating influence. The resulting hot days and cool nights benefit heat-loving red grape varieties such as cabernet sauvignon and zinfandel, which in the right hands can be turned into intensely colored, distinctively fruity wines.

★ Schramsberg Vineyards   *map page 107, A/B-3*
On the southern edge of Calistoga, tucked into an idyllic dell on the slope of a mountain, is Schramsberg, a famed maker of sparkling wines. Founded in 1965 by Jack and Jamie Davies, the winery occupies the 19th-century cellars, stone

Annie Schram (seated right) poses with vineyard workers and family members in front of a new wine cellar.

winery, and home of Jacob Schram. Schram had founded a winery here in 1862, a year after Charles Krug started his, the first in the valley.

The Davies family's excursion into sparkling-wine production was unique not because they made their wine by the traditional *méthode champenoise*—others had done that before—but because they insisted on using the traditional grapes of Champagne: chardonnay and pinot noir, very few of which had been planted in the Napa Valley at that time. Schramsberg has not looked back since President Richard Nixon served Schramsberg sparkling wine to the Chinese premier Chou En-lai in Beijing in 1972 at the "Toast to Peace." Production has increased, but the quality is still as good as ever.

You'll need an appointment to take a tour and taste at this especially charming winery, where the rustic wood buildings at the end of the narrow, winding lane feel far away from the traffic of Highway 29. The tour includes a glimpse of the original Schram home, constructed entirely without metal fastenings, using only dowels, pegs, and dovetail joints. You'll get to walk through a portion of the caves, where an astounding 2.5 million bottles are housed, stacked from floor to ceiling in a way that seems to defy physics. The guide also demonstrates the way bottles are riddled before you're seated for a generous tasting of three very different bubblies and their lone still wine, a Bordeaux-style blend. If you're smitten with their sparklers, ask about their periodic harvest camps (in fall) and blending camps (in spring). In these hands-on weekend sessions, you can participate in the harvest or learn about blending techniques—*see* the Crush Camp box in the Northern Sonoma County chapter. *1400 Schramsberg Road; 707-942-4558.*

Sterling Vineyards   *map page 107, A/B-2/3*

The huge, white hilltop building here looks more like an Aegean monastery than a winery. When it first opened in 1969, locals thought of it more as a tourist attraction than a place for serious wines. The red wines were quite good; after a few bumpy decades under various ownership, the winery's in corporate hands and is turning out notable merlot, chardonnay, and cabernet. To reach the tasting room, you'll need to hop on an aerial tram, which gives great views of the vineyards below. (The tram's a big hit with kids, hence Sterling's popularity as a family-friendly winery.) Once up top, you can follow a short self-guided walking tour, with more impressive views over the valley. *1111 Dunaweal Lane; 707-942-3344.*

Clos Pegase   *map page 107, A/B-2/3*
Just after the valley had gotten used to Sterling's white monastery-like presence, art book publisher Jan Shrem raised everybody's blood pressure with his plan for an Egyptian temple of a winery across the street from Sterling. The plans of post-modernist architect Michael Graves originally called for an art museum to be next to the winery, but local regulations squashed that game plan. No matter, for now the owners' art collection is integrated with the winery grounds and the tasting room itself. A curvaceous Henry Moore sculpture and a 19th-century marble fountain share the courtyard; inside, you'll see surrealist paintings from the 1940s to 1960s.

Outrageously individual, Clos Pegase is a refreshing palate cleanser after visiting one too many tasting rooms with the same faux French or imitation Italian style. Best of all, the wines are as interesting as the art and architecture, and they're getting better with every vintage. The chardonnay and sauvignon blanc both emphasize fresh fruit flavors, and the reds—mostly cabernet, pinot noir, and merlot—tend to have soft, round tannins, so they're best drunk while still young. *1060 Dunaweal Lane; 707-942-4981.*

The Henry Moore sculpture at Clos Pegase represents Gaia, the ancient Greek "Mother Earth."

CHAMPAGNE AND SPARKLING WINES

If you don't like dry Champagne say so. A moderately sweet (or moderately dry)
Champagne is a human kind. A Brut is not. It is an acquired taste.

—*Hilaire Belloc*

Sparkling wines are, despite the mystique surrounding them, nothing more or less than wines in which carbon dioxide is suspended, making them bubbly. Sparkling wines were perfected in Champagne, France's northernmost wine district, where wines tend to be a bit acidic because grapes do not always fully ripen. That's why sparkling wines have traditionally been naturally tart, even austere.

Because of their progenitor's birthplace, many sparkling wines are often called "Champagne." However, this term designates a region of origin, so it really shouldn't be used for American sparkling wines. That's not to say that Napa and Sonoma county sparkling wines are in any way inferior to French ones—some are even better. The French Champagne houses are fully aware of the excellence of the California product and have been quick to cash in on the laurels gathered by such pioneers as Hanns Kornell, Schramsberg, and Iron Horse by establishing sparkling-wine cellars in Sonoma and Napa with American partners.

Keep in mind that although we no longer need to drink pricey imported Champagne, quality American sparklers don't come cheap. Good sparkling wine will always be expensive because a great amount of work goes into making it.

Harvest

It starts with the harvest. White sparkling wines are made from white and black grapes, which allows them to achieve complex flavors. Growers pick the black grapes carefully to avoid crushing them. The goal is to minimize contact between the inner fruit and the skins, where the purply-red color pigments reside. The grapes are rushed to the winery, crushed very gently, and the juice is strained off the skins right away, again, to prevent the juice from coming in contact with pigments and turning red. (The juice of the black grape's inner fruit is usually white.) Even so, some sparklers have more of a pink tinge to them than the winemaker intends.

Sparkling wines are traditionally made from pinot noir (and, in France, from pinot meunier as well) and chardonnay grapes. In California, pinot blanc, riesling, and other white wine grapes may also be used.

In the disgorging process, the lees are removed from the bottle.

Fermentation

The freshly pressed juice and pulp, or must, is fermented with special yeasts that preserve the wine's fruit, the characteristic fruit flavor of the grape variety used. Before bottling, this finished "still" wine (wine without bubbles) is mixed with a *liqueur de tirage,* a blend of wine, sugar, and yeast. This mixture causes the wine to ferment again—in the bottle, where it stays for 6 to 12 weeks. Carbon dioxide, a by-product of fermentation, is produced and trapped in the bottle, where it dissolves in the wine (instead of escaping into the air, as happens during fermentation in barrel, vat, or tank). This captive carbon dioxide transforms the still wine into a sparkling wine. The second fermentation also raises the wine's alcohol content by about one percent. This is one reason why grapes for sparkling wines are picked at low sugar levels: they must ferment out initially to 11 percent alcohol instead of the 12 percent (or more) of regular wines.

Aging

Bottles of new sparkling wine are stored on their sides in deep cellars. The wine now ages *sur lie,* or "on the lees" (the dead yeast cells and other deposits trapped in the bottle). This aging process enriches the wine's texture and embellishes the complexity of its bouquet. The amount of time a sparkling wine ages *sur lie* bears a direct relation to its quality: the longer the aging, the more complex the wine.

Riddling

The lees must be removed from the bottle before a sparkling wine can be enjoyed. This is achieved in a process whose first step is called "riddling." In the past, each bottle, head tilted slightly downward, was placed in a riddling rack, an A-frame with many holes of bottleneck size. Riddlers gave each bottle a slight shake and a downward turn, every day if possible. This continued for six weeks, until each bottle rested upside down in the hole and the sediment had collected in the neck, next to the cork. Simple as this sounds, it is actually very difficult to do. Hand-riddling is a fine art perfected after much training. Today, most sparkling wines are riddled in ingeniously designed machines called gyro palettes, which riddle up to 500 or more bottles at one time, though at some wineries the work is still done partially or entirely by hand.

Disgorging

After riddling, the bottles are "disgorged." The upside-down bottles are placed in a deeply chilled solution, which freezes the sediments in a block that attaches itself to the crown cap sealing the bottle. The cap and frozen plug are removed, the bottle is topped off with a wine-and-sugar mixture called "dosage" and recorked with the traditional champagne cork. The dosage determines the final sweetness of a sparkling wine.

. . . and ends with the signature cork.

Brut to Doux

Sparkling wines with 1.5 percent sugar or less are labeled "brut"; those with 1.2 to 2 percent sugar are called "extra dry"; those with 1.7 to 3.5 percent are called "sec"; and those with 3.5 to 5 percent, "demi-sec." "Doux" (sweet) sparkling wine has more than 5 percent sugar. Most sparkling-wine drinkers refuse to admit that they like their bubbly on the sweet side, and this labeling convention allows them to drink sweet while pretending to drink dry. It's a marketing ploy invented in Champagne at least a century ago. A sparkling wine to which no dosage has been added will be bone dry (and taste "sour" to some) and may be called "extra-brut" or "natural."

Vintage Dating

Most sparkling wines are not vintage dated but are "assembled" (the term sparkling-wine makers use instead of "blended") to create a *cuvée,* a mix of different wines and sometimes different vintages consistent with the house style. However, sparkling wines may be vintage dated in very great years.

Bulk or Charmat Process

Sparkling wine may also be made by time- and cost-saving bulk methods, although this is not done with Champagne. In the bulk or Charmat process, the secondary fermentation takes place in large tanks rather than individual bottles. Each tank is basically treated as one huge bottle. After the bubbles have developed, the sediments are filtered from the wine and the wine is bottled. But at a price: such sparkling wine has neither the complexity nor the bubble quality of the more slowly made sparklers. In the United States, sparkling wine made in this way must be labeled "Bulk Process" or "Charmat Process."

Sparkling wines made in the traditional, time-consuming fashion may be labeled *méthode champenoise* or "wine fermented in this bottle." But read carefully. One sparkler labels itself "wine made in the bottle." There's quite a difference in methodology here between "this" and "the." The latter is sparkling wine made in the transfer process, in which the second fermentation of the wine takes place in a bottle, but in which all the bottles of a particular batch—instead of being disgorged individually— are emptied into large tanks, under pressure. The sediments are filtered out, the wine is rebottled, corked, and shipped to market.

The different processes of making sparkling wine have an effect not only on the quality and complexity of the wine itself but also on the quality of the bubbles. Filtered wines are not as complex as unfiltered ones: their bubbles are more sparingly distributed, and they do not last very long. But that doesn't really matter, since most wines made like this are drunk quickly, at parties or weddings.

Castello di Amorosa   *map page 107, B-3*

Looking for all the world like a medieval castle, complete with drawbridge, stables, and secret passageways, the Castello di Amorosa even has a chapel where mass is performed in Latin every Sunday. Opened in 2007 after 14 years of construction, this brainchild of Dario Sattui, who also owns several properties in Tuscany, shows his passion for medieval Italian architecture. Some of the 107 rooms contain replicas of 13th-century frescoes, and the dungeon has an actual iron maiden from Nuremberg, Germany. You must sign up for a tour to see most of the extensive property, although paying for a tasting allows you some access, as well as samples of several of their excellent Italian-style wines. *4045 North St. Helena Highway; 707-967-6272.*

■ CALISTOGA   *map page 107, A-1/2*

From Lincoln Avenue, Calistoga's main street, you can see Mount St. Helena rising to the north, some 4,000 feet above the valley floor, along with other mountains to the west and east. The false-fronted shops, old hotels, and stone buildings look like those of a cattle town tucked into a remote mountain valley. A hundred years ago there were holdups of the stagecoach line that ran across the shoulder of Mount St. Helena to Clear Lake carrying the payroll for the quicksilver mines dotting the mountains. There was even a gold mine here, high above Calistoga, but the town's true claim to fame came from its waters, which bubbled from natural hot springs.

When Sam Brannan—Mormon missionary, entrepreneur, and vineyard developer—learned in 1859 that a place in Napa Valley called Agua Caliente by the settlers did indeed have hot springs and even an "old faithful" geyser, he bought up 2,000 acres of prime property and laid out a resort. Planning a place that would rival New York's famous Saratoga Hot Springs, he built an elegant hotel, bathhouses, cottages, stables, an observatory, and a distillery. The distillery proved to be the only moneymaker; its brandy was shipped as far as Europe.

The resort remained unprofitable even after the railroad reached Calistoga in 1868, and the town never became a world-class resort. But Californians kept coming to "take the waters," supporting a sprinkling of small hotels and bathhouses built wherever a hot spring bubbled to the surface. These getaways are still going, and you can come for an old-school experience of mud baths (mixed from mineral water, peat, and volcanic ash) or naturally warm mineral baths.

(previous pages) Barrels large and small at Sterling Vineyards.

Low-key Calistoga sits atop natural hot springs.

Calistoga remains an understated sort of place, with quiet, tree-shaded back streets and mellow bed-and-breakfasts. And, if you've been shocked by the big crowds and high prices farther down the valley in St. Helena and Yountville, casual Calistoga might be the place for you to set up your home base while exploring the valley. The Napa River flows right through town, but you'll be hard-pressed to find a sign directing you to the places where you can dangle your feet in its cold waters. Park at Pioneer Park on Cedar Street, just north of Lincoln Street, walk past the white gingerbread bandstand, and take the short trail down to the river.

The trail continues across the river—merely a creek at this point—on a concrete walk that leads to two worthwhile sites: the **Sharpsteen Museum** (1311 Washington Street; 707-942-5911) and the adjoining **Sam Brannan Cottage.** The museum was founded by Ben Sharpsteen, a Walt Disney animator, after Sharpsteen had retired to Calistoga. It contains detailed dioramas showing how the resort looked in its heyday. Other permanent and rotating exhibits cover the region's past, from the indigenous Wappo people who once lived here to World War II. The cottage, one of three in town to survive from town founder Sam Brannan's day, has been restored to its original appearance.

A GREAT DRIVE IN NORTHERN NAPA

You'll need some prior planning for this suggested day's drive; a few of the wineries require reservations. Starting in St. Helena, get an early start and head south on Highway 29 a few miles until you see the Rubicon Estate sign on your right. This will start your day with a glamorous locale and robust cabernets from historic local vineyards. From Rubicon, return along the driveway and go straight across Highway 29 onto Rutherford Road. About 1½ miles past Highway 29 you'll see a driveway on your left for Round Pond. If you've made a reservation, you can stop at Round Pond for a tour and tasting at the olive mill. Picnic lunches are also available here by reservation.

After lunch, head back to Highway 29. Two wineries off this stretch are particularly worth visiting, and both require reservations. If you've made an appointment at Schramsberg, turn right off Highway 29 on Peterson Road, and then another quick right on Schramsberg Lane. The road is very narrow and winding; you'll have to pull to the side if another car is coming in the opposite direction. After visiting, return to Highway 29 and turn right (south), to continue toward St. Helena. If you've booked a visit at Stony Hill instead, take Highway 29 south until you pass Bale Lane on your left. Start looking for the turnoff to the Bale Grist Mill Historic Park on your right. Turn right, drive past the parking lot for the park, and follow the winding unmarked road up the hill for about five minutes until you see the small sign for Stony Hill. After your visit, return to Highway 29 the way you came, turn right, and continue south for another couple of miles to return to downtown St. Helena.

Shops and restaurants along Lincoln Avenue in downtown Calistoga tend to cater to locals rather than visitors, and you'll find few of the high-priced boutiques popular in places like St. Helena. If you haven't picked up too many bottles at the wineries already, you might want to stop at the **Enoteca Wine Shop** (1348B Lincoln Avenue; 707-942-1117), where extensive tasting notes are posted for most of the wines they sell. At the edge of downtown Calistoga, the **Wine Garage** (1020 Highway 29; 707-942-5332) attracts bargain-hunting oenophiles with its policy of stocking only wines that cost $25 a bottle or less. The wine buyers seek out small vintners producing undervalued wines, so you'll always discover something new and exciting here.

At 4,344 feet, Mount St. Helena is the region's highest peak.

NAPA VALLEY
COUNTRY ROADS

What could be more romantic than driving along a winding Wine Country back road, past development-free oak forests, vineyards, and horse pastures? When planning a tour of Napa Valley wineries, consider setting aside a day or two to explore some that are off the beaten path. You'll need to change your mindset for this. Don't be in a hurry. Be patient with lumbering pieces of farm machinery and with the occasional herd of cattle slowly mooing down the road. These pauses will give you time to see the sights: strange rock formations, uncommon trees such as tanbark oak and cypress, vivid wildflowers. The relaxed pace continues at the wineries, where you might be the only visitor in sight.

Watch for wildlife in unexpected places. Deer, for example, have a way of popping up behind blind curves, and hawks and eagles in pursuit of prey will skim across the road at breakneck speed. On several back roads you might venture down steep trails to creeks and rivers. Beware of poison oak, rattlesnakes, and "No Trespassing" signs. Stay on established trails, being careful not to trample fragile vegetation, and never pick wildflowers since some of them will not grow back.

■ OUTSIDE CALISTOGA

Even if you don't have time to travel as far afield as Mount St. Helena, you can get a taste of the sleepy pace and dramatic scenery of Napa's northern border just a 5- to 10-minute drive north of Calistoga. Here the Mayacamas and Vaca ranges hem in the valley floor—welcoming turf for warm-weather grapes like zinfandel and cabernet sauvignon. The following wineries are in the newly created AVA, approved in 2009 after years of legal wrangling.

★ Storybook Mountain Vineyards *map page 147, A-2*

Although this tiny winery is barely visible, tucked into a rock face in the Mayacamas range, the vineyard is one of the most beautiful in the Wine Country, with vines rising steeply from the winery in dramatic tiers. Zinfandel is king here, and those produced by Jerry and Sigrid Seps are deep red in color, full-flavored, and richly complex, with a unique peppery spiciness. These well-structured wines age beautifully. They even make a Zin Gris, an unusual dry rosé of zinfandel grapes. (Traditionally, in Burgundy, vin gris is made from pinot noir grapes.)

Tastings (reservations required) are preceded by a low-key tour, during which visitors walk into the picture-perfect vineyard and learn how zinfandel grapes, usually prone to mildew because the grapes grow in such tight clusters, thrive on their eastern-facing slopes. Next comes a visit to the atmospheric tunnels, parts of which have the same rough-hewn look as they did when Chinese laborers painstakingly dug them around 1888. *3835 Highway 128; 707-942-5310.*

Chateau Montelena   *map page 147, A-2*

Chateau Montelena is the architectural equivalent of a mash-up; its French-style, gray stone château rises above an artificial lake dotted with ornate red Chinese pavilions. The man behind the château was California senator Alfred L. Tubbs, who had it constructed in 1882, when the California wine industry was booming because the phylloxera root louse had sucked France's vines dry. The lake and Chinese touches came in the late 1950s, added by a Chinese engineer who

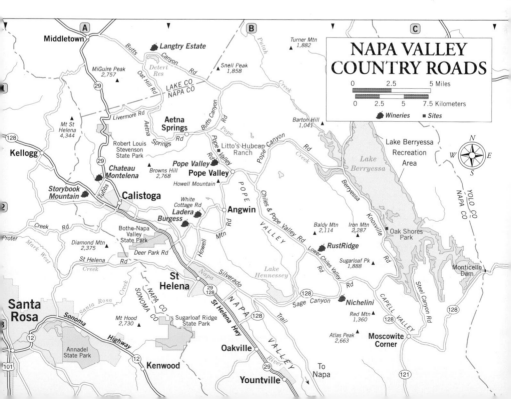

bought the property as a retirement home. You'll get the best view of this quirky combination as you walk up the hill from the driveway, past the duck-filled pond. From here the château, with its ivy-covered facade, little turrets, and ornamental crenellations, looks like it's straight out of a fairy tale.

Los Angeles attorney Jim Barrett rescued the property from hard times in the early 1970s, restored the winery, and hired Miljenko "Mike" Grgich as winemaker. Enlisting Grgich proved to be a stroke of genius: his 1973 chardonnay took first place in the famous 1976 Judgment of Paris tasting of top French and Californian wines. (The events at Château Montelena leading up to the competition are depicted in the largely fictional 2008 movie *Bottle Shock,* portions of which were filmed here. Call ahead if you're interested in taking a tour featuring some of the movie locations.) Grgich has since left to open his own winery, but the Chateau Montelena wines, now made by Bo Barrett, are still world-class. Be sure to taste the chardonnay, whose bright citrus and green apple flavors shine through since the wine doesn't undergo malolactic fermentation. The estate-grown cabernet sauvignon has lots of big berry and cassis flavors. *1429 Tubbs Lane; 707-942-5105.*

■ OVER MOUNT ST. HELENA TO GUENOC LAKE

At 4,344 feet, Mount St. Helena is the tallest peak in the Bay Area, and the curving road across it is splendidly scenic. If you drive slowly, you can take note of the changing vegetation and the variety of rock formations. **Middletown**, at an altitude of about 1,100 feet, lies exactly midway between Lower Lake and Calistoga, in the heart of the Loconoma Valley. Though there's not much reason to dawdle in Middletown, where feed stores and hardware stores line the streets, it's a good place to stop for gas and lunch. The **Cowpoke Cafe** (21118 Calistoga Road; 707-987-0661) is hard to miss, painted inside and out like a black-and-white Holstein. At the north end of town, Butts Canyon Road leads east through grassy fields, where cattle graze in the pastures. Keep an eye out for wild boars, which abound in this valley. The white plumes rising in the hills to the west are steam plumes from volcanic fumaroles, which operate in principle much like a geyser, except that the water turns to steam before it reaches the surface. As Butts Canyon Road approaches Detert Reservoir, often called Guenoc Lake, you might spot ducks, geese, and perhaps even a blue heron or bald eagle.

(above) This house was occupied by the British actress Lillie Langtry when she owned Guenoc Ranch, from 1888 to 1906. (following pages) The view from Langtry House.

Langtry Estate & Vineyards   *map page 147, A-1*

A long driveway leads to this hilltop winery, built to resemble the old Langtry barn that still stands about 2 miles south of the winery, but with a difference—it's the size of a football field. Langtry owns a whopping 21,000 acres and produces about 250,000 cases a year. Still, it feels like a much smaller operation, and the few visitors in the tasting room are likely to be friends and neighbors of the staff. Many of their wines are modest, but they are likeable and well balanced. Standouts include a Lake County petite sirah with big berry and spice flavors, as well as a port of petite sirah.

When visiting, be sure to pick up a brochure for the self-guided tour near the entrance; it explains a bit about the layout of the vast property, so you'll know which vineyards you're seeing as you look across the Guenoc Valley floor. The white manor in the distance, half-hidden by huge valley oaks, is the house where the British actress Lillie Langtry stayed when she owned Guenoc Ranch in the late 19th century. *21000 Butts Canyon Road; 707-987-9127.*

■ POPE VALLEY AND CHILES VALLEY

Grapes were first planted in the valleys just east and over a ridge from the Napa Valley floor in 1854, when stagecoaches ran from St. Helena across the ridges separating the Guenoc and Napa valleys. Today, the forest has reclaimed formerly cultivated land, but you can still tell the course of the old road by the moss-covered stone walls along its margins. Here and there in the woods you'll discover the ruin of an abandoned winery, and you may stumble over an ancient vine hanging in among the oaks, laurels, and pines. South of Guenoc Lake, Pope Valley narrows dramatically and becomes densely overgrown with oaks, laurels, cypresses, gray pines, and chaparral scrub.

Another few miles to the southeast, Pope Valley Road enters a grassy glen, arid and golden outside the few rainy months in winter and early spring. For more than 100 years some of Napa County's best grapes have been grown here in the Pope Valley. Though not technically part of the Napa Valley, Pope Valley growers are nevertheless entitled to label their wines "Napa Valley AVA." Higher in elevation than the Napa Valley proper—and thus hotter in summer and colder in winter— Pope Valley is best know for sauvignon blanc, as well as sangiovese, cabernet sauvignon, and merlot grapes, many of which are snapped up by Napa winemakers such as St. Supéry, who are attracted by prices that are sometimes half what they are for grapes grown around Rutherford.

Slightly above Pope Valley lies Chiles Valley, which constitutes its own AVA. The climate in Chiles Valley, a rugged, narrow slice in the Vaca Mountains, is similar to that in Oakville and Rutherford, and like those regions, Chiles has a reputation for big cabernets and zinfandels. Because of the higher elevation, though, it's a bit colder here in the winter, so the grapes are harvested later..

Although there are few signs of civilization in Pope Valley, it does have at least one quirky tourist attraction: **Litto's Hubcap Ranch** (Pope Valley Road, near Pope Valley Winery), a private home where every fence, tree, and building is plastered with hubcaps. The creator of this odd folk art project, Emanuele "Litto" Dimonte, died in 1985, but his family has kept the thousands of hubcaps he spent years collecting. Though the property is strictly off limits to visitors, you can appreciate Litto's handiwork glinting in the sun as you drive by.

Pope Valley Winery   *map page 147, B-2*
You may have to peek into the barrel room to find someone to pour wines for you in this simple tasting room with a corrugated tin roof. That's because this

Trail Up Mount St. Helena

Although the hike to the top of Mount St. Helena isn't exactly a walk in the park—the steep trail tends to get even steeper just when you're wishing it wouldn't—the views are a wonderful payoff. As you near the peak, you'll get a sudden, dramatic look at the Napa Valley stretching south from the foot of the mountains to the salt marshes of San Pablo Bay. The hills of Sonoma County ripple to the west.

To reach the trailhead, drive up Highway 29 north of Calistoga to the crest of the road, where there are two large dirt parking areas on either side of the highway (a small sign reading "Robert Louis Stevenson State Park" will warn you it's coming up). A trail starting at the eastern parking area leads to the palisades—steep-sided cliffs of volcanic origin—and into very scenic backcountry. A grassy flat above the western parking area was the site of a tollhouse used in the days when the highway was a toll road frequented by stagecoaches, miners, and highwaymen. Stairs mark the trail leading to the top of the mountain. This trail passes the site of the cabin occupied by Robert Louis Stevenson and his bride, Fanny Osbourne, in the summer of 1880. A monument, carved in the shape of an open book, commemorates the couple's stay. The 5.1-mile trail continues uphill to connect with the well-traveled dirt fire road that runs all the way to the top. Much of the trail lacks shade, so bring plenty of water. In summer it gets glaringly hot, but if you come in another season, bring an extra layer to keep you warm on the windy summit.

rustic little winery producing about 4,000 cases a year doesn't get that many visitors. If you visit from Thursday to Sunday, however, you'll be warmly welcomed with free tasting of their wines, which include a dry chenin blanc; Bella Rosa, a dry rosé of sangiovese that has a bit more oomph that your average rosé; and a merlot. They also make chenin blanc, zinfandel, and more. Though tours are not regularly scheduled, ask whether anyone has time to show you around the small, rough-hewn cave dug into the hillside next to the tasting room. *6613 Pope Valley Road; 707-965-1246.*

RustRidge Winery   *map page 147, B-2*

Though it's only a 20-minute drive from the Napa that most visitors know, secluded RustRidge feels more like Oklahoma or Montana than the California Wine Country. Signs on Lower Chiles Valley Road point you toward their property, where you'll wind your way past fairly arid land, barns, horse paddocks, and farm equipment before finding the tasting room. The property—now owned by Susan Meyer and her husband, Jim Fresquez—was purchased by the Meyer family in 1972 as a Thoroughbred horse ranch, and Jim continues to breed and train horses here; you're likely to see some of his foals right outside the tasting room. You can even stay overnight here: there's a five-room bed-and-breakfast.

Their chardonnay, which undergoes partial malolactic fermentation, has lively acidity that makes it very food-friendly, and their flagship Racehorse Red, a zinfandel, cabernet sauvignon, and petite sirah blend, is particularly attractive. *2910 Lower Chiles Valley Road; 707-965-9353.*

Nichelini Winery   *map page 147, B/C-3*

Opened around 1890 by the Swiss-Italian immigrant Anton Nichelini, this winery is still owned and run by his descendants and their families, making Nichelini the oldest family-owned and continuously operated winery in the Napa Valley. The old winery buildings cling to a steep embankment where the road skirts a cliff, making it one of the more scenic properties in the area. (Luckily, there's a picnic area here.) The wines to taste are the zinfandel and the crisp and very refreshing sauvignon vert. The latter grape, often grown in Bordeaux, where it is known as muscadelle, is usually blended with other grapes, but here it makes a delightful single-varietal wine redolent of tropical fruit. The winery is open for tastings on weekends only, though they can sometimes make time for visitors on weekdays, so it pays to call ahead. It is so small, there is no need for tours. The tasting counter is in a barrel room, and most of the equipment sits outside. *2970 Sage Canyon Road; 707-963-0717.*

■ HOWELL MOUNTAIN APPELLATION

The rugged heights of the Howell Mountain AVA spread out over 14,000 acres, but a mere 600 or so are planted with vines. This will surely change in the next several years, though, as vintners vie for coveted permits to clear the dense forests of the high, rolling plateau and plant vines. The soil is skimpy on the nutrients (no rich alluvial dirt here). The stressed vines thus yield small, flavor-packed grapes with thick skins that yield firm tannins. Wineries throughout Napa have been buying grapes grown here for years, although in recent decades the region has largely flown under the radar and received little press and even fewer visitors. Though visitors are still few and far between here—in part because many of the wineries are not open to the public—Howell Mountain seems poised to become the next big thing.

Burgess Cellars   *map page 147, B-2*
This old stone winery, built in 1875 by a Swiss winemaker named Carlo Rossini, is a real cliff-hanger, hugging the steep western flank of Howell Mountain. It is the site of the original Souverain Cellars, which opened here in 1942 and shared in the post-Prohibition Napa Valley wine resurrection. Tom Burgess bought the winery in 1972, just in time to share in another renaissance, and he has consistently made superb merlot, cabernet sauvignon, and syrah. The wines became less tannic and more elegant in the mid-1980s, but that did not diminish their aging capability. A mature Burgess red is truly a great experience. Luckily for those who didn't stock their cellars with Burgess wines decades ago, the winery sets aside 10 percent of each of their cabernets to re-release at least ten years later, and you can taste and purchase these library wines—some of them up to 30 years old—at the winery. Tastings are by appointment only, but they also pour their wines at the tasting room Wineries of Napa Valley, in downtown Napa (see the Southern Napa Valley chapter). *1108 Deer Park Road; 707-963-4766.*

Ladera Vineyards   *map page 147, B-2*
Ladera means "hillside" in Spanish, and that alone tells you a lot about this winery, which harvests its grapes from two vineyards on far sides of the Napa Valley: one on rugged and steep Mt. Veeder, on the west side of the valley, and the other on Howell Mountain to the east. Both yield the intensely flavored grapes that are characteristic of well-drained hillside vineyards. Though full-bodied cabernets are Ladera's claim to fame, it also produces a bit of sauvignon blanc, merlot, malbec, and syrah.

A GREAT DRIVE ON NAPA'S COUNTRY ROADS

From Calistoga, drive north on Highway 29 to Tubbs Lane. Turn left and you'll soon see the entrance to Chateau Montelena on your right (the sign is small and the driveway easily missed, so drive slowly). After visiting the winery, return to Highway 29 and turn left. The routes winds steeply up the slopes of Mount St. Helena until you reach the crest, where dirt parking lots on either side of the road invite you to park and hike in Robert Louis Stevenson State Park. After your hike, continue on Highway 29 north, this time winding downhill to Middletown. You might want to stop in Middletown for lunch, as you won't be seeing any more restaurants until you return at the end of the day.

At the end of town, turn right onto Butts Canyon Road, where you'll wind past endless white wooden fences and pastureland. When you see Guenoc Lake in front of you, veer left onto Canyon Road and look for the sign for Langtry Estate on your left. A highlight of the visit is the splendid views down over the valley from the terrace. Return to Canyon Road and turn left. Eventually Butts Canyon Road turns into Aetna Springs Road; here turn left onto Pope Valley Road. Soon you'll see Litto's Hubcap Ranch on your left. Stay right at the Y to follow Chiles and Pope Valley Road. When you come to the Y, stay left to follow Lower Chiles Valley Road rather than right to stay on Chiles and Pope Valley Road. In about a mile you'll see a sign on leading you left to RustRidge Winery. After your visit, return to Lower Chiles Valley Road, turn right, then turn left on Chiles and Pope Valley Road in about a mile. As the road rounds Lake Hennessey, veer left onto Highway 128, which will return you to the Silverado Trail. Turning right on the Silverado Trail will return you to Calistoga.

The Howell hillside also has a hand in the crushing process. Though Ladera has been producing wines here only since 2000, their splendid three-story stone winery dates back to1886. Because of the sloping land, each story of the building has its own ground-level entry. The grapes could then be put on the top floor for crushing, and gravity would do its work to get the juice down to the bottom floor. This gravity-flow system is still used today. Tours of the historic property, which include a glimpse of the underground caves, are available by appointment only on every day but Sunday. *150 White Cottage Road South; 707-965-2445.*

Carneros District vineyards.

CARNEROS DISTRICT

Los Carneros American Viticultural Area, established in 1983, stretches across the cool lower reaches of Sonoma and Napa counties. The word *carneros* means "sheep" in Spanish, and the slopes now covered with vines were once thought to be good only as pasture. Today, however, the only sheep you're likely to see are the metal sheep sculptures grazing in front of the museum and art preserve di Rosa, as winemakers have snapped up almost every available acre, sending land values through the roof. Though vintners have clearly wised up to the value of the Carneros region, visitors have been slower to catch on. Most zip right through in their haste to get to big-name spots to the north—but if you check out a few of these places, odds are you'll become a convert.

To understand how different the Carneros is from the other California wine-producing regions, you must approach it from the roads that border the water. From San Francisco, travel north on U.S. 101 to Novato and take the Highway 37 turnoff to the east, which will take you along the northern reaches of San Francisco Bay, at this point called San Pablo Bay. On a gray day, the flat marshes and low hills near the bay look bleak indeed, more like a Scottish moor than a California shore. During summer and autumn, strong west winds blow in from the ocean each afternoon, tempering the hot days.

The soils here are shallow and not particularly fertile, which means that the vines struggle to produce fruit. Though it seems that this would be a drawback, in fact it's a plus. Vines that grow slowly and yield less fruit tend to produce very concentrated, high-acid grapes that are ideal for winemaking. Grapegrowers in the mid-19th century recognized this and planted vast tracts here. Because of the low yields, some of the land was allowed to revert to sheep pasture after phylloxera destroyed the vines in the 1890s. But the reputation of the grapes survived, and shortly after the repeal of Prohibition, vines once again began to spread across the hills.

Pinot noir and chardonnay grapes are considered king here, as they thrive in the moderate temperatures of the exposed, windy slopes. These days, however, wine-makers are also trying out merlot and syrah, which are also considered well suited to the cool winds, thin soil, and low rainfall. (Carneros generally gets less rain than elsewhere in Napa and Sonoma.) Even warm-climate grapes such as cabernet

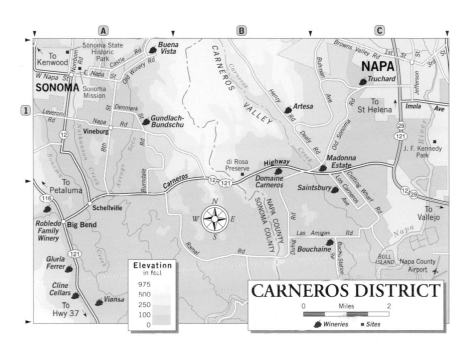

sauvignon can ripen well in favored Carneros locations. Though many of these grapes are cultivated by small Carneros wineries that use them to make estate wines, many are instead purchased by wineries elsewhere in Napa and Sonoma. High-profile places like Robert Sinskey, Domaine Chandon, and Beaulieu Vineyard have all tapped the Carneros grape supply to make wines of great complexity and depth.

■ SONOMA COUNTY WINERIES

Viansa Winery *map page 159, A-2*

If you're traveling to Sonoma County from San Francisco, one of the first wineries you'll pass is Viansa (which perhaps explains the crowds and occasional tour buses). The winery building, with its red-tile roof and ochre walls, has that Tuscan-villa look, and the extensive grounds encompass an olive grove, picnic facilities, and a spacious marketplace. Better yet, they overlook wetlands that are an important stopover for birds traveling along the Pacific Flyway, a major route for birds migrating along the West Coast, from South America to Alaska.

This plaque and sculpture celebrate the wetlands surrounding Viansa Winery.

Italian varietals hold sway in the vineyards: nebbiolo, sangiovese, and pinot grigio, in addition to lesser-known grapes such as vernaccia and tocai friulano. The market reaches far beyond the usual tasting room, selling cookbooks, housewares, and light meals like focaccia sandwiches, pasta salads, and gelato. The picnic tables, some of which are shaded by olive trees, overlook the wetlands below, where you might spot one of the many species of birds that pass through here, including egrets, Canada geese, and red-tailed hawks. *25200 Arnold Drive/Highway 121; 707-935-4700.*

Cline Cellars   *map page 159, A-2*

If you visit here on a summer day, you'll likely get a blast of the wind for which the Carneros region is known. The stiff breeze is the result of the Petaluma Gap, a sort of wind tunnel created by a break in the mountains. Although Cline has planted vineyards here, most of the grapes it uses come from old vines grown in the Oakley area of Contra Costa County. Both areas produce some less-familiar Rhône varietals, making this a good place to surprise your palate.

Zinfandel and heat-loving Rhône varieties such as marsanne, mourvèdre, and carignane thrive in the Oakley climate. Here in the Carneros, Rhône varietals such as syrah, roussanne, and viognier fill most of their vineyards, rather than the pinot noir and chardonnay grapes more common in the region. The marsanne has an uncommonly zesty citrus flavor, and the mourvèdre has a slightly more exotic, spicier flavor than the more familiar cabernet sauvignon. Be sure to taste the dark-red carignane, but there are also syrah and zinfandel for more traditional palates. The 1850s farmhouse that houses the tasting room has a pleasant wraparound porch for enjoying the weeping willow trees, ponds, and rosebushes on the property. Tastings and tours are offered daily. *24737 Arnold Drive/Highway 121; 707-940-4030.*

Gloria Ferrer Champagne Caves   *map page 159, A-2*

The Spanish hacienda style of this winery makes it look sunny even on a gray Carneros day. The Spanish sparkling-wine maker Freixenet was the first winery to start producing Carneros fizz, establishing this site in 1982. Vintner Bob Iantosca crafts superb sparkling wines from his beloved chardonnay and pinot noir grapes, but still finds the time to make a small quantity of still wines, making him something of a rarity among winemakers. Tours here, which include the caves and a glimpse of some antique wine-making equipment, are offered daily. You can enjoy the tastings either seated indoors or, weather permitting, out on the terrace. *23555 Highway 121; 707-996-7256.*

Robledo Family Winery   *map page 159, A-1*

Founded by Reynaldo Robledo, Sr., a former migrant worker from Michoacán, Mexico, this relative newcomer to the Carneros region is truly a family affair. You're likely to encounter one of the charming Robledo sons in the tasting room, where he'll proudly tell you the story of the immigrant family while pouring sauvignon blanc, pinot noir, merlot, cabernet sauvignon, and other wines, including a chardonnay that comes from the vineyard right outside the tasting room's door. All seven Robledo sons and two Robledo daughters, as well as matriarch Maria, are involved in the winery operations. If you don't run into them on your visit, you'll see their names and pictures on the bottles of wine, such as the Dos Hermanas late-harvest dessert wine, or one of the ports dedicated to Maria Robledo. *21901 Bonness Road; 707-939-6903.*

■ NAPA COUNTY WINERIES

★ Domaine Carneros   *map page 159, B-1/2*
As you travel from Sonoma County to Napa County on Highway 121, you will see a majestic château on the right side of the highway. If you think it looks like it belongs in France, you're right: It's a copy of the Château de la Marquetterie, an 18th-century mansion owned by the Taittinger family in Champagne, France. This is home to Domaine Carneros, established in 1987 by the Taittinger Champagne house along with a few American partners. The sparkling wines made here are austere, the perfect accompaniment for fresh oysters. Instead of offering tastings like most wineries, Domaine Carneros sells tasting flights, full glasses, and bottles of their bubbly treat and serves them with hors d'oeuvres to those seated in the Louis XV–inspired salon or on the terrace. Though this makes a visit here a tad more expensive than most stops on a winery tour, it's also one of the most opulent ways to enjoy the Carneros District. There is a visitors center that's open daily, and tours are offered. *1240 Duhig Road; 707-257-0101.*

Madonna Estate   *map page 159, B/C-1*
Winemaker Andrea Bartolucci, whose family has been growing grapes in Napa since 1922, oversees the 160 gently rolling acres of vines here. He uses organic and dry farming techniques to grow nearly a dozen kinds of grapes. (Dry farming, which leaves established vines to rely on rainwater, stresses the plants, resulting in a smaller yield but more intensely flavored grapes.) Though the winery's location right on Highway 121 is less scenic than some and the tasting room is modest, it's worth a visit for a taste of their crisp, lean pinot grigio, with a fresh melony aroma; the smoky, creamy chardonnay aged in French oak; and the earthy pinot noir. The muscat canelli, gewürztraminer, and riesling, produced in small quantities, are available only at the winery. Tastings are offered daily and tours are offered by appointment. *5400 Old Sonoma Road; 707-255-8864.*

Saintsbury   *map page 159, C-1/2*
Back in 1981, when Saintsbury released its first pinot noir, conventional wisdom was that only the French could produce great pinot. No matter that a few cutting-edge winemakers, like Beaulieu's André Tchelistcheff, had been making pinot from Carneros grapes since the late 1930s. But what a difference a few

Gloria Ferrer Champagne Caves, the source of the first Carneros sparkling wine.

ORGANIC WINES

If, as many grapegrowers insist, a wine is only as good as the vineyard it comes from, those who have adopted sustainable, biodynamic, or organic viticulture methods may be onto something. These approaches have exploded in popularity since the 1990s.

But what do vintners mean by "organic"? Although governmentally recognized and regulated (by the State of California as well as by the United States and the European Union), organic viticulture is vaguely defined and its value is hotly debated—just like the rest of organic farming. It boils down to a rejection of chemical fertilizers, pesticides, and fungicides. Partly because it is difficult and expensive to qualify for official certification, partly because organic vineyards have smaller yields, and partly because it is hard to grow grapes organically except in warm, dry climates, organic viticulture remains the exception rather than the rule in the industry.

Even rarer than wines produced from organically grown grapes are completely organic wines. To make an organic wine, not only do the grapes have to come from organic vineyards, but processing must use a minimum of chemical additives. Most winemakers argue that it is impossible to make truly fine wine without using at least some additives, such as sulphur dioxide (sulfites), an antioxidant that protects the color, aroma, bright flavors, and longevity of wine. And of course, organic winemaking is more expensive.

Many wineries that might qualify as partially organic resist the label, wary of its impact on their reputation. Still the movement is gaining momentum. Many major players, even if they are not certified organic, have taken steps to reduce their use of pesticides or implement other eco-friendly policies. Others like Frog's Leap, Hess, Pipestone Vineyards, and Tablas Creek grow some or all of their grapes organically. Very few producers make completely organic wine; they include Bonterra Vineyards, Coturri Winery, Organic Wine Works, Frey Vineyards, and Coates Vineyards. As demand for organic products grows, supply will no doubt follow. In the meantime, if you want organic wine, read the label carefully. To be labeled "organic," a wine must contain 100 percent certified organic grapes and have no added sulfites. Wines that contain sulfites can indicate that they are made from certified organic grapes.

decades make: the Carneros region is now thought to produce some of the best pinots in the world. If you're still in doubt, try Saintsbury's earthy, intense Brown Ranch pinot noir. Their other pinot noirs are lighter in style and more fruit-forward. Named for the English author and critic George Saintsbury (he of *Notes on a Cellar-Book* fame), the winery also makes chardonnay, syrah, and a delightful vin gris. The quality of the wine makes Saintsbury well worth a visit, but you must make an appointment to do so. *1500 Los Carneros Avenue; 707-252-0592.*

★ **Artesa Winery**   *map page 159, B-1*

Artesa is a monument to the old saying that if at first you don't succeed, try, try again. Opened in 1991, the winery made sparkling wine but failed to find its stride, so its owners changed its name and its product. Artesa released its first still wines in 1999. Now very successful, the winery consistently turns out strong wines, primarily cabernet sauvignon, chardonnay, merlot, and pinot noir.

Though burrowed into a steep hillside, the winery is strikingly sleek. A long staircase flanked by waterfalls, sculpture, and reflecting pools leads to the entrance. Inside, large-scale artworks, including dramatic glass and metal sculptures, continue the modern look. Huge windows in the airy tasting room frame views of the vineyards below and the San Pablo Bay beyond. Tours and tastings are offered daily. *1345 Henry Road; 707-224-1668.*

Truchard Vineyards   *map page 159, C-1*

Diversity's the name of the game at this family-owned winery, which has plenty of prime acreage in the rolling hills of Carneros. Although they sell most of their grapes to others vintners (including big players like Far Niente, Nickel & Nickel, and Frog's Leap), they save some of the best for their own bottles, producing mostly 100 percent varietal versions of everything from roussanne, zinfandel, merlot, syrah, petit verdot, and cabernet sauvignon to the chardonnay and pinot noir the region is known for.

You have to reserve a tour and tasting, but if you go to the trouble you'll be rewarded with a casual but informative experience tailored to your interests. You might choose to hear about the experience of Tony and Jo Ann Truchard, the owners, who purchased their first parcel of land (formerly a plum orchard) here in 1974, or you can climb the small hill for a picture-perfect view of the pond and the pen of angora goats over the ridge. In either case you'll end up tasting their wines in a restored turn-of-the-century barn. *3234 Old Sonoma Road; 707-253-7153.*

Bouchaine Vineyards *map page 159, C-2*
Somewhat off the Highway 121 trail of wineries, these vineyards lie between the Carneros and Huichica creeks and the tidal sloughs of San Pablo Bay. The alternately breezy and foggy weather works well for the Burgundian varietals pinot noir and chardonnay, which account for most of their vines. From the lovely back patio you're likely to see hawks or even golden eagles soaring above the vineyards; they even have to place netting over the vines to keep the birds away from the grapes. Their commitment to sustainable practices is evident everywhere, from the birdhouses installed in the vineyards to the winery's redwood façade, made from their original wine tanks. Tastings are offered daily, and a brochure describes a $\frac{7}{10}$-mile self-guided tour through the vineyard behind the tasting room. *1075 Buchli Station Road; 707-252 9065.*

■ AWAY FROM THE WINERIES

For a break from wine tasting, grab a picnic lunch and take Cuttings Wharf Road south to the Napa River, stop at the public boat ramp, and dangle your feet in the river. Keep a lookout for white egrets, great blue herons, wood ducks, and other waterfowl. But beware: these waters are tricky and rise and fall with the tide. If the bleak marshes to the south look familiar, there's a reason: Francis Ford Coppola shot some of the Mekong Delta scenes for *Apocalypse Now* here.

You can also relax by the river and hike through wildflower meadows and marshes in **J. F. Kennedy Park,** just south of Napa on Highway 29. For a more rugged hike, climb the wooded knoll in **Westwood Hills Wilderness Park** (Browns Valley Road, Napa), a city-owned tract that is truly wild. **Skyline Park** (Imola Avenue, east from Highway 121) is more bucolic, with open meadows garlanded with blue and white lupines and California poppies in the spring. Wild turkeys strut their stuff uphill, where the meadows merge into the oak woods. Farther up, the banks are densely covered with small ferns, and giant chain ferns grow from the stone walls of long-abandoned buildings. The trail ends above woodsy Lake Marie, whose placid waters are shielded by the oak and madrone woods of 1,630-foot Sugarloaf Mountain.

(opposite) Domaine Carneros is a copy of the 18th-century Château de la Marquetterie.

Dramatic Artesa Winery has a small wine museum.

■ DI ROSA *map page 159, B-1*
The 20th century's last three decades were as productive for northern California artists as they were for the region's vintners. One man who participated in both realms was Rene di Rosa, vineyard owner, art collector, and (as was his late wife, Veronica), an artist. When di Rosa sold his Winery Lake Vineyard to Seagram in 1986, he withheld some of the acreage to create this stunning art and nature preserve. One of the Wine Country's best-kept secrets, this brilliant resource displays thousands of works from di Rosa's hoard, many of them figurative or abstract expressionist works. Some appear in a 130-year-old stone winery-cum-residence and barnlike galleries. Others appear where you might not expect them: in an olive grove, in a sculpture meadow, and even on the lake itself.

Some of the works were commissioned especially for the preserve, such as Paul Kos's meditative *Chartres Bleu,* a video installation in a chapel-like setting that replicates a stained-glass window of the cathedral in Chartres, France. Other highlights include Mark di Suvero's sculpture *For Veronica* (di Rosa), Veronica di Rosa's own *Endless Summer,* and numerous works by San Francisco Bay Area stalwarts

Is it art or is it nature? Veronica di Rosa's Endless Summer (1989) at di Rosa.

Robert Arneson, William T. Wiley, Viola Frey, Roy De Forest, Beth Hird, David Best, and Nathan Oliveira. The Gatehouse Gallery is open Wednesday through Friday, but to tap into the art, architecture, and landscape beyond the gatehouse, you must reserve space on a tour. The hour-long tour gives you a quick overview of the property, but it doesn't give you much time to appreciate the many works in the large main gallery. Serious art lovers should book the longer "Discovery Tour." *5200 Sonoma Highway; 707-226-5991.*

A Great Drive in Carneros

Heading up to Carneros from San Francisco, drive north on Highway 121. If you like red wines, look for Cline Cellars on your left, just after you pass Viansa. If sparkling wine is more your thing, continue past Cline less than a mile until you see the entrance for Gloria Ferrer on your left. After either visit, continue north on Highway 121, which is also called Arnold Drive along this stretch. Soon Highway 121/Highway 12 will veer to your right. Follow this road, also know as the Carneros Highway, to cross the entire length of the region.

Wineries line the rolling hills on either side of the highway, and bits of shiny reflective tape, tied to the vines to keep the birds away, flicker in the sunlight. When you see the grand French-style château on your right, turn into Domaine Carneros. Here you can sit on the terrace and order caviar or a cheese plate accompanied by a glass of bubbly. Turn right on the Carneros Highway as you leave Domaine Carneros. At Old Sonoma Road, turn left. After about a third of a mile, turn left onto Dealy Lane. Dealy Lane turns into Henry Road, which takes you right up to Artesa. After your visit, return to the Carneros Highway the way you came, then turn left. In a few miles the road intersects with Highway 29, the main thoroughfare through the Napa Valley, and from here you can continue on to any destination in Napa.

Olive trees grow on a ridge above a Sonoma Valley vineyard.

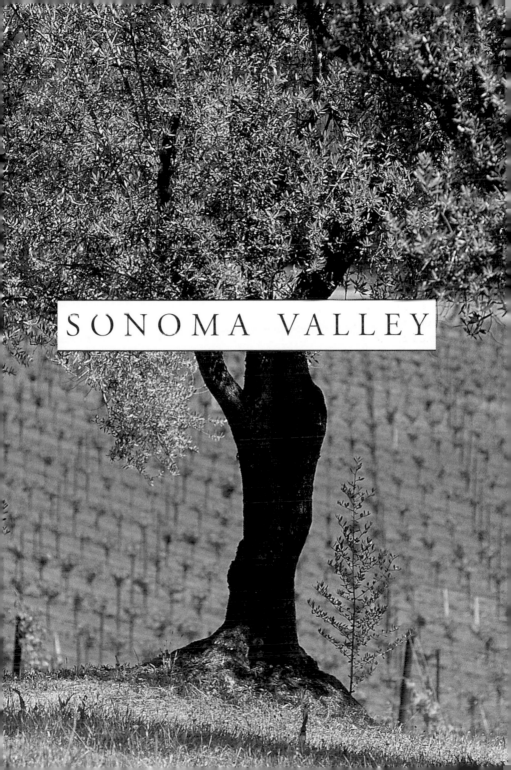

SONOMA VALLEY

Although the Sonoma Valley doesn't have quite the name recognition of its neighbor just over the Mayacamas Mountains to the east, it's hardly undiscovered territory. Once visited by oenophiles seeking smaller crowds, a less commercial, low-key atmosphere, and lower winery tour and tasting fees, Sonoma now has its own moments of Napa-esque luxury.

Along the main corridor through the Sonoma Valley, Highway 12 from Sonoma to Santa Rosa, you'll spot sophisticated inns and spas between the ubiquitous wineries. In high season, the towns of Glen Ellen and Kenwood are filled with well-heeled wine buffs. Still, the pace of life is a bit slower here than in Napa—you'll see as many bicyclists as limos zipping from one winery to the next. And the historic Sonoma Valley towns offer glimpses of the past.

There are several kinds of growing conditions and soil types crammed into this relatively compact area, so you'll find many different grape varietals growing here. The Sonoma Valley, like the Napa Valley, starts in the south on the cool, windswept, and fogbound shores of the Carneros, where chardonnay, pinot noir, merlot, and gewürztraminer vines are in great supply. Unlike the Napa Valley, however, the Sonoma Valley is open to the north as well, allowing cool marine air to funnel south from the Russian River Valley via the Santa Rosa Plain. In between, cabernet sauvignon and zinfandel are just a few of the many varietals that thrive in the relatively warm spots on the slopes of the mountains and the valley floor. The Sonoma Mountain subappellation, on the western border of the Sonoma Valley AVA, benefits from a sunny mountain location and poor rocky soil, producing deep-rooted vines and intensely flavored grapes that are made into unique, complex red wines.

■ **TOWN OF SONOMA** *map page 173*

The town of Sonoma, the valley's cultural center, is the oldest town in the Wine Country and the place where the first wine north of San Francisco was made. Founded in the early 1800s, when California was still part of Mexico, it is built around a large, tree-filled plaza that is surrounded by historic buildings, hotels, restaurants, and shops. There's plenty to keep you busy for a couple of hours here before you head out to tour wineries.

If you enter town from the south, on wide Broadway (Highway 12), you'll be retracing the last stretch of what was once California's most important road—El Camino Real, or "the king's highway," the only overland route through the state. During California's Spanish and Mexican periods, this road ran past all of the state's missions: beginning at San Diego de Alcala (1769), the first, and ending at San Francisco Solano de Sonoma (1823), the 21st and last. You can still see this last mission in the center of Sonoma.

Most of the town's historic sites, as well as its best restaurants and interesting shops, are clustered around **Sonoma Plaza**, where a staffed visitors center on the east side doles out helpful information on the town. American rebels proclaimed California's independence from Mexico here on June 14, 1846, the event marked by a statue on the northeast side of the plaza. The rebels' Bear Flag flew over the plaza until July 9, when the U.S. flag was raised and Sonoma became an American garrison town. Across the street from the statue is the site of the Mission San

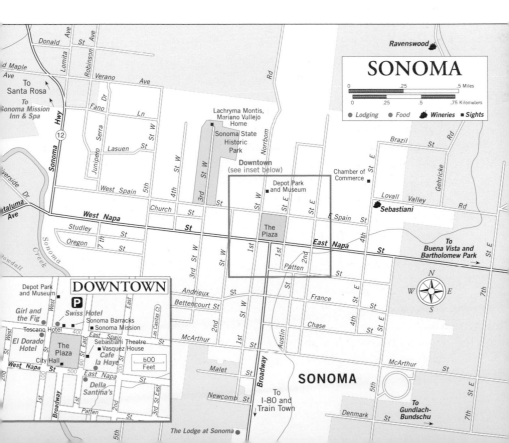

The adobe barracks of General Vallejo's Sonoma fortress.

Francisco Solano Sonoma, or **Sonoma Mission** (114 Spain Street East; 707-938-9560), most of which has been restored. Although the original mission church and its plaza are gone, the mission chapel and the adobe barracks of Mariano Vallejo's Sonoma fortress still stand. Behind the barracks is the municipal parking lot, which has unlimited free parking—there's a two-hour limit on the plaza. On the lot's north side you'll find Depot Park and the **Depot Park Museum** (270 First Street West; 707-938-1762), worth a quick stop for its local history exhibits.

Other surviving historic buildings are clustered along Spain Street, on the north side of the plaza. Notable examples include the now-empty Blue Wing Inn (133 Spain Street East), which was built by Vallejo as a guesthouse and became a notorious saloon during Gold Rush days, when the scout Kit Carson, the bandit Joaquin Murietta, and the army officer Ulysses S. Grant were patrons. The **Toscano Hotel** (20 East Spain Street) dates from the 1850s; step inside the front door to see a musty-smelling re-creation of the hotel's lobby and bar. The nearby **Vasquez House** (414 First Street East), in the El Paseo passageway off the east side of the plaza, was built in 1856 by "Fighting" Joe Hooker before he became a Union hero during the Civil War, and is open Monday, Wednesday, and Saturday from 1 to 4.

A view looking north up Sonoma Valley. In the foreground is Sonoma's town plaza.

Italian immigrant Samuele Sebastiani, who founded a local wine dynasty at the turn of the 20th century, made a major mark on the town. He refurbished the plaza's **Sonoma Hotel** (110 Spain Street West), which dates from the 1880s. He was also behind the elaborate **Sebastiani Theatre** (476 1st Street East; 707-996-2020), built in 1934 on the plaza's east side—easily spotted by its swooping marquee. You can still check out a show here, either a first-run movie or an occasional live music performance. Sebastiani built homes for his workers, donated a parochial school, built streets for the town, and contributed to many other civic projects. **Sebastiani Vineyards** is four blocks east of the plaza.

The Salvador Vallejo Adobe on the west side of the plaza (home of Mariano's brother) dates from 1846. It has been the **El Dorado Hotel** on and off for nearly 160 years (see the Where to Stay in Wine Country chapter). The building's past life was pretty gritty, with time as a brothel and boardinghouse, but you'd never guess it now, as it's a swanky modern hotel.

Although Sonoma has more than its share of historic adobes from the city's Mexican period, this is not at all a musty museum town. Nor is the plaza a museum piece—it's a place where people hang out on the shady benches, have picnics, and listen to musical performances at the small amphitheater. Two small playgrounds on the plaza ensure that every Sonoma visitor with kids stops here to play. There's also a fantastic farmers' market on Tuesday evening (April through October) and Friday morning (year-round).

The stone **City Hall** was erected on the plaza in 1906. Wonder why it looks the same from all angles? Its four sides were purposely made identical so that none of the merchants on the plaza would feel that city hall had turned its back to them. Plenty of businesses still ring the plaza, including shops, restaurants, and of course, wine-tasting rooms. Be sure to walk into the courtyards **El Paseo** and the **Mercato** on the west side of the plaza, where cafés and boutiques line the passageways.

Some of the town's best browsing will get your mouth watering. Get a head start at tasting local wines at the **Wine Exchange of Sonoma** (452 First Street East; 707-938-1794). For picnic fixings, head to the **Sonoma Cheese Factory** (2 Spain Street; 707-996-1931), which, in addition to stocking more varieties of Sonoma Jack cheese than you probably knew existed, also sells a fine selection of wines and breads. There's a coffee and gelato bar in back. A block east of the plaza, **Vella Cheese Company** (315 Second Street East; 707-938-3232) has been making

Catch a first-run movie at the old-school Sebastiani Theatre.

cheese since 1931; try their superb dry jack or sharp raw milk cheddar. For delicious—and tremendous—sandwiches and fresh-baked goods, pop into **Basque
Boulangerie** (460 First St. E; 707-935-7687), where locals line up every morning
for hot-out-of-the-oven baguettes. Nearby, the quirky **Baksheesh** (423 First St. W;
707-939-2847) sells hand-crafted gifts from the developing world, such as baskets,
art prints, and artifacts.

■ WINERIES IN TOWN

Sebastiani Vineyards   *map page 184, C-7*
Although Samuele Sebastiani established a vineyard in Sonoma in 1904, he
made only bulk wine until 1944, when his son, August, decided the wines were
good enough to carry the family name on the label. Sebastiani was soon by far the
largest winery in Sonoma County. Sebastiani was among the pioneers planting
grapes in Carneros (in the Schellville area). Lately, traditional varieties such as barbera, cabernet sauvignon, and zinfandel have been joined by roussanne, mourvèdre, and other intriguing varietals such as a hybrid that's a cross between muscat
and grenache. Although the winery is known for its hearty reds, it also produces
several white wines, including an unusual white pinot noir. When you enter the
tasting room, you might feel like you've stumbled into a housewares store rather
than a winery, it's so chockablock with porcelain serving pieces, bath products, and
even socks with pictures of grapes on them. Press on to the back of the room,
where the wines are poured. *389 Fourth Street East; 707-938-5532.*

Ravenswood   *map page 184, C-6/7*
The Ravenswood winery building looks like a hillside bunker. You almost get
the feeling these Sonomans are digging in to ward off a threatened invasion
from Napa, on the other side of the ridge. As you wind your way up Gehricke
Road, chances are you'll be following zinfandel pilgrims en route to their mecca,
for Ravenswood is adored by many for its bold zins, which generally live up to the
winery's motto "no wimpy wines."

Their zinfandel grapes, often blended with other varietals such as carignane and
petite sirah, come from vineyards as far flung as the Alexander Valley and Dry
Creek Valley AVAs to Lodi, as well as a number of plots in the Sonoma appellation.
But try their other wines as well, especially the Bordeaux varietals. Several times
each summer, Ravenswood organizes barbecues, serving up the hearty foods that

The 1871 harvest at Buena Vista was one of many wine-related images in the Napa and Sonoma valleys captured on film by Eadweard Muybridge.

pair with zinfandel so well; call ahead for a schedule. Tours are offered daily, but you can also just enjoy views up their steeply sloping hillside from the windows of the tasting room. *18701 Gehricke Road; 707-933-2332.*

Buena Vista Carneros Estate   *map page 184, D-7*

The old Buena Vista winery got off to a tough start. Founded by the innovative Agoston Haraszthy in 1857 (see the Wine Country Then and Now chapter), it suffered heavy losses in the late 19th century when phylloxera devastated its vineyards, and then experienced a second blow when the great 1906 earthquake collapsed its cellars and destroyed the stored wine. The winery lay idle until the 1940s, when Frank Bartholomew, a war correspondent, bought the old edifice, reopened the tunnels, and replanted the vineyards. When Bartholomew sold the winery in 1968, he kept the vineyards, forcing the new owners to look for vineyard land elsewhere. They found it in the budding Carneros District of southern Sonoma and Napa counties—hence the winery's new name.

Buena Vista's best wines are the limited-production estate vineyard wines produced from the Ramal Vineyard in Carneros, planted with pinot noir, chardonnay, merlot, and syrah. Its production facility in the Carneros is closed to the public, but this Sonoma winery has a tasting room inside the atmospheric 1862 Press

House, plus a shady courtyard for picnicking. The daily tours are especially good if you're a history buff, as they discuss Haraszthy and the saga of winemaking in the valley. *18000 Old Winery Road; 707-252-7117.*

★ **Bartholomew Park Winery**   *map page 184, D-7*
Although this winery is a newbie, founded only in 1994 by Jim Bundschu, grapes were grown in some of its vineyards as early as the 1830s, and some of the land it encompasses was part of the original Buena Vista winery. The emphasis here is on small lots of hand-crafted, single-varietal wines whose grapes—cabernet, merlot, zinfandel, and sauvignon blanc—are all harvested from the same vineyard. Organic farming methods are used whenever possible, and because terroir is such an important consideration, as little manipulation as possible occurs during the wine-making process.

The wines themselves make Bartholomew Park worth a stop, but another reason to visit is its museum, with exhibits about the history of the winery and the Sonoma region in general. Displays on different methods of pruning vines and different types of soil that actually incorporate real vines and soil are particularly vivid. Another plus is the beautiful, slightly off-the-beaten-path location. Though the winery's only a short drive from the middle of Sonoma, the town seems far away when picnicking on their woodsy grounds. *1000 Vineyard Lane; 707-935-9511.*

Gundlach-Bundschu   *map page 184, C-8*
Gundlach-Bundschu, like Ravenswood, looks a bit like a large gun bunker, but don't let that scare you away. This 1970s incarnation may not be pretty, but it's a heck of a lot of fun. Jazz, pop, or rock-and-roll play over the sound system as you walk into the tasting room, instead of the light classical music permeating the air at more staid establishments. Next to the winery, there's a small stage for summer theater and music performances, and nearby there are lots of attractive picnic spots. And one of the Bundschus started a promotional group called the Wine Brats.

But behind the casual exterior lies a serious history of noteworthy wine. Like many wineries in northern California, Gundlach-Bundschu, established in 1858, closed its doors during Prohibition, but the property did not change hands. Great-great-grandson Jim Bundschu replanted the family's Rhinefarm Vineyard, one of California's oldest vineyards, at the crossroads of the Sonoma Valley, Carneros, and Napa Valley appellations. These days, the winery is lauded for its red wines. A

Attendees sample the goods at a Sonoma Valley olive oil festival.

recent pinot noir had a nose of rose petals, and the 1996 Vintage Reserve cabernet sauvignon is particularly complex.

A short, breathtaking hike up the hill from the tasting room takes you to a viewpoint from which you'll be treated to a panorama of the lower valley and the Carneros. You'll likely see a lot of Sonomans picnicking here: this spot is a favorite local hangout. *2000 Denmark Street; 707-938-5277.*

■ GLEN ELLEN *map page 184, C-3/4*

The Sonoma Valley Highway, Highway 12, runs north from Sonoma through tract homes and strip malls with a hangdog look. After the valley opens up, oaks and stone fences dominate the landscape, as the road heads toward Glen Ellen, 9 miles up Sonoma Creek from Sonoma.

Tucked among the trees of a narrow canyon, where Sonoma Mountain and the Mayacamas pinch in the valley floor, Glen Ellen looks more like a town of the Sierra Foothills gold country than a Wine Country village. Its main street, narrow and crooked, runs past houses climbing steep slopes. Several old buildings have been reclaimed as up-to-date shops and restaurants. Two tree-lined creeks, the Sonoma and the Calabazas, merge in the center of town, just above the point where the main road turns sharply to cross the bridge.

Sonoma Mountain rises west of town, much of its eastern flank covered by the forests of **Jack London State Historic Park,** once the author's Beauty Ranch, where he lived, wrote, and died in a small white farm cottage. Following his death, London's wife, Charmian, operated it as a dude ranch. After she died, in 1955, she willed the ranch to the state parks system.

The park's 2-mile hiking trail through oak woods is an excellent one. It takes you to London's grave and to the ruins of Wolf House, which burned under mysterious circumstances in 1913, a month before the couple were to move into it. Shaded by huge redwood trees, the remains of London's house look like an ancient castle from a European fairy tale. The author's grave, though, is a simple affair: a small picket fence and a plaque mark the spot where his ashes rest. The setting is about as perfectly 19th-century as you can experience anywhere in the Wine Country. *2400 London Ranch Road, off Arnold Drive; 707-938-5216.*

Wine has been part of Glen Ellen since the 1840s, when a French immigrant, Joshua Chauvet, planted grapes and built a winery and the valley's first distillery. The winery machinery was powered by steam, and the boilers were fueled with

On the trail at Jack London State Historic Park.

wood from local oak trees. In 1881, Chauvet built a stone winery to house his operations. Other valley farmers followed Chauvet's example, and grapegrowing took
off. Wine was even made during Prohibition, when the locals took a liberal view of
the 200 gallons each family was allowed to produce for personal consumption.

Glen Ellen and neighboring Kenwood have several excellent inns and restaurants. When you check into one of the utterly comfortable local bed-and-breakfasts
such as the Gaige House, you're following in the footsteps of the countless visitors
who have traveled to this sunny region to give their congested lungs a much-
deserved rest from San Francisco's foggy air. Though dozens of wineries in the area
beg to be visited, it's hard not to succumb to Sonoma's slow pace and simply
lounge poolside at your lodgings or stock up on picnic supplies at Glen Ellen's
Village Market (13751 Arnold Drive; 707-996-6728) for a leisurely lunch. The
renowned cook and food writer M.F.K. Fisher, who lived and worked near Glen
Ellen for 22 years until her death in 1992, would surely have approved.

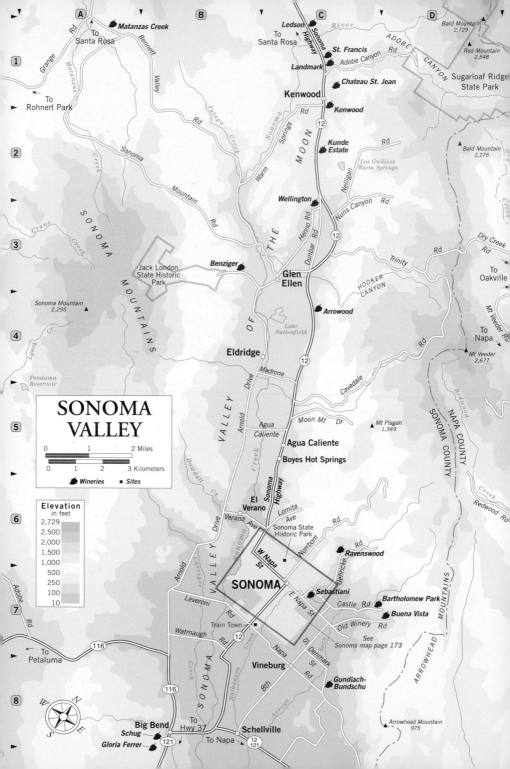

■ GLEN ELLEN WINERIES

The wineries of this hilly region make excellent wines, albeit no longer from local grapes alone. Most wineries here are open daily for tastings, but a few require appointments and a small number are closed to visitors. Among the latter is the excellent **Laurel Glen**, whose rich, supple reds can be sampled at the tasting room Locals in Geyserville (see the Northern Sonoma chapter).

Arrowood Vineyards & Winery   *map page 184, C-4*
Right on Highway 12, just outside Glen Ellen, is Arrowood, a small winery with a big reputation. Richard Arrowood made great wine when he was the winemaker at Chateau St. Jean, and he continues making great wine at Arrowood, once his own place but now owned by Robert Mondavi. A veranda with wicker chairs wraps around the gray-and-white building that looks like it would be at home on Cape Cod. In the tasting room, which is open daily, try the big but approachable cabernet sauvignons and excellent, inky syrahs. Fans of white wine might appreciate the Côte de Lune Blanc, a blend of marsanne, roussane, and viognier. Tours are by appointment only. *14347 Sonoma Highway; 707-935-2600.*

★ Benziger Family Winery   *map page 184, B-3*
A mile or so outside Glen Ellen is Benziger, which since it sold off its Glen Ellen label to a bulk wine producer in the 1990s has been making memorable wine from its surrounding estate vineyards. And along with the serious pours comes a seriously good tour.
Opened in 1981, this winery in the Sonoma Mountain AVA is known for cabernet sauvignon, merlot, sauvignon blanc, and chardonnay. A tractor-pulled tram takes you through the vineyards, where signs point out grape varieties and a guide thoroughly explains their farming practices and what's happening in the vineyards at the moment. Space on the tram can be hard to come by during summer and early fall, so try to come before lunchtime to get a seat. Near the tasting room is a demonstration vineyard and garden that explains more about the biodynamic farming practices used on site. *1883 London Ranch Road; 707-935-3000.*

★ Matanzas Creek Winery   *map page 184, A-1*
Just a 10- to 15-minute drive from Glen Ellen via curvy Bennett Valley Road, Matanzas Creek, in the Sonoma Valley AVA's northwestern corner, has an especially aromatic calling card. In front of the tasting room building stretch

Lavender gardens stretch in front of the Matanzas Creek tasting room.

gardens with literally thousands of lavender plants. When the lavender's in bloom, typically in June and July, it's truly a feast for the senses (and the bees). Even in the dead of winter, the tasting room is notably lovely, with its understated Japanese aesthetic and its koi pond.

Sandra McIver opened Matanzas Creek in 1977 on the site of an old dairy farm in Bennett Valley. In 2003, Bennett Valley was formally recognized as Sonoma's newest AVA. Surrounded by the Sonoma, Bennett, and Taylor mountains, the land is cooled by a maritime breeze coming through the Petaluma Wind Gap, a break in the mountains, resulting in a longer growing season than elsewhere in Sonoma. The winery is known for merlot, sauvignon blanc, and chardonnay, though in 2005 they added to their lineup a dry rosé of merlot—a wine that's very fashionable in Sonoma and Napa at the moment. The tasting room is open daily, and tours are offered by appointment every day except Sunday. *6097 Bennett Valley Road; 707-528-6464.*

■ KENWOOD WINERIES

The Sonoma Highway winds north from Glen Ellen to the small town of Kenwood, whose vineyards and wineries occupy the flat bottom and slopes of the valley's northern section. The wines from this area aren't really all that distinct from those of other Sonoma Valley regions, but the landscape is very pretty, with meadows and woods bordering the highway.

Several wineries in the Kenwood area are small operations, some of them started within the last decade or so, that do not have tasting rooms of their own. At **Family Wineries of Sonoma Valley** (9380 Sonoma Highway; 888-433-6555), you can sample the output of four wineries. Since the tasting room is staffed by the owners and winemakers of the wineries represented, you can count on learning a lot about the wines being poured. It's open daily.

Kunde Estate Winery *map page 184, C-2*
As growers, the Kundes go back five generations, starting with Louis Kunde, who bought Wildwood Vineyards in 1904. The family continued making wine during Prohibition (no one says whether this was sacramental or under-the-counter wine) but stopped making wine in 1942, when the eldest son went off to war. The family returned to winemaking in 1990, and these days their sprawling 2,000-acre estate, with about 800 acres planted with vineyards, produces some of the finer wines in Sonoma. Though they make only a few whites, their chardonnays are well regarded; typically, they will pour a flight, allowing you to taste the marked difference between a crisp chardonnay aged entirely in stainless steel, to a richer one that has undergone malolactic fermentation. Their estate-grown wines include a large range of reds, including the Italian varietals primitivo and barbera, Bordeaux-style blends, and an excellent zinfandel crafted from vines more than 120 years old. Although old vines yield far fewer grapes than younger ones, many believe that the wines produced from them are super-concentrated.

Outside the tasting room a rock wall frames a wooden door built into the side of the hill. Behind that door are the tunnels where the wine is aged. Take a guided tour to enjoy a walk through these cool caves, or simply walk a few steps up the hillside into the demonstration vineyards for a look at the vines of different varietals. In season, you can help yourself to a taste, comparing the flavors of, say, zinfandel and sauvignon grapes. *9825 Sonoma Highway; 707-833-5501.*

Kenwood Vineyards *map page 184, C-1/2*

Back in California's Tortilla Flat days, when wine was sold by the barrel instead of the bottle, this winery was owned by the Pagani brothers. When the Martin Lee family and friends bought out the Paganis in 1970, the wines were upgraded to the sipping variety, but even now Kenwood makes some good basic red wine, as well as its more showy cabernet sauvignons and zinfandels, many poured in the tasting room housed in one of the original barns on the property. The best of these come from Jack London's old vineyard, in the Sonoma Mountain appellation, above the fog belt of the Sonoma Valley. (Kenwood has an exclusive lease.) But what the wine connoisseurs keep coming back for is Kenwood's crisp sauvignon blanc. Tastings are available daily. *9592 Sonoma Highway; 707-833-5891.*

Chateau St. Jean *map page 184, C-1*

At the foot of the Mayacamas Mountains stretch the grandiose grounds of Chateau St. Jean, an old country estate once owned by a family of midwestern industrialists. (A couple of ponds in the shape of Lakes Michigan and Huron speak to their loyalties.) The wines are good, and winemaker Margo Van Staaveren was named 2008 Winemaker of the Year by *Wine Enthusiast* magazine. The reserve chardonnay and the La Petite Etoile fumé blanc, however, are worth seeking out. Take some time to explore the impeccably maintained formal gardens, whose style harmonizes with the Mediterranean-style villa. The gardens are open daily, but tastings are by appointment only. *8555 Sonoma Highway; 707-833-4134.*

Landmark Vineyards *map page 184, C-1*

Fleeing from subdivisions north of Santa Rosa, Landmark decamped to the foothills of Sugarloaf Ridge in 1990. Rich, round chardonnay used to be the winery's main claim to fame, but in recent years critics have been taking note of its pinot noir as well. Stop here to taste the wines, but also take a close look at the building, which is a faithful reconstruction of a mission-period rancho—right on up to the shingle roof. Ask to borrow their bocce balls if you want to take advantage of the court in the picnic area. If you'll be visiting on a summer Saturday, call in advance to reserve a spot on the short horse-drawn wagon tour of the vineyard. *101 Adobe Canyon Road; 707-833-0218.*

(opposite) The welcome sign is out at Kenwood Vineyards.

The red soils of the Kunde Estate Winery produce some of the finest zinfandel in the region.

★ **St. Francis Winery**   *map page 184, C-1*
Named for Saint Francis of Assisi, founder of the Franciscan order, which established missions and vineyards throughout California, this winery has one of the most scenic locations in Sonoma, nestled at the foot of Mount Hood. The visitors center beautifully replicates the California Mission style, with its red tile roof and dramatic bell tower. Out back, a slate patio overlooks vineyards, lavender gardens, and hummingbirds flitting about the flowerbeds.

The charm of the surroundings is matched by the wines, most of them red. Their reserve wines are all vineyard designates, made from grapes harvested from a single vineyard; the Pagani Vineyard Reserve Zinfandel is a particularly fine example. Yet their other wines, many more modestly priced, are worth tasting too, like a peppery petite sirah and a lively cabernet franc. If it's available (typically hourly on weekends and once a day on weekdays), consider paying a bit more for a food and wine pairing to taste one of their reserve wines with an inventive dish. *100 Pythian Road; 800-543-7713.*

The Spanish mission–style St. Francis bell tower appears on the winery's labels.

Ledson Winery and Vineyards *map page 184, C-1*

The strange purple-brick château of Ledson Winery sits incongruously amid vineyards. The winery was originally designed by Steve Ledson as a home for his family. When the outrageously ornate building, usually called "the castle" by locals, started gaining intense interest during its construction, the family decided it made more sense to transform the building into a winery and tasting room for their wines, first released in 1994.

Ledson produces a great number of varietals, including the obligatory pinot noir, syrah, zinfandel, and cabernet sauvignon, but also malbec, barbera, mourvèdre, primitivo, and several others. Particularly worth tasting are their chardonnay, a fine late-harvest zinfandel, and their fruity pinot noirs. The estate merlot—the first wine they released—continues to impress. A large deli next to the tasting room provides all you'll need to picnic under the oak trees. *7335 Sonoma Highway; 707-537-3810.*

A Great Drive in Sonoma Valley

It's easy to zip through the Sonoma Valley in a day—the drive from Sonoma at the south end to Kenwood to the north can be done in about 25 minutes—but once you start stopping at Sonoma's historic sites and the valley's wineries, your visit could easily be spread over two days. For a day trip of the highlights, start in the town of Sonoma. Do a lap around the historic plaza, then pick up picnic supplies at the Sonoma Cheese Factory. Once in your car, drive southeast on Napa Street West, which turns into Napa Street East. Turn right on 8th Street East and left onto Denmark Street, where you'll see the Gundlach-Bundschu winery sign. After a tasting, hike up the GunBun hill for your picnic.

Back in the car, head back to Sonoma Plaza and continue along West Napa Street (also Highway 12), following the signs north on Highway 12. About half an hour later, you'll pass the tiny town of Kenwood. Just north of Kenwood, on the right side of Highway 12, is St. Francis Winery, a very photogenic spot and a must for red-wine fans. Returning south on Highway 12, look for Kunde Estate just south of Kenwood, just a few minutes down the road. If you've managed to wrap up your wine tasting before 4 P.M., continue south on Highway 12 and take the Arnold Drive exit into the picturesque town of Glen Ellen. From Arnold Drive turn right on London Ranch Road. After winding your way uphill for a few minutes you'll reach Jack London State Historic Park. Take a short stroll through the grounds and a gander at some of the historic buildings near the parking area before the park closes at 5 P.M. Return to Highway 12 and continue south to the town of Sonoma for dinner.

Well-tended gardens surround the Dry Creek Valley's opulent Ferrari-Carano winery.

N O R T H E R N
SONOMA COUNTY

Northern Sonoma County is a study in contrasts. In urban Santa Rosa, bypassed by almost all Wine Country visitors, bland office parks take the place of vineyards, while 15 miles to the north, the ritzy little town of Healdsburg buzzes with luxe hotels, hip wine bars, and some of the Wine Country's hottest restaurants. Just outside these towns, however, it's all rolling hills, with only the occasional horse ranch, orchard, or stand of oak trees interrupting the vineyards.

The quickest route north to northern Sonoma from San Francisco is straight up U.S. 101 to Healdsburg, but the back roads offer the best rewards. Highway 116 (also called the Gravenstein Highway), west of 101, leads through the little towns of Forestville and Graton (both with a handful of great restaurants), before depositing you along the Russian River near Guerneville. A popular destination for weekending San Franciscans, Guerneville doesn't have any notable wineries itself, but it is a convenient place for picking up River Road, then Westside Road, which passes through pinot noir paradise on its way to Healdsburg. Highway 128, east of 101, passes through some of the prettiest countryside in Sonoma, past rolling farmland and a few country stores, before ending up in Calistoga, at the north end of the Napa Valley.

The Northern Sonoma AVA covers a large area and overlaps much of the three AVAs that meet at Healdsburg: the Russian River AVA, which runs southwest along the lower course of the river; the Dry Creek Valley AVA, which heads northwest from town; and the Alexander Valley AVA, which runs east and north of Healdsburg. Also in this area are the Knights Valley, Chalk Hill, Green Valley, and Sonoma Coast AVAs. Although each of the regions claims its own microclimate, soil types, and most-favored varietals, they do have something in common: peace and quiet. Northern Sonoma is far less crowded than the Napa Valley and the larger tasting rooms in southern Sonoma. Though Healdsburg, with its wealth of chic restaurants and hotels, is hardly a stranger to overnight visitors, it's rare to bump into more than a few others in most of northern Sonoma's tasting rooms.

Iron Horse, best known for its sparkling wine, also produces an excellent chardonnay.

■ RUSSIAN RIVER APPELLATION

The Russian River AVA has a unique, grape-friendly climate. Because of its low elevation, sea fogs push far inland to cool the land, yet in summer they burn off, giving the grapes enough sun to ripen properly. The cool climate is perfect for fog-loving pinot noir grapes as well as chardonnay. The namesake river does its part by slowly carving its way downward through many layers of rock, depositing a deep layer of gravel that in parts of the valley measures 60 or 70 feet. This gravel forces the roots of grapevines to go deep in search of water and nutrients. In the process, the plants absorb a multitude of trace minerals that add complexity to the flavor of the grapes. In California as in France, such gravelly soils produce some of the world's greatest wines.

Iron Horse Vineyards   *map page 197, A-3*
At the end of a meandering country road off Highway 116 is Iron Horse, whose sparkling wines smoothed the way of glasnost. Ronald Reagan served them at his summit meetings with Mikhail Gorbachev; George Herbert Walker

Bush took some to Moscow for the signing of the START Treaty. Iron Horse also makes excellent chardonnay and pinot noir.

Despite its fame, Iron Horse, founded in 1979, has avoided pretense—the winery buildings are of the simple Sonoma redwood-barn style—but an access road lined with olive trees, wildflowers, and acres of fruit orchards and vegetable gardens makes this a beautiful place. Enjoy views out over the predominantly cool and foggy Green Valley while you taste their deeply flavored sparklers with a long, rich finish. Also look for their Joy! Sparkling Cuvée, a unique blend that was produced only in magnums and aged 10 to 15 years on yeast in the bottle. In 2004 Iron Horse released its first dessert wine, a bright late-harvest viognier that's worth watching. Tours are by appointment on weekday mornings, and the tasting room is open daily. *9786 Ross Station Road, off Highway 116; 707-887-1507.*

Korbel Champagne Cellars   *map page 197, A-2*

Back in the 19th century, when the Korbel brothers logged the redwood forests of the Russian River, they planted crops among the stumps. Through trial and error, they found that grapes grew best. So in 1882 they established a winery and began making "champagne." Thus began the life of the go-to $10 bubbly.

Technically, Champagne is made only in the French region of that name and all other bubbly is "sparkling wine." (See the Champagne and Sparkling Wine box in the Northern Napa Valley chapter.) Whatever you choose to call it, Korbel's wine is quite good and reasonably priced. The Natural, a pinot and chardonnay blend, is best. And the winery is a delight to visit, with its 19th-century buildings, a deli and microbrewery, and extensive rose gardens. The tour—considered by many the best in Sonoma County for its enthusiastic, well-informed tour guides and the beauty of the lush, historic grounds—will give you a good idea of how sparkling wine is made. *13250 River Road; 707-824-7000.*

■ WESTSIDE ROAD WINERIES

Although Highway 101 gives you a straight shot from Santa Rosa to Healdsburg, if you have enough time you should consider taking the long way 'round, following River Road to the west and then Westside Road back east to Healdsburg. Scenic Westside roughly follows the curves of the Russian River, wandering through vineyards, woods, and meadows—and thankfully, it's rarely busy. There are more wineries along this road than we have space to mention. Stop at as many as you can—they all tend to be uncrowded and relaxed—and pinot noir fans in particular will find a lot to love here.

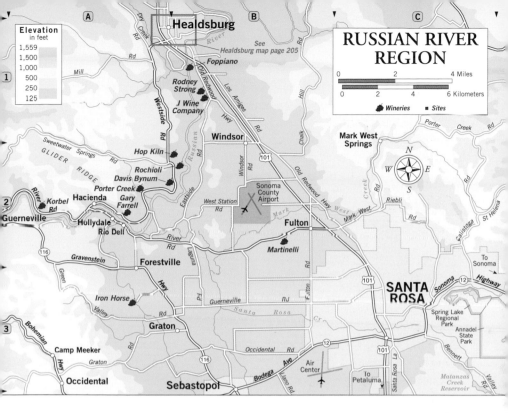

Healdsburg

See
Healdsburg map page 205

Foppiano

Rodney
Strong

J Wine
Company

Windsor

Mill

Sweetwater Springs

GLIDER

RIDGE

Hop Kiln

Rochioli
Davis Bynum

Porter Creek

Korbel

Hacienda

Gary
Farrell

Guerneville

Hollydale

Rio Dell

Gravenstein

Forestville

Iron Horse

Graton

Camp Meeker

Graton

Occidental

Sebastopol

West Station
Rd

Sonoma
County
Airport

Fulton

Martinelli

Guerneville

Santa   Rosa

Occidental   Rd

Bodega   Ave

Air
Center

To
Petaluma

Mark West
Springs

Riebli

Riebli

SANTA
ROSA

Spring Lake
Regional
Park

Annadel
State
Park

Matanzas
Creek
Reservoir

RUSSIAN RIVER REGION

0   2   4 Miles

0   2   4   6 Kilometers

● Wineries   ■ Sites

N
W   E
S

★ **Gary Farrell Winery**   *map page 197, A-2*

Once you turn through the striking stone-and-metal gate at Gary Farrell, the westernmost Westside Road winery, a super-steep drive snakes up to the sleek, modern tasting room. From here, the views down the precipitous slope are the most gobsmacking in Sonoma. The wines are equally impressive: Farrell made his mark with a 1985 pinot noir from grapes grown at nearby vineyards, including Rochioli, and he continues to make restrained pinots that are particularly food-friendly. In the 1990s, he turned his attention to zinfandel, garnering high praise for his work with that varietal—his full-bodied, spicy zin from the Maple Vineyard in the Dry Creek Valley is a triumph. Farrell also makes chardonnay, sauvignon blanc, merlot, and a cabernet sauvignon. *10701 Westside Road; 707-473-2900.*

Porter Creek Vineyards   *map page 197, A-2*

This place is about as down-home as you can get. Look closely for Porter Creek's sign; the driveway is in a sharp bend in the road. Opened in 1982, the winery is truly low-key—there's just a simple little redwood-beam tasting room out behind a small home. It may be a modest family farm, but it happens to make notably good wine with estate-grown chardonnay, pinot noir, syrah, and zinfandel grapes. Its vineyards climb up steep hillsides, where cover crops must be planted between the vines to limit erosion. The volcanic soil imparts a slight mineral note to the well-balanced chardonnay, and the rich zinfandel explodes with berry flavor. Tastings are available daily, but there are no tours. *8735 Westside Road; 707-433-6321.*

Davis Bynum Winery *map page 197, A/B-2*

From the road, Davis Bynum looks more like a summer retreat than a serious winery, but once you have made it past the white entrance cottages and tasted the wines, you'll agree that this winery's reputation is well deserved. The namesake founder got into winemaking in 1951 when he bought 50 pounds of grapes from Robert Mondavi and made a few gallons of petite sirah. The current winery opened in 1973. Bynum was the first to make pinot noir exclusively from Russian River grapes and has championed local grapes ever since, making wines that emphasize fruit rather than oak. Quality has kept up with the expansion of production. In addition to the pinot noir, be sure to taste the merlot, the fumé blanc, and the chardonnay. There are no tours here, but the tasting room is open daily. *8075 Westside Road; 707-433-5852.*

Rochioli Vineyards & Winery *map page 197, A/B-2*

The Rochioli family started growing grapes in 1933, tending vineyards planted in the 19th century and planting new vines on gravelly benchlands above the Russian River. After decades of selling grapes to local wineries, the Rochiolis started making their own wine in 1982. Production is small—about 14,000 cases annually—but the wines are worth stopping for. Because of the cool growing conditions in the Russian River Valley, the flavors of their estate chardonnay and sauvignon blanc are intense and complex. Their pinot, though, is largely responsible for the winery's stellar reputation and has helped cement the Russian River's reputation as a pinot powerhouse. Fans on the winery's mailing list snap up most of the somewhat pricey single-vineyard bottles, which vary from soft and berry-rich to crisp and tannic. The tasting room patio, shaded by roses, is a great place for sipping wine and enjoying the view across the Russian River vineyards. *6192 Westside Road; 707-433-2305.*

★ Hop Kiln Winery *map page 197, A/B-2*

As you wind along Westside Road it's hard to miss the odd-looking Hop Kiln winery, where three chimney-ish stone towers rise from a barnlike building

CRUSH CAMP

Are your winery visits making you eager to pitch in and get your hands dirty? Are you starting to look longingly at the pruning shears and rows of vines? Consider signing up for one of the short, hands-on winemaking programs offered by a few local wineries, usually in September and October. You'll see the inner workings of harvest and even blend your own bottle. Below are top options for these "crush camps."

Camp Schramsberg. Three-day sessions at Schramsberg Vineyards, focusing on making sparkling wines. Campers pick grapes in the vineyards and follow them to the crusher. Winemakers explain and teach traditional methods such as riddling—and as a dramatic finish, the art of opening a bottle of bubbly by slicing its neck with a sabre. *707-942-4558; www.schramsberg.com.*

Crush This! Three-hour crash course at Ravenswood Winery. Staff members show how to assess grapes' ripeness, how to punch down fermenting juice, and how to blend wine. You'll create your own zinfandel blend to cork and bring home. *707-933-2349; www.ravenswood-wine.com.*

Sonoma Valley Portworks. Every autumn, this small, boutique port-maker in downtown Petaluma invites wine club members (and guests) behind the scenes, where they climb ladders, descend into a homemade grape-stomping contraption, and crush away with bare feet. All participants receive a bottle of wine. *707-769-5203; www.portworks.com.*

that was originally built for the production of America's *other* favorite beverage—beer. Built in 1905, the structure housed kilns for drying hops and a baling press. Today, wine is stored in those old kilns, whose thick stone walls help keep the wine cool. Poke around the tasting room and you'll see original equipment such as odd pipes and railcar tracks running through the building.

Though the building alone would be worth a visit, most people, of course, come for the wines, which include big, fruity zinfandels and chardonnays. Their popular Thousand Flowers is a sauvignon blanc, chardonnay, chenin blanc, gewürztraminer, and muscat canelli blend with a faint aroma of flowers and tropical fruit. The rustic grounds, with shaded picnic tables and a duck pond, are a good place for a picnic with a bottle of their aptly named Big Red. Tastings are offered daily. *6050 Westside Road; 707-433-6491.*

■ EAST OF THE RUSSIAN RIVER

Just south of Healdsburg, a few wineries dot the area between the Russian River to the north and west and U.S. 101 to the east. Though the wineries are more far-flung, and the area may not have quite the bucolic, backcountry feel as the Dry Creek or Alexander valleys, you can find some excellent wines here.

Foppiano Vineyards *map page 197, B-1*

Established in 1896, Foppiano made primarily bulk wine until 1970, but has recently proven that it can produce quality wines under the "rock-and-roll wine-maker," Bill Regan. (Regan's known for playing music by Eric Clapton and Jeff Beck as he works.) In the unassuming tasting room be sure to taste Foppiano's flag-ship wine, a hearty petite sirah, and the zinfandel, a good, modestly priced wine that just begs for a pizza or plate of pasta. The winery also produces sangiovese, cabernet sauvignon, pinot noir, and merlot. Tastings are available daily, and there is a self-guided vineyard tour. *12707 Old Redwood Highway; 707-433-7272.*

Rodney Strong Vineyards *map page 197, B-1*

Although Rodney Strong, who founded this place in 1959, passed away in 2006, the winery promises to continue producing intensely flavored reds. The 1970s cement building doesn't look particularly enticing from the exterior, but inside is an attractive octagonal tasting room ringed by a balcony overlooking the production facilities. An excellent self-guided tour leads along the balcony for a good view of the fermentation tanks and other machinery, but twice-daily guided tours are also available.

Back at the bar, you can taste the fruits of the winery's high-tech labors. Symmetry, a red Bordeaux-style blend, is one of their most impressive offerings, but also taste the excellent pinot noir. (Strong was one of the first to plant pinot noir in the Russian River Valley.) The winery sponsors outdoor concerts on the grounds during summer. *11455 Old Redwood Highway; 707-431-1533.*

★ J Vineyards and Winery *map page 197, B-1*

There's no doubt about J's raison d'être: the tasting room's bar is brightened by a fiber-optic light sculpture of bubbly spraying from a bottle. It sets the tone for a cheerful visit, and your tasting fee also covers a few bites of beautifully presented hors d'oeuvres designed to complement each of the wines they're pouring. A simi-lar but even more opulent tasting experience is available in the Bubble Room,

Harvest time at J Vineyards.

where older vintages and smaller production wines are poured for a slightly higher fee. Though the sparkling wine in those distinctive J bottles is their strong suit, they've also recently produced still wines, including chardonnay, pinot gris, and pinot noir. Tours are by appointment only, but the tasting room is open daily. *11447 Old Redwood Highway; 707-431-5410.*

★ **Martinelli Vineyards & Winery**   *map page 197, B-2*
This winery, in a 100-year-old hop barn with the telltale triple towers, has the feel of an old country store, with a wood-beam ceiling and an antique stove in the corner. The warm welcome you'll get from the tasting room staff might also remind you of another era. The Martinelli family has been growing grapes and other fruits in the Russian River Valley since the late 1800s, and one spot, Jackass Hill, has been producing grapes since 1899. Still, there's nothing old-fashioned about these sophisticated wines. Crafted by the acclaimed winemaker Helen Turley since 1993, the wines are typically big, complex, well balanced, and high in alcohol. Martinelli currently makes sauvignon blanc, chardonnay, muscat Alexandria, pinot noir, syrah, and an incredibly rich zinfandel, the wine that typically brings visitors to this back road in Windsor. The tasting room is open daily, and there's a picnic area at the edge of the vineyard, overlooking the tasting room and winery. (Unfortunately, due to licensing restrictions, alcoholic drinks are not allowed at the tables.) *3360 River Road; 707-525-0570.*

■ **HEALDSBURG**   *map page 205*

As you park your car on the Healdsburg plaza, you'll get a heady whiff of southern magnolias. The magnolias grow next to tall Canary Island date palms that are in turn dwarfed by towering California redwoods, making the plaza a shady haven. When the nearby vineyards are a hurricane of activity, and the wine buffs are starting to circle, this plaza is the eye of the storm.

Former Healdsburg resident Millie Howie describes the town as "straight out of a Norman Rockwell painting," and she's right. The flower beds are tidy, the bandstand always looks freshly painted, and the businesses are dressed up in style. But Healdsburg also has a buzz about it these days. Around the old-fashioned plaza you'll find fashionable boutiques, hip new tasting rooms, and some of the best restaurants in the Wine Country. Healdsburg has long had a strong dining scene, but now restaurants like the ultra-luxe Cyrus and the trendy Barndiva are kicking things up a notch.

Beer Country

All over California, winemakers happily admit that "it takes a lot of beer to make fine wine." Lucky for them, there's no shortage of good beer in Wine Country.

The 1976 opening of the New Albion Brewery in Sonoma marks what many consider to be the renaissance of American craft-brewing. It went under six years later, but not before inspiring other pioneers throughout the state. With California in the forefront, the microbrewery movement took off. Today, you can find distinctive local beer throughout Wine Country.

Ales of every description—from blond to stout—predominate at California microbreweries, but lagers are another favorite. Many of California's brewers take their inspiration from old British or European styles, tweaking them to sometimes extreme levels of intensity (and alcohol content). You'll find monstrously malty porters, deep-golden lagers, and hefty wheat beers, plus lots of generously hopped—even triple-hopped—pale ales that start with a floral nose and finish with an ultra-bitter kick.

Many breweries operate tasting rooms and tours just as wineries do. Look for brewpubs and local beer festivals to try more of the state's finest. Below are some of the best California breweries to visit.

Anderson Valley Brewing, Inc. Brewery tours, tasting room, and 18-hole disc golf course at the home of Deep Enders Dark Porter, Boont Amber Ale, and other consistent medal-winners. *17700 Highway 253, Boonville; 707–895–2337.*

Bear Republic Brewing Co. Hops rule the Racer 5, XP Pale Ale, and specialty draft brews at this brewpub. There's also a limited—and mediocre—food menu. *345 Healdsburg Avenue, Healdsburg; 707–433–2337.*

Firestone Walker Brewing Company. Superb barrel-fermented ales in the brewery tasting room. *1400 Ramada Drive, Paso Robles; 805-238-2556.*

Lagunitas Brewing Co. Hopheads' dreams come true in the India Pale Ale (IPA) and limited-release seasonal beers poured in the tasting room. Brewery tours available. *1280 N. McDowell Boulevard, Petaluma; 707–769–4495.*

Mendocino Brewing Company. The beer, such as the amber Red Tail Ale, is made in Ukiah, but you can taste it at the company's tap room, in an old brick saloon that was the original brewery. *13351 S. Highway 101, Hopland; 707–744–1361.*

Russian River Brewing Co. It's all about the double IPA and Belgian-style ales in this brewery's large pub. *725 4th Street, Santa Rosa; 707–545–2337.*

Healdsburg's food fetish extends from the restaurants to the specialty grocers and markets—you'll be spoiled for choice when shopping for edibles. At the **Oakville Grocery** (124 Matheson Street; 707-433-3200), visitors and locals alike line up at the wine bar, the espresso bar, and the take-out counter that doles out huge sandwiches, hearty soups, and salads. At **Costeaux** (417 Healdsburg Ave., 707-433-1913), which, in 2009, was named by *Modern Baking* magazine as Retail Bakery of the Year, sample authentic French baguettes or stock up on cookies and cupcakes for later. If it happens to be Saturday morning from May through November, head to the open-air **Farmers' Market** (North and Vine streets, one block west of the plaza), where local producers of cheese, olives, and olive oils, along with growers of the freshest of vegetables, gather to sell their wares. (A smaller market takes place on the plaza itself on Tuesday evenings.)

You could also easily spend an afternoon poking around the galleries and shops fringing the plaza. At **Saint Dizier Home** (259 Center Street; 707-473-0980), beautiful furnishings such as tables, couches, and hand-carved cabinets share the space with contemporary items like hand-painted silk pillows. Across the square, the **Plaza Arts Center** (130 Plaza Street; 707-431-1970) displays work by local artists who also staff the gallery. In addition to the larger-scale paintings and photography, look for suitcase-friendly fine crafts, such as jewelry.

But to truly catch the Healdsburg spirit, go to the plaza early in the morning, before the sun bears down, and order a fragrant sticky bun and a cup of coffee at the **Downtown Bakery & Creamery** (308 Center Street; 707-431-2719), a local cult favorite. The bakery uses local dairy products and fruit in their breads and decadent pastries. If you come back on a weekend evening, you might be treated to a free concert—anything from jazz to Sousa marches.

Since there are several tasting rooms in the town center, you could sample wine all day without ever getting in your car. An outlet for **Gallo** (320 Center Street; 707-433-2458) is on the plaza, and **Kendall-Jackson** (337 Healdsburg Avenue; 707-433-7102) has a tasting room just to the north. By far the most stylish tasting room, however, is **Thumbprint Cellars** (102 Matheson Street; 707-433-2393). With its leather chairs, brown velvet curtains, and chic light fixtures, it could be the living room of some very hip friends in San Francisco. You will have to get in your car to head north on Healdsburg Avenue to **Tip Top Liquor Warehouse** (90 Dry Creek Road; 707-431-0841), a nondescript-looking spot that stocks an interesting selection of wines at fair prices. Though it's strongest in bottles from

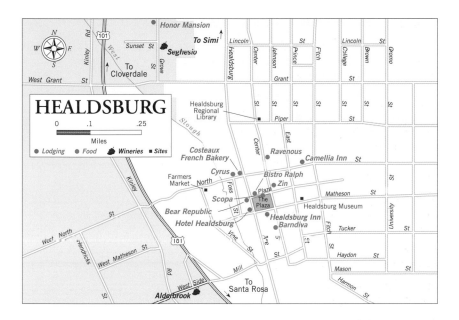

Sonoma, you'll also find a few Napa wines here too, including some cult cabernets that are particularly hard to find.

The **Healdsburg Museum** (221 Matheson Street; 707-431-3325) displays a collection of local historical objects, including baskets and artifacts from native tribes. Other exhibits cover the Mexican Rancho period, the founding and growth of Healdsburg in the 1850s, and the history of local agriculture (grapes, hops, prunes).

■ WINERIES IN HEALDSBURG

Alderbrook Winery   *map page 205, B-2*
Head out to the edge of Healdsburg to find this cluster of olive-green buildings. A fire warms the spacious but homey tasting room on chilly days. The standouts here include excellent Russian River Valley pinot noirs, which tend to sell out shortly after they're released, and dense Dry Creek Valley zinfandels. A small selection of picnic fixings and, conveniently, single glasses of wine, are available if you'd like to linger on the veranda or sit at one of the picnic tables in the grassy back yard. Tours are by appointment only, but the tasting room is open daily. *2306 Magnolia Drive; 707-433-5987.*

Seghesio Family Vineyards *map page 205, A-B-1*

Italian immigrant Edoardo Seghesio and his wife, Angela, planted zinfandel vineyards here in 1895 and added a winery in 1902. For years they and their descendants sold wine in bulk to other wineries, including Paul Masson and Gallo, but they finally began bottling wines under their own name in the 1980s. The majority of the grapes used by Seghesio are estate grown, in vineyards in the Alexander, Dry Creek, and Russian River valleys. Even though winemaker Ted Seghesio prefers his wines to be immediately drinkable, they have surprising depth and aging potential. Be sure to try the old vine zinfandel and the chianti, as well as their super-Tuscan blend called Omaggio, a blend of cabernet sauvignon and sangiovese. *14730 Grove Street; 707-433-3579.*

Simi Winery *map page 210, B-3*

The Simi brothers, two Italian émigrés, founded a winery at the northern edge of Healdsburg in 1876 and named it Montepulciano. When this proved too difficult for non-Italian locals to pronounce, the brothers changed the name to Simi Winery. Now owned by French investors Möet-Hennessy–Louis Vuitton, Simi's on an upswing under current winemaker Steve Reeder, who arrived in 2003 after winning great acclaim for his work at Chateau St. Jean. He looks mostly to the Alexander and Russian River valleys for grapes. Simi has long been known for crisp chardonnays, but these days its spicy, jammy cabernet sauvignons are getting attention. The winery also produces modest amounts of sauvignon blanc and merlot. You can glean plenty of info here too, as the twice-daily tour is thorough and the tasting room staff readily discusses the vintages. *16275 Healdsburg Avenue; 800-746-4880.*

■ DRY CREEK VALLEY APPELLATION

If you follow Healdsburg Avenue from downtown Healdsburg to Dry Creek Road and turn northwest, you'll soon feel like you've slipped back in time. Healdsburg looks totally urban by comparison—this is pure, unspoiled countryside. Although the Dry Creek Valley has become renowned for its wines, it has preserved a rural simplicity rarely found in California's Wine Country today.

Dry Creek Road and the parallel West Dry Creek Road, brightened by wildflower-strewn shoulders in spring and early summer, offer tantalizing vineyard views as they skirt the hillside on the east side of the narrow valley. The winding

(opposite) A stroll through Healdsburg.

Canoeing on the Russian River.

roads can be quite narrow in places, forcing you to slow down—a good thing for the many bicyclists who navigate this route.

The valley's well-drained, gravelly floor is planted with chardonnay grapes to the south, where an occasional sea fog creeping in from the Russian River cools the vineyards, and with sauvignon blanc to the north, where the vineyards are warmer. The red decomposed soils of the benchlands bring out the best in zinfandel—the grape for which Dry Creek has become famous—but they also produce great cabernet sauvignon. And these soils seem well suited to Rhône varieties such as cinsault, mourvèdre, and marsanne, which need heat to ripen properly. Grapes like this valley so much that they grow wild in roadside thickets, the way blackberries cluster elsewhere in the West.

The Dry Creek Valley is so picture-perfect it would be a shame to pass up the opportunity to picnic at one of the wineries. For prepared sandwiches, bread, terrific cheeses, and other picnic supplies, stop by the **Dry Creek General Store** (3495 Dry Creek Road; 707-433-4171), established in 1881 and still a popular spot for locals to hang out on the porch.

At work in the vineyards of Seghesio.

Dry Creek Vineyard *map page 210, A/B-2*
Along Lambert Bridge Road, which connects Dry Creek Road and West Dry Creek Road, sits Dry Creek Vineyard, often touted as the first local winery opened since Prohibition. The historical record shows that this is not exactly true, but Dry Creek's founder David Stare played a key role in putting the valley's wines onto the oenological map. Opened in 1972, his winery offers the usual assortment of wines, from big reds to light and fruity whites, but it stands out for its fumé blanc, its zesty dry chenin blanc, and its zinfandel. Dry Creek has a delightful grassy picnic area brightened by flowers and is a perfect place to hang out on a hot summer's day. There are no tours given, but it is open for tastings. *3770 Lambert Bridge Road; 707-433-1000.*

Quivira Vineyards *map page 210, A-2*
Named after a legendary kingdom sought by Spanish explorer Vasquez de Coronado after he was told its streets were paved with gold, Quivira blends the old and the new. Its winery looks like a plain wooden barn, but in 2005 it was covered with solar panels. Founders Henry and Holly Wendt first purchased property here in 1981, coming out with the first small experimental batches of zinfandel

and sauvignon blanc in 1983. More than twenty years later zin and sauvignon blanc are still mainstays, but the winery also produces an excellent grenache and a mourvedre to boot. If the weather's warm, take the self-guided tour around the gardens out front, and be sure to visit the resident pig. *4900 West Dry Creek Road; 707-431-8333.*

★ **Preston Vineyards** *map page 210, A-2*

One of the more remote Dry Creek wineries, Preston Vineyards is nonetheless worth seeking out for its wonderfully homespun feel. Once you wind your way down their private road, flanked by vineyards and punctuated by the occasional olive tree, you'll be welcomed by the sight of a few farmhouses encircling a shady yard prowled by several friendly cats. In summer, a small selection of organic produce grown in their gardens is sold from an impromptu stand on their

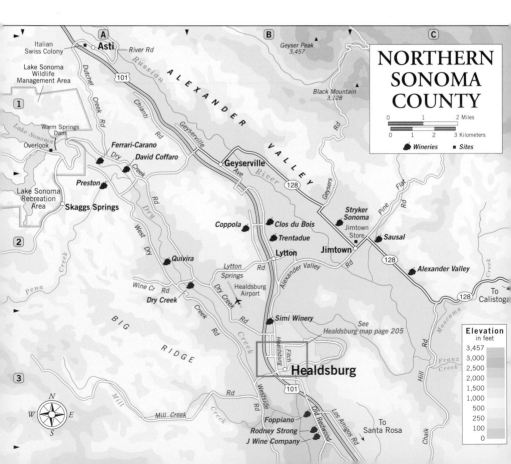

The Dry Creek Valley's gravelly soil has become renowned for producing quality zinfandel.

front porch, and house-made bread and olive oil are available year-round. Their down-home style is particularly in evidence on Sundays, the only day of the week that tasting room staffers sell a three-liter jug of Guadagni Red, a zinfandel, cinsault, and carignane blend filled from the barrel right in front of you.

Owners Lou and Susan Preston are committed to organic growing techniques and use only estate-grown grapes in their wines. Sauvignon blanc, barbera, and zinfandel are standouts, and the excellent L. Preston is a blend of syrah, cinsault, carignane, and mourvèdre, the heat-seeking grapes that tend to do so well in the Dry Creek Valley. They only produce 8,000 or so cases of wine a year, most sold at the winery, so be sure to stock up if you find something you like. *9282 West Dry Creek Road; 707-433-3372.*

David Coffaro Estate Vineyard *map page 210, A-1/2*
Some of the more interesting wines in the Dry Creek Valley today are being concocted by David Coffaro, who takes his cue from French blends. Here zinfandel, for example, might be mixed with tannat, a varietal popular in the Basque region and Uruguay but not often found in the United States. The results are typi-

cally big, complex, fruit-forward wines that are easily drunk shortly after bottling, but can also be aged for several years.

The tasting room resembles an enormous garage where barrels take the place of cars, and Coffaro's beloved Raider memorabilia lines the wall behind the bar. The amiably gruff pouring staff aren't as chatty as some of the gregarious tasting room employees elsewhere, but once you ask a few questions, they'll share their deep knowledge of the wines. When wine is in the barrels, they're happy to allow visitors a taste, since most of the wines are sold according to a futures program, before it makes its way into the bottle (you can even purchase their wine while the grapes are still on the vine). *7485 Dry Creek Road; 707-433-9715.*

Ferrari-Carano   *map page 210, A-1*
Villa Fiore, this winery's visitors center, is Dry Creek's oddball. The pink confection looks like a shiny, Disney-esque re-creation of a grand Tuscan villa, complete with a lush garden and endless stretches of neatly manicured lawns. The wines here are a bit less grand than the setting, although the chardonnay and Trésor, a Bordeaux-style blend, are as good as they come.

(opposite) Vines frame the tasting rooms at Quivira Vineyards. (above) The summer festival season always includes some grape-stomping contests.

Preston Vineyards has a friendly, homespun appeal.

The owners have vineyards in the Alexander and Knights valleys as well as Dry Creek, plus vines in the Napa part of the Carneros. Winemakers Aaron Piotter and Sarah Quider believe in blending, so it's tough to figure out where exactly the grapes for a wine labeled "Sonoma County" come from. A zinfandel made from Dry Creek grapes is excellent; a cabernet-sangiovese blend named Siena is also worth trying. Downstairs the Enoteca Lounge pours reserve wine. There's also a spectacular view of the grand barrel room. You must call ahead to reserve a spot on the single daily tour, but the tasting room and gardens are open all day. *8761 Dry Creek Road; 707-433-6700.*

■ ALEXANDER VALLEY APPELLATION

The Alexander Valley AVA covers both sides of the upper Russian River Valley from northeast of Healdsburg to the Mendocino County line north of Cloverdale. Its landscape varies from flat bottomlands to hills more than 1,500 feet high. It is warmer than the Russian River appellation, and its small side valleys become very hot in summer. Sea fogs only occasionally drift in from the Santa Rosa Plain, and though they cool the land, they burn off more quickly than on the lower river.

A view of Ferrari-Carano, Dry Creek, Sonoma County.

There's a lot going on climatically and geologically. Soils include loam, gravelly loam, and gravelly sandy loam, as well as well-drained gravel flats near the river. But because as recently as the 1980s the valley was mostly planted to walnuts, pears, prunes, and bulk grapes—except for the sections left in scrub and pasture—one might argue that experimentation here has hardly begun. So far, chardonnay, sauvignon blanc, zinfandel, and cabernet sauvignon seem to do well in places. Italian grapes such as sangiovese or the Rhône varieties, which do so well in the Dry Creek Valley, may make great wines in the warmer parts of the Alexander Valley. Stay posted for a decade or two. This is a valley full of surprises.

■ **GEYSERVILLE** *map page 210, B-1/2*
Not long ago, Geyserville was a dusty farm town with little to offer wine tourists besides a grocery store and a large mural depicting regional roadside attractions. This is still little more than a crossroads, with a few small markets and a good restaurant or two, but the storefront tasting room **Locals** (21023 Geyserville Avenue; 707-857-4900) is definitely worth a stop for serious wine tasters. Local winemakers, critics, and tourists come here to taste wines produced by nine small

wineries that do not have tasting rooms of their own, including Laurel Glen Winery, Dark Horse, Ramazzotti Wines, and others. There's no fee for tasting, and the extremely knowledgeable staff is happy to pour you a flight of several wines so you can compare, say, several different cabernet sauvignons.

■ UPPER ALEXANDER VALLEY
West of U.S. 101, wineries of the Dry Creek and Alexander Valley appellations mingle. That's because the dividing line runs along Dry Creek Ridge, and wineries in the canyons are closer to the Russian River than to Dry Creek.

Trentadue Winery   *map page 210, B-2*
When Leo and Evelyn Trentadue decided to move to a truly rural location in 1959, they found their new home in a neglected Alexander Valley prune and pear orchard. True to their Tuscan heritage, the family planted classic Italian grape

During the Russian River Wine Road Barrel Tasting, you can "preview" wine before it's bottled.

varietals such as sangiovese and carignane on their property. They still produce wines that are 100 percent tempranillo and mourvedre, something of a rarity in the area, but now they've added merlot, cabernet sauvignon, cuvée, and zinfandel to their lineup, and they have earned a reputation for making big, beefy red wines.

When visiting their ivy-covered Tuscan-style villa, be sure to taste their Old Patch Red, a blend of zinfandel, petite sirah, carignane, and syrah with a long, lingering finish. Fans of port should ask about the merlot-based port with chocolate essence, available for an additional fee. Tours, by reservation only, include a short ride through the vineyards in a tractor-pulled wagon, and the tasting room is open daily. *19170 Geyserville Avenue; 707-433-3104.*

Clos du Bois   *map page 210, B-2*

There's no fancy French connection here; the name was suggested by the first owner's children, who thought the ho-hum title "Woods Vineyard" would sound better rephrased in French. Now Constellation Brands company holds the reins, and they farm more than 900 acres in the Alexander Valley and buy grapes from several other locations, including the Dry Creek and Russian River valleys. Although the large, airy, modern tasting room and gift shop here aren't particularly atmospheric, the winery is worth a stop for its friendly staff and an in-depth tour that takes you through a demonstration vineyard and usually includes a barrel tasting in the cellar. (Make an appointment for the twice-daily tours.)

Though you may be familiar with their inexpensive, approachable "Classic" wines, also look for their more intense Proprietary Series, especially the top-of-the-line Marlstone Bordeaux blend, which has been superb in past years. Their shop sells the full range of wines, and half bottles are good bets for picnickers who want to pick up some cheese from the deli case and take a seat at the tables under the gazebos outside. *19410 Geyserville Avenue; 707-857-1651.*

Francis Ford Coppola's Winery   *map page 210, B-2*

After several years fine-tuning his work at his Napa property, Rubicon Estate, filmmaker-winemaker-publisher-hotelier Francis Ford Coppola decided to branch into the Alexander Valley. In 2006, he snapped up this majestic French-style château, formerly of Chateau Souverain, to showcase his less-expensive wines. Where the Napa winery (see the Northern Napa Valley chapter) will focus on the high-end vintages, this winery has a more casual approach.

At this writing, the winery was undergoing significant construction. When all is said and done, the new facility is expected to have a pool and family day passes. A casual café is expected to serve pizzas and salads, as well as other light fare.

Tours were not yet available at this writing but were in the works. In the meantime, the tasting room staff was keeping visitors happy with generous pours of wines from their well-priced Rosso & Bianco line, as well as samples of the sauvignon blanc, merlot, zinfandel, and pinot noir from the more complex Diamond Collection. A new line of wines under development will focus on grapes grown in the Sonoma Valley. *300 Via Archimedes; 707-857-1400.*

■ LOWER ALEXANDER VALLEY

The lovely lower Alexander Valley is one of Sonoma's least-visited regions. Driving through the rolling rills along Highway 128, you're more likely to have to slow down for tandem bicyclists than for other drivers. And you might find you're the only visitor in the tasting room at some of the small, family-owned wineries. This, of course, means that it's a particularly good destination for picnicking. Luckily, the **Jimtown Store** (6706 Highway 128; 707-433-1212) has great espresso and a good selection of deli items, including their signature brie-and-chopped-olive sandwich. While you're here, take a few minutes to browse through their gifts, which include both housewares and old-fashioned toys like sock monkeys.

★ Stryker Sonoma Winery and Vineyards   *map page 210, B-2*

You can catch a tempting glimpse of the Stryker tasting room from Highway 128, and the building becomes even more intriguing as you approach it. Dramatic horizontal concrete louvers frame the barrel room. Inside the tasting room, vaulted ceilings and seemingly endless walls of windows onto the vineyards suggest you've entered a cathedral to wine. The architecture isn't too show-offy, though. It integrates well with the landscape, with a stone wall framing the building and earthy colors predominating.

The wines might not be *quite* as dramatic as the building, but they are definitely worth checking out. Most of their bottles—which generally tend toward the dry and fruit-forward—are single-varietals, such as chardonnay, petit verdot, merlot,

Harvesting the bounty of Sonoma County: red-hot chili peppers (above) and Alexander Valley grapes (below).

The hibiscus tea is good hot or cold at Jimtown Store near Healdsburg.

zinfandel, and cabernet sauvignon. The two exceptions are Bordeaux-style blends, including the powerful E1K Red Blend, which, unfortunately, is not usually poured in the tasting room. (Though it never hurts to ask if there might be some open.) The tasting room is open daily, but there are no tours. *5110 Highway 128; 707-433-1944.*

Sausal Winery   *map page 210, C-2*
Founded in 1956, family-run Sausal lures you in with an excellent cabernet and truly outstanding zinfandel, the best of which comes from vines more than 100 years old, resulting in a strong brambly flavor. Buy a bottle, grab a table on the patio, and enjoy a picnic lunch and the view of vines and oak trees stretching all the way to the hills. Sniff the air. If the wind is right, the breeze carries a heady aroma of grapes and wild laurel. Tastings are offered daily. *7370 Highway 128; 707-433-2285.*

Alexander Valley Vineyards is a terrific picnic spot.

Alexander Valley Vineyards   *map page 210, C-2*

Off Highway 128 is the 1841 homestead of Cyrus Alexander, for whom the valley is named. The Wetzel family bought part of the land homesteaded by Cyrus Alexander from his heirs in 1963 and restored the historic Cyrus Alexander Adobe to serve as their family home. But the Wetzels also planted vineyards, and in 1975 they built a winery with adobe blocks and weathered wood.

Today when you visit the winery, the yellow labs belonging to Hank Wetzel, who oversees the vineyard and winery operations, are likely to lope up to meet you. Head into the tasting room to taste the splendid Sin Zin, which is fairly low in alcohol for a California zinfandel and full of ripe cherry flavor. Their estate chardonnay will please fans of round, rich incarnations of the grape. After tasting, you can wander up a grassy hill behind the winery to the cemetery of the Alexander family or grab a bottle and head for the picnic tables. Alexander Valley is open for tastings daily; you will need an appointment to tour the wine caves. *8644 Highway 128; 707-433-7209.*

A Great Drive in Northern Sonoma

Healdsburg is the area's hub, so plan on starting a day's drive here, nabbing an early breakfast in the town plaza. From downtown Healdsburg, take Healdsburg Avenue to Dry Creek Road and turn west. Almost as soon as you pass under the U.S. 101 freeway bridge, you'll feel like you're in the true countryside, free of urban sprawl. Turn left on Lambert Bridge Road, then right on West Dry Creek Road, taking your time on this scenic track. Drive past the "No Outlet" sign and veer right on the narrow lane alongside Peña Creek until you see an old barn on your left and the Preston Vineyard sign on the right. After visiting Preston, return the way you came until you reach Yoakim Bridge Road. Turn left there, then right on Dry Creek Road and left on Canyon Road. Just after Canyon Road crosses U.S. 101, turn right on Highway 128, which will lead you through Geyserville to Jimtown. Pick up picnic fixings at the Jimtown Store, then backtrack along Highway 128 less than a mile to the dramatic tasting room at Stryker Sonoma, where you can taste their wines and enjoy your picnic.

Next return southeast on Highway 128; at the Jimtown Store, turn left on Alexander Valley Road. Veer left at Healdsburg Avenue to return to downtown Healdsburg, where you can taste wine at one of its many tasting rooms before dinner.

If you're lucky enough to have a second day, stock up on sandwiches at the Oakville Grocery before leaving Healdsburg. Drive south on Healdsburg Avenue and turn right on Mill Street. After it crosses U.S. 101 it turns into Westside Road. Wind along Westside Road, looking out for the many cyclists along this route, for about 20 minutes to Gary Farrell, where you can see much of the Russian River Valley below you from the tasting room. Return to Healdsburg by winding back the way you came along Westside Road, stopping to taste at whichever of the many tasting rooms appeals to you: Porter Creek is small and rustic, for instance, while Hop Kiln is housed in an unusual historic building.

Poppies and grapes at Madroña Vineyards, in the Sierra Foothills.

BEYOND NAPA AND SONOMA

To many a visitor, "California Wine Country" is synonymous with the grape-growing areas of the Napa Valley and Sonoma County, but within the state lie several other regions with splendid wineries. In this chapter we slip north of Napa and Sonoma to Mendocino County's Anderson Valley and head east to the Clarksburg, Lodi, and Sierra Foothills AVAs. In the next chapter we visit the best of California's Central Coast.

■ ANDERSON VALLEY APPELLATION

Time for the road less traveled. If you turn off U.S. 101 at Cloverdale to wind their way west along Highway 128, you'll discover a Wine Country that's worlds away from the tour buses and faux French châteaus of Napa. Some combination of distance from San Francisco (the drive from the city takes about 2½ hours on a good day) and the hairpin switchback roads seems to have preserved the unpretentious, rustic nature of this region.

A drive here takes you through chaparral and oak forests, pastureland and apple orchards. Restaurants and B&Bs are relatively few and far between. Although the increasing attention to Anderson Valley wines has brought an uptick in tourism, this is still the spot to enjoy life in the slow lane.

At the western end of the valley, known to locals as the "Deep End," cool fog and significant rainfall create ideal conditions for growing certain northern European varietals like chardonnay, riesling, gewürztraminer, and the Anderson Valley AVA's star, pinot noir. Farther inland, where summer temperatures can be up to 15 degrees warmer than those of the Deep End, chardonnay and sauvignon blanc are the favored varietals. Many of the grapes grown throughout the region are sold to winemakers elsewhere, but there's an increasing tendency to hold onto the goods. Locals who are tired of seeing Napa and Sonoma wineries get the credit for wines produced from Anderson Valley grapes are taking matters into their own hands—and their own crushers. The latest locally produced wines are slowly moving beyond the valley's reputation for modestly priced but unspectacular vintages and are winning a new fan base.

The valley's wine boom dates from only the early 1970s, when Tony Husch of Husch Vineyards and Ted Bennett of Navarro Vineyards planted gewürztraminer

Boonville's Anderson Valley Brewing Company opened in the 1980s, before many local wineries.

vines in what they considered to be the perfect climate for this finicky Alsatian grape. But Husch found that chardonnay and pinot noir grew even better here, and every year since the number of acres dedicated to pinot noir increases.

It was John Scharffenberger who, in 1981, firmly placed the Anderson Valley among America's top producers. The French were so impressed with his bubbly that, in 1982, the Champagne producer Roederer moved in next door instead of settling in the Napa Valley as other French wine entrepreneurs had done. Today, the sparklers of these neighboring wineries consistently rank among the top half dozen produced in North America.

■ BOONVILLE *map page 226, A-4*

At the center of the Anderson Valley is Boonville, a small farming town once so isolated its residents invented a lingo all their own, known as Boontling, or Boont, for short. Few traces of this unique language survive, though you'll still find Boontling dictionaries sold in local shops. Boonville, whose other regional claims to fame are the annual Apple Show in September and two or three annual sheep dog trials, is a

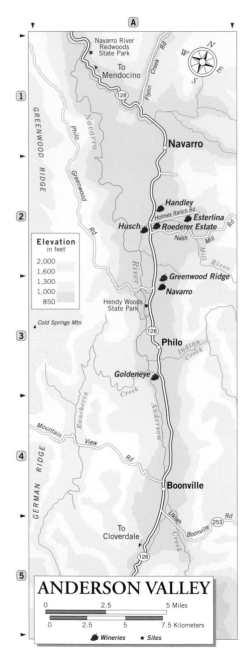

ANDERSON VALLEY

| 0 | 2.5 | 5 Miles |
| 0 | 2.5 | 5 | 7.5 Kilometers |

🍷 Wineries   ■ Sites

less lonely place these days, thanks largely to the stream of Bay Area weekenders passing through town en route to the Mendocino Coast.

Anderson Valley grapegrowers have played a big role in ending the valley's isolation, but despite wineries moving into the valley and fancy restaurants popping up, Boonville hasn't changed much. Like the local wines, the food here is of high quality yet down to earth— for instance, the **Boonville Hotel** (see the Where to Stay in Wine Country chapter) serves marvelous roadhouse meals. You can also hit the **Boonville General Store** (17810 Farrer Lane; 707-895-9477) for delicious baked goods and organic deli food. Or for a change of pace from winery touring, you can visit the **Anderson Valley Brewing Company** (17700 Route 253, at Highway 128; 707-895-2337), which has a beer tasting room and offers tours twice daily.

■ PHILO   *map page 226, A-3*
Northwest of Boonville, Highway 128 cuts through a low ridge, which is just high enough to impede the fog creeping up the Navarro River from the ocean. North of here the land is much cooler than in the southern valley—making it perfect for redwoods, apples, and grapes. The town of Philo, which is little more than a

Navarro Vineyards sits amid rolling hills of redwoods and other trees.

wide spot in the road, has long been an apple-growing center. If you're visiting in summer or fall, stock up at one of the many fruit stands along the highway. One of the best is **Gowan's Oak Tree** (6600 Highway 128, 707-895-3353), about seven miles northwest of Philo.

Northwest of the few businesses that constitute "downtown" Philo, almost to the town of Navarro, the **Floodgate Store & Deli** (1819 Highway 128, 707-895-2870) is a great lunch stop for its chili and Mexican food. A couple of miles farther north stand the magnificent giant trees of **Navarro River Redwoods State Park** (Highway 128, 2 miles east of Highway 1; 707-937-5804), a lovely spot for a shady stroll.

From east to west, below are some of Anderson Valley's best wineries to visit.

Goldeneye Winery   *map page 226, A-3*

Don't get any James Bond ideas: this winery takes its name from the Goldeneye duck, whose migratory flyway is nearby. The owners of the Napa Valley's well-respected Duckhorn Vineyards have been making pinot noir here from local grapes with very satisfying results. Leisurely tastings take place in a restored farmhouse, where you can sit at the Arts and Crafts–style dining table

while the staff discusses the relative merits of their various styles of pinot noir. Or you can take your glass to the shady back patio, which overlooks a vineyard. *9200 Highway 128; 800-208-0438.*

★ **Navarro Vineyards**   *map page 226, A-3*
If you're looking for multiple choices, Navarro is a good bet since it typically has a very long list of vintages ready for tasting. The winery, started in 1973 by Ted Bennett, produces an unusually diverse array of wines for the region, including cabernet sauvignon, chardonnay, a dry rosé, and, of course, pinot noir. The unusual Alsatian-style gewürztraminers, though, are the winery's most impressive offering. The cheeses and smoked salmon for sale inspire more than a few picnics at the tables overlooking the vineyards. Navarro prides itself on its sustainable business practices, including worker benefits (most of its labor force gets health insurance and vacation, a rarity in California's wine industry) and eco-friendly policies, such as reduced use of fossil fuels. *5601 Highway 128; 707-895-3686.*

Greenwood Ridge   *map page 226, A-3*
Though Greenwood's octagonal, redwood tasting room is smack in the middle of the Anderson Valley, the grapes for the wines are grown several miles away in the Mendocino Ridge AVA, above the fog that often blankets the area. Zinfandel and cabernet sauvignon are the stars here, but the sauvignon blanc and white riesling— the first wine that winemaker Allan Green ever produced—have also won multiple gold medals. The late-harvest riesling has a full and fruity yet remarkably clean taste. This winery is green in more than name alone; in 2006, it became the first solar-powered winery in the Anderson Valley. *5501 Highway 128; 707-895-2002.*

★ **Roederer Estate**   *map page 226, A-2*
From the looks of this unassuming tasting room, which blends into the hillside, it would be hard to guess that this is an outpost of a renowned French Champagne-maker. Lured by the cool, foggy conditions perfect for growing pinot noir and chardonnay grapes, Roederer opened its American operation here in 1981. Only estate-grown grapes go into the sparkling wines, which are generally considered among the very best sparklers made in the United States. They share

(previous pages) Harvesters really hustle—for both the good of the grapes and their compensation. (They're often paid per bin.)

characteristics of the finest Champagne, with a creamy, full-bodied character and fine, tiny bubbles, and they're remarkably consistent from year to year. A tasting here (which has a small fee) includes their flagship L'Ermitage Brut, a chardonnay–pinot noir blend. *4501 Highway 128; 707-895-2288.*

Husch Vineyards *map page 226, A-2*
The setting here—a converted late-19th-century barn, with a rusted antique car in the yard and picnic tables spread out under the trees—makes a tasting feel particularly down-home. Established in 1971, this is the oldest winery in the Anderson Valley. The zesty estate-grown gewürztraminer is about as good as it gets, and the pinot noir demonstrates that elusive aroma and flavor characteristic of the best wines made from this varietal. But don't neglect the top-notch chardonnay. *4400 Highway 128; 800-554-8724.*

Handley Cellars *map page 226, A-2*
Milla Handley caught the wine bug while studying at the University of California at Davis, and she and her husband, Rex McClellan, opened Handley Cellars in 1982. The winery produces a splendid chardonnay from Anderson Valley grapes, a delicately blushing pinot gris, an exotically fruity gewürztraminer, and some very good sparkling wines. Your attention may also be caught by the

---

A GREAT DRIVE IN ANDERSON VALLEY

All of the Anderson Valley wineries covered here are just off Highway 128, which means navigating here is a cinch. From U.S. 101, take Highway 128 west at Cloverdale. You'll wind through the woods and vineyards for about 30 miles before reaching the town of Boonville, where you might want to get out, stretch your legs, get lunch or stock up on picnic supplies before continuing west to the wineries. (If you're keen to picnic with a vineyard view, Navarro's visitors area is your best bet.) Continuing west along Highway 128, Roederer is a must-stop for fans of bubbly. You can pick and choose from among the remaining wineries in the chapter; all are visible from the highway with the exception of Esterlina (reservations required), which is about 2 miles from the highway. Highway 128 eventually connects with the coastal Highway 1.

winery's impressive, large-scale works of international folk art collected by Milla and her father, such as a 14th-century granite Ganesh figure. *3151 Highway 128; 707-895-3876.*

Esterlina Vineyards and Winery   *map page 226, A-2*
One of the few African-American–owned wineries in California, the former Pepperwood Springs was bought by the Sterling family in 2000. They've got plantings in several promising areas, including the Russian River Valley, the Alexander Valley, and the nearby Cole Ranch region, the smallest of the AVAs at less than one-quarter square mile, where the family grows pinot noir, merlot, riesling, and cabernet sauvignon. The gravelly soil of their Alexander Valley land produces grapes for luscious cabernet sauvignons and award-winning pinot noirs. The winery is open by appointment only, so call ahead. *1200 Holmes Ranch Road; 707-895-2920.*

■ LIVERMORE VALLEY AND LODI APPELLATIONS

Livermore and Lodi may not have the name recognition (yet) or the natural beauty of other California wine regions, but these two appellations could be the sleeper hits of your wine tour. They're particularly easy to reach if you're coming from San Francisco, and they're both refreshingly untrampled by tourists. Most importantly, these rich agricultural regions are turning out noteworthy, locally grown and vinted wines.

Local wine production wasn't always something to crow about—even though both Livermore and Lodi have grown excellent grapes since the 1800s. Instead, growers here often sold their grapes to their big-name neighbors up north, and Napa and Sonoma vintners turned some of those crops into prizewinning wines. What didn't get sold to these better-known vintners was shipped in bulk. The Lodi and Livermore names thus became synonymous with cheap California jug wine—if they were recognized at all.

The tide began to turn in 1979, after the already famous Robert Mondavi bought the Woodbridge wine company. (His parents had once been Lodi growers.) Other Lodi producers followed suit, and in the 1980s the premium wine industry picked up in the Livermore Valley too.

Livermore Valley, just east of San Francisco Bay, is a patchwork of housing developments and vineyards, ringed by mountains and crisscrossed by freeways and high-tension wires. Lodi sits south of Sacramento in the broad, flat Central Valley, which is planted with vineyards, orchards, and vegetable fields. Both AVAs blister in summer; the weather is relatively mild the rest of the year. Because of its suburban setting so close to San Francisco, the Livermore Valley sees a very active tasting scene on weekends, with locals and day-trippers flowing in and out of about 35 tasting rooms. Lodi remains quiet—it's still very much a farming community. Its 60-plus wineries draw Bay Area weekenders, Sacramento locals, and vacationers traveling between the Sierras and the coast.

■ LIVERMORE VALLEY APPELLATION

A quick shot east of San Francisco on the interstate, the Livermore Valley AVA lies at the edge of the East Bay area, south of I 580, between I-680 and I-5. The sunny, warm valley cuts east–west, by night channeling in ocean breezes that cool the air by 30 degrees or more. It's ideal grape weather, and the rocky soil provides stressful growing conditions that, along with a long, hot growing season, make grapes sweeter and wines more complex. Livermore Valley winemakers have had success especially with petite sirah, chardonnay, and sauvignon blanc, but they continue to experiment with different varieties.

Robert Livermore planted the valley's first commercial vineyards in the 1840s, and C.H. Wente and James Concannon built the region's wine industry, both establishing wineries in 1883. The valley's fifty pre-Prohibition wineries pioneered large-scale viticultural methods such as overhead irrigation and machine harvesting. But the Livermore Valley faded into obscurity during Prohibition even though it continued to grow large quantities of grapes. Its comeback, sparked in the 1990s, is attracting some top talent, and the region appears poised to produce its first modern blockbusters.

Many of the Livermore Valley's tasting rooms line up along Tesla Road; others are secluded along quiet back roads that curve through rolling vineyards.

Wente Vineyards Estate Winery *map page 234, C-2*

By far the Livermore Valley's largest producer—each year they make 1 million cases of wine—family-owned Wente is also among the state's oldest. Their reputation stands on the shoulders of chardonnay. In a typical year good acidity does much to balance toasty oak notes in the chardonnay, and the sauvignon blanc is aromatic and crisp. The reds—cabernet sauvignon, syrah, and merlot—tend to deliver almost too much smooth, round fruit. You can taste estate, single-vineyard, and small-lot wines at the brick-walled main Estate Tasting Room in the original winery, which is always busy. From here you can also take a tour of the production facility.

Tastings are also held at the Vineyard Tasting Room (5050 Arroyo Road; 925-456-2305). It's farther out of town and is part of a landscaped Wente complex that includes a white-tablecloth restaurant, a golf course, and an event space. On weekends, guided educational tastings are offered in the sandstone caves below. *5565 Tesla Road; 925-456-2405.*

Workers prune vines in preparation for a new growing season.

The Steven Kent Winery *map page 234, B/C-2*
This is the kind of wine that wins the fierce devotion of groupies. Meticulously crafted in tiny lots, the hard-to-find bottlings of velvety cabernet sauvignon, chardonnay, and Bordeaux-style blends exemplify intense California style: concentrated fruit and oak unapologetically fill the mouth and nose. The sleekly designed barrel room is meant as much for worship as for commerce. *5443 Tesla Road; 925-243-6440.*

Concannon Vineyard *map page 234, B/C-2*
Still family-run, Concannon was founded by an Irish immigrant and for many decades specialized in sacramental wine. Its recent efforts have centered around petite sirah, a Rhône-based grape that Concannon claims to have created in 1961. Since then, the boldly flavored red wine, rich with spicy blackberry flavors, has been the winery's trademark. In the barn-like tasting room, whose walls are hung with historical photographs and clippings, the staff also pours current releases of cabernet sauvignon, syrah, and sauvignon blanc grown in Concannon's Central Coast vineyards. The Livermore-grown wines, including the best of the petite sirah, are sold only to wine club members, but if you're lucky there might just be a bottle open. *4590 Tesla Road; 925-456-2505.*

Mitchell Katz Winery at Ruby Hill   *map page 234, A/B-2*
A precise reconstruction of the 1887 Ruby Hill Winery, this thoroughly up-to-date visitor facility is built of bricks and keystones reclaimed when the original place was torn down. The building, which has the stern look of a Victorian-era factory, stands at the end of a palm-lined drive just east of the Livermore town line in Pleasanton. Big red wines, such as cabernet sauvignon, petite sirah, and zinfandel, dominate the winery's repertoire, but a few respectable renditions of sangiovese offer a lighter touch of oak. The tasting room is open Thursday through Sunday only. *1188 Vineyard Avenue, Pleasanton; 925-931-0744.*

★ Thomas Coyne   *map page 234, B-2/3*
Amid stacked barrels of aging wine and idle bits of wine-making equipment, Tom and Emilie Coyne pour their own creations in an impossibly picturesque 1881 winery. At the end of a long dirt drive, you'll find the timber-roofed building, its heavy, weathered oak door usually open to the view. The surrounding vineyards are scattered with the sagging outbuildings of the old Chateau Bellevue wine operation, but the scenery is just icing on the cake here. Consistently outstanding, earthy Rhône-style reds—grenache, syrah, mourvèdre, and several blends—plus juicy whites such as viognier, have made Thomas Coyne one of the Livermore Valley's most respected vintners. The winery is open on weekends only; Wednesday through Sunday you can sip a sample at Tesla Vintners (5143 Tesla Road; 925-606-9463), a cooperative tasting room. *51 East Vallecitos Road; 925-373-6541.*

■ LODI APPELLATION

Along the Mokelumne River south of Sacramento, the Lodi AVA leads all California in grape production. Here, growers harvest more zinfandel, merlot, cabernet sauvignon, sauvignon blanc, and chardonnay than in any of the state's other AVAs. The numbers are staggering: about 750 growers, more than 90,000 vineyard acres, 600,000 tons of grapes annually. All of this action goes on 35 miles from the state capital and a 100-mile drive northwest of San Francisco. You can get here easily via I-5 or Highway 99; wineries ring downtown Lodi.

What makes this such a super-fertile spot? The wide, flat plain on which Lodi sits owes its exceptional fertility to a thick build-up of eons-old sediment that washed down many rivers from the Sierra Nevada. Farms and ranches have been

(previous pages) Coastal fog creates perfect conditions for Roederer's sparkling-wine grapes.

reaping the soil's riches for generations; Lodi's first vineyards were planted in the 1850s. For more than a century, grapes were just another crop—albeit a major driver of the local economy. Lodi finally earned AVA status in 1986, but winemakers here have had to fight for respect. Many of the early vineyards still produce, including some that yield potent zinfandel. Rhône, Italian, and Spanish varieties are making an appearance. In 2006, seven subappellations were named within the Lodi appellation, marking the area's progress as a premium wine region.

Since the early 1990s, Lodi has led the way in the sustainable viticulture movement. The Lodi-Woodbridge Winegrape Commission, the local industry association, achieved a California first in 2006, with the publication of *The Lodi Rules for Sustainable Winegrowing,* a set of environmentally friendly viticulture standards for the appellation. The forward-looking organization also operates the **Lodi Wine & Visitor Center,** open daily, where you can see excellent exhibits on sustainable grape-growing, winemaking, and Lodi's wine history. The tasting room pours a

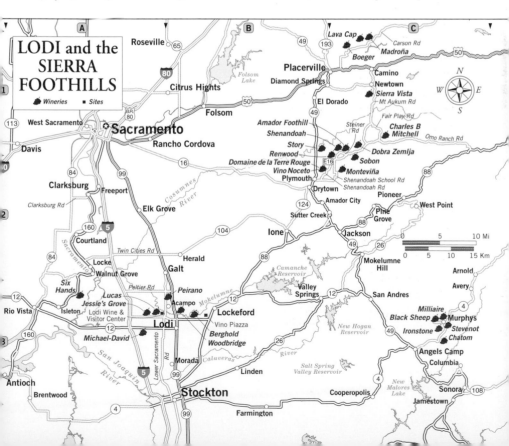

LODI and the SIERRA FOOTHILLS

🍇 Wineries   ■ Sites

The Lodi visitors center has eye-opening exhibits on sustainable viticulture.

wide selection of area wines and sells them by the bottle. *2545 West Turner Road (east off I-5); 209-367-4727.*

Another interesting Lodi stop is **Vino Piazza**, an old grape-processing plant now occupied by the tasting rooms of about a dozen micro-wineries. Wander from building to building and taste barbera and zinfandel from Macchia or mourvèdre and cabernet franc from Stone Garden Vineyards. The wines may be of uneven quality, but where else have you seen a tasting room in a concrete fermenting vat? Check out the schedule of weekend special events, live music, and theater performances. *12470 Locke Road, Lockeford; 209-727-9770.*

Berghold Vineyards & Winery   *map page 239, B-3*
A hint of Lodi's future? Perhaps, if Lodi is the "next Napa." This glitzy visitor facility showcases the deep pockets and antiques collection of Joe Berghold as much as it does his wine. Opened in 2005, the tasting room recalls an earlier wine era with its vintage Victorian interior, including restored, salvaged mantelpieces, leaded glass, and a 26-foot bar. All of the respectable, estate-grown wines, such as syrah and late-harvest viognier, pay homage to French wine styles. You can gift-shop for high-end wine doodads too. *17343 North Cherry Road; 209-333-9291.*

Oak-barrel aging takes place on a grand scale at Woodbridge.

Woodbridge Winery   *map page 239, B-3*
Although Woodbridge may sound too familiar to you (overexposure to their chardonnay at your grocery store?), a visit to the facility is fascinating. Woodbridge may be one of the top-selling wines in the U.S., but the tasting room is surprisingly small and humble. Its Mission-style building lies incongruously in front of a massive factory of giant tanks, pipelines, and warehouses. Twice-daily tours take visitors into vast aging rooms, past speeding bottling lines, and to sparkling laboratories.

Woodbridge's high-profile success helped shape the entire industry in Lodi. When Robert Mondavi bought the old co-op in 1979, he turned out some of Lodi's first single-label premium wines. In 1986, this winery started to produce and vintage-date varietally labeled wines. Such innovations encouraged other local wineries to move away from bulk to higher-quality wines. You can sample the best-sellers here; they're competent but unsurprising. Instead, look for the hard-to-find and tasting room–exclusive offerings such as the Lodi Old Vine Zinfandel and a well-aged port. *5950 East Woodbridge Road; 209-365-8139.*

Peirano Estate Vineyards *map page 239, A/B-3*
The Lodi vineyards planted by Italian immigrant Giacomo Peirano have been in continuous production since the early 1880s. Today, great-grandson Lance Randolph grows chardonnay, cabernet sauvignon, merlot, and most notably zinfandel from old vines that are head-trained (pruned like miniature trees, instead of being trained along trellising wires). The wines are rich and full-flavored, but they also have a good complexity and a crisp acid backbone. The tasting room is open only Saturday and Sunday, and there is a picnic area among the vines. *21831 North Highway 99, Acampo; 209-369-9463.*

Lucas Winery *map page 239, A-3*
David Lucas was one of the first local producers to start making serious wine, back in 1978, and labeling it with the Lodi name. Today, his are among Lodi's most sought-after wines, especially the ripely fruity zinfandel. In addition to zin, Lucas makes a light chardonnay with subtle oaky flavors. The tasting room here is open from Thursday through Sunday; have a look around before or after you sip, or take the hour-and-a-half tour for $55. *18196 North Davis Road; 209-368-2006.*

Michael-David's tasting room shares space with the family's produce stand.

Jessie's Grove *map page 239, A-3*

For a glimpse of 19th-century life in the San Joaquin Valley, stop at this ranch and poke around the outdoor display of decommissioned farm equipment. Shaded by ancient oak trees, a ramshackle 1870s outbuilding houses the tasting room, whose raw wood walls are covered with framed historical photos and memorabilia. The friendly staff pours a popular, zesty zinfandel called Earth, Zin & Fire, a boldly oaked chardonnay, and other offerings. If a current release of their Ancient Vine Carignane is available, check out what 120-year-old vines can do. *1973 West Turner Road; 209-368-0880.*

★ Michael–David Vineyards *map page 239, A-3*

Fifth-generation farmers-turned-winemakers Michael and David Phillips operate their very laid-back tasting room at Phillips Farms, a rustic roadside fruit stand where they still sell their family's gorgeous produce. They've been making zinfandel, syrah, viognier, chardonnay, merlot, and cabernet sauvignon since 1984; the Rhône-style wines labeled Incognito are especially worth a try. Shop for picnic provisions and homemade jam, sit at one of the round tables at the Farm Café for a real burger and truly killer pie, and step out back to visit the herb gardens and farm animals. *4580 West Highway 12; 209-368-7384.*

■ SIERRA FOOTHILLS APPELLATION

The winemaking scene across California's Gold Rush country exemplifies that cliché, "oldie but goodie." Several of the vineyards here have vines dating back to the early 20th century, and the region is known for potent, high-alcohol wines made from these tough old-timers. It's a great chance to try some liquid history.

The Sierra Foothills AVA (which overlaps the El Dorado and Shenandoah Valley AVAs) teems with pocket-size, distinctly different vineyards. Its microclimates vary depending on the elevation, so the Foothills produce everything from barbera and sangiovese to chardonnay and riesling. Of the 100-plus wineries now spreading along Highway 49, roughly from Nevada City in the north to Angels Camp in the south, most remain very small, producing only a few thousand cases a year.

John Muir strolls a Sierra Foothills vineyard he planted.

Vines were planted here shortly after the Gold Rush of 1849, when tens of thousands of fortune-seekers swarmed into the mountains and created a massive insta-market for everything from soap to wine. According to naturalist John Muir, who explored the mountains later in the 19th century, pockets of the area were "settled mostly by Italians and Germans, who plant a few vegetables and grape-vines at odd times, while their main business is mining and prospecting." Vineyards were well established by the 1870s and wineries were going full-steam by the 1890s. Most of these operations fell victim to Prohibition, but many of the abandoned vines survived.

The local wine industry lay dormant until the 1970s, when the California wine boom spilled east from Napa and Sonoma. Growers planted new vines and winer-ies opened up in the central Sierra counties of El Dorado, Amador, and Calaveras. Winemakers rediscovered the gnarled old vines too—more than one Foothills vintner claims that some of the zinfandel vines John Muir saw still grow here. You can identify these veterans easily by their knobby heads (which form when vines are head-trained to grow as freestanding plants). The resulting old-vine zin has become the region's signature.

Spring is a great time to visit the Foothills. The rolling land is green with velvety grass, and wild turkeys strut their new feathers beneath stout oak trees. Sacramento's suburban sprawl has begun to encroach, but in the historic districts of former mining towns like Nevada City and Sutter Creek, the white-railed balconies of Old West storefronts still shade the raised sidewalks. Landmark hotels, some built of stone, still serve their original purpose, and Victorian homes have been converted into B&Bs.

It's relatively easy to get around the Foothills wineries: Take U.S. 50 from I-5 at Sacramento to reach El Dorado County, and highways 16 and 49 from Sacramento to reach Amador and Calaveras counties. Once you get off the freeways, roads can be winding and hilly, so don't expect to get anywhere quickly.

■ EL DORADO COUNTY

El Dorado County vineyards are the coolest in the Foothills, since they're the highest—as much as 3,000 feet above sea level, with one vineyard at 3,600 feet. Vintners here claim that altitude and cool growing conditions lend their wines a special elegance, and, indeed, some excellent chardonnay and riesling come out of this AVA and its sub-region, the Fair Play AVA.

★ Boeger Winery *map page 239, C-1*
Greg Boeger, scion of a Napa Valley wine family, resurrected a Gold Rush–era vineyard in the 1970s and turned it into one of El Dorado County's leading wineries. Planted on steep hills, the estate vineyards supply a wide variety of grapes, from zinfandel to nebbiolo to tempranillo. Boeger is best known for his snappy barbera but he has a flair for blends, such as a spicy zinfandel-primativo-petite sirah combo. The tasting room, open daily, has a couple of pleasant picnic spots and a collection of antique cars and trucks. *1709 Carson Road, Placerville; 530-622-8094.*

Sierra Vista Vineyards & Winery *map page 239, C-1*
Back in 1972, founder John MacCready determined that these steep 32 acres on Red Rock Ridge (2,800 to 2,900 feet above sea level) should be dedicated to grapes of the northern Rhône Valley. The result is Fleur de Montagne, a smooth and fruity blend of syrah, grenache, mourvèdre, and cinsault; Belle Rose, a substantive dry rosé; and the golden dessert wine Viognier Doux. Another interesting offering is the crisp, bright, unoaked chardonnay. The tasting room is open daily, and there's a picnic area with a lovely mountain view. *4560 Cabernet Way, Placerville; 530-622-7221.*

Madroña vineyards fly at exceptionally high altitudes.

Lava Cap Winery   *map page 239, C-1*
In the Apple Hills area, northeast of Placerville, Lava Cap's vineyards are high-fliers: they range in elevation from 1,500 feet to 2,900 feet, among California's highest. Founded in 1981, the winery produces chardonnay, sauvignon blanc, viognier, and a number of reds, including a superb zinfandel that is full-bodied yet surprisingly elegant and complex. *2221 Fruitridge Road, Placerville; 530-621-0175.*

Madroña Vineyards   *map page 239, C-1*
In the hills west of the village of Camino, at an elevation of 3,000 feet, family-run Madroña ranks as one of the highest-altitude California wineries. The hot days and cooler nights at this elevation produce fruit with good balance and intense character. The truly mountain-grown wines include zinfandel, merlot, chardonnay, and gewürztraminer, as well as a late-harvest zinfandel and other dessert wines. The tasting room's open daily. *2560 High Hill Road, Camino; 530-644-5948.*

(opposite) Boeger is one of El Dorado County's largest wineries.

Charles B. Mitchell Vineyards *map page 239, C-1*

Winemaker Charles Mitchell finds his inspiration in French wines, and his unpretentious, wood-paneled tasting room feels like someplace in the French countryside. His is one of about a dozen wineries in the Fair Play AVA, which lies entirely within El Dorado County. Among Mitchell's locally grown wines, the sauvignon blanc stands out for its floral nose and mellow finish. Two non-vintage red blends, Monsier Omo's Red Sunshine and Bella Rossa, have a fresh lightness hard to find in Foothills reds. Cellar tours and barrel tastings are available on request. Open daily. *8221 Stoney Creek Road, Fair Play; 530-620-3467.*

■ AMADOR COUNTY

Amador County has the lowest (1,200 to 1,600 feet above sea level) and thus the warmest of the Foothills vineyards, notable for their weighty, alcoholic, and multi-faceted zinfandels. Its prime vineyard region, the Shenandoah Valley AVA, is not a valley at all—it's actually a gently rolling mesa above the deep canyons of the Cosumnes River and Dry Creek. The vineyards cluster along country roads east of Plymouth, about 20 miles south of Placerville on Highway 49.

Story Winery *map page 239, B/C-1*

Founded in 1973, Story is a big zin booster. The vines in its Picnic Hill vineyard are over a century old and produce one of the most enjoyable of the winery's very powerful zinfandels. Story is also one of the few wineries still to use mission grapes, the *criolla* variety brought to California by Spanish missionaries in the 18th century; it goes into a mission-zinfandel blend. You can picnic here under huge oak trees that survived the Gold Rush; the view is one of the best in the Shenandoah Valley. *10525 Bell Road, Plymouth; 209-245-6208.*

Renwood Winery *map page 239, C-2*

One of the largest wineries in Amador County, this is one of the few that is not a family operation. Renwood's strength lies in its varied zinfandels (check out the Amador Ice Zinfandel, a dessert wine), some of them from vines dating back as far as the 1880s. Syrah, barbera, and viognier round out the offerings. The tasting room, open Thursday through Sunday, can get crowded on weekends. *12225 Steiner Road, Plymouth; 209-245-6979.*

Sierra Foothills towns like Amador City attract many weekenders with cafés, country stores, and bed-and-breakfast inns.

Shenandoah Vineyards

map page 239, C-1/2

Certified organic, Shenandoah grows its grapes without using chemical pesticides, herbicides, or fertilizers. (The wine itself is not organic, because a minimum amount of sulfites are used in vinification.) ReZerve selections such as a plummy barbera and an almost chocolaty zinfandel top Shenandoah's repertoire, but you can also try a contrastingly crisp sauvignon blanc. Attached to the lofty tasting room is a large gallery with artwork for sale. For more by this wine-making family, head a few miles away to their historic Sobon Estate (below). *12300 Steiner Road, Plymouth; 209-245-4455.*

Zinfandel grapes at Sobon Estate.

Amador Foothill Winery   *map page 239, C-1/2*

This hilltop winery is known for its vineyard-designated zinfandel and convincingly Tuscan-style sangiovese. Striving for balance and food-friendliness, winemaker Katie Quinn has a lighter touch with oak than do many California vintners. Her sémillon and sauvignon blanc are worth a try. Open Friday through Sunday. *12500 Steiner Road, Plymouth; 800-778-9463.*

★ Dobra Zemlja   *map page 239, C-2*

You might have more fun here than at any other Foothills winery, in large part thanks to the irrepressible owner-winemaker, Milan Matulich. At the bottom of a long, long winding drive, a barn stands amid eucalyptus trees. Open a massive wooden door and step into a dimly lit cave where wine ages in stacked barrels. Presiding over a counter at one end, Matulich cheerfully extols the virtues of gigantic red wine, a faint Croatian accent filtered through his drooping white moustache. Syrah, zinfandel, sangiovese, and blends of these three affirm the winery's Croatian name (pronounced "do-brah zem-yah"), which translates "good earth." *12505 Steiner Road, Plymouth; 209-245-3183.*

Amador County is known for powerful zinfandels.

Sobon Estate Winery *map page 239, C-1/2*
The winery here was established in 1856 by a Swiss immigrant, Adam Uhlinger, and run by the D'Agostini family from 1911 until the 1980s. Exhibits at the on-site Shenandoah Valley Museum, in the original cellars and winery building, include huge wine casks and early farming and wine-making implements. The rustic tasting room, in a creaky barn, pours several of Sobon's zinfandels, a variety of other reds (including syrah and sangiovese), and a couple of Rhône-style whites (viognier, roussanne). You can also taste Shenandoah Vineyards wines here. *14430 Shenandoah Road, Plymouth; 209-245-4455.*

Monteviña Winery *map page 239, C-2*
There are so many wines to taste here—from a simple white blend to a zinfandel port—that you may want to limit yourself to the limited release and reserve categories. The Trinchero family has owned Monteviña since 1988, but the winery has been here since 1970 and was a major contributor to the Foothills wine renaissance. It is by far the region's largest winery, but it has managed to maintain some of the spirit of a boutique operation. Red wine, especially zinfandel, is the star; taste the muscular, spicy zin from the Terra d'Oro reserve list. There are also big

red Italian varieties on the limited release list, among them aglianico and terodelgo. With its covered picnic patios, the winery is a favorite picnic spot. *20680 Shenandoah School Road, Plymouth; 209-245-6942.*

★ Vino Noceto   *map page 239, B/C-1*

Vino Noceto is a yummy example of the benefits of doing one thing, and doing it well. Since 1987, Suzy and Jim Gullett have devoted themselves to making the best sangiovese possible, and now they produce several versions in different styles. You can taste everything from a light, fruity quaffer to a rich, hearty sipper. The winery also does sangiovese-based rosé, blends, and grappa. The doggie head outside the tasting room—a seven-foot-tall bust of a dachshund wearing a chef's hat—has nothing whatsoever to do with the wine. *11011 Shenandoah Road, Plymouth; 209-245-6556.*

Domaine de la Terre Rouge   *map page 239, B/C-2*

This winery has two labels with different wine-making styles. The Terre Rouge label focuses on Rhône varietals, while the Easton label covers old-vine zinfandel and barbera. A leader in the popularity explosion of Rhône varietals in California, the winery has had good results with inky, soft syrah and a big marsanne-viognier-roussane blend. The jury is still out on the zinfandel. The winery is open only on Friday through Monday. *10801 Dickson Road, Plymouth; 209-245-4277.*

■ CALAVERAS COUNTY

At elevations of 1,550 to 2,400 feet, Calaveras County works well with Mediterranean grape varieties such as barbera, dolcetto, marsanne, mourvèdre, nebbiolo, syrah, and tempranillo. Many of the area's wineries are near the Gold Rush hamlet of Murphys or have tasting rooms along the town's Main Street. Murphys lies a few miles east of Highway 49 (at Angels Camp) via Highway 4.

★ Chatom Vineyards   *map page 239, C-3*

Gay Callan makes wine exclusively from grapes grown in her own vineyards, and her secluded winery feels like a place apart. Among more than a dozen varietals, her syrah, cabernet sauvignon, and zinfandel stand out for their inky, velvety quality. Whites, such as chardonnay and sauvignon blanc, are aromatic

Monteviña Wines, a red wine house, is a major player in the Foothills wine bloom.

and fruity. Tucked away in the sunny Esmeralda Valley, between Murphys and Angels Camp, the woodsy winery stands amid flower gardens and has a peaceful picnic area. The small, friendly tasting room is open daily. *1969 Highway 4, Douglas Flat; 209-736-6500.*

Ironstone Vineyards   *map page 239, C-3*
Modeled after a 19th-century gold-stamp mill (used to extract gold from ore and quartz), Calaveras County's largest winery is about as close to a Napa Valley–style wine theme park as you'll find in the Foothills—and it attracts Napa-style throngs. Besides the tasting room, there's a lakeside park (where you can learn to pan gold on weekends), an amphitheater, a jewelry shop, an antiques collection, and (deep breath) the Ironstone Heritage Museum and Gallery, which celebrates the history of Sierra Foothills gold and viticulture in displays such as a 44-lb hunk of crystalline gold. The music room contains a 767-pipe organ from a 1927 movie palace in Sacramento. Winery tours are offered daily. A juicy, medium-bodied cabernet franc, a cabernet sauvignon with well-balanced tannins, and a soft, easy-drinking merlot please the crowds. *1894 Six Mile Road; 209-728-1251.*

Milliaire Winery   *map page 239, C-3*
Founded in 1983, Milliaire is a down-home street-front winery in a former gas station at the southern end of Murphys. Who needs glitz, though, when the wines speak for themselves? Rich, full-bodied zinfandels anchor the list, which also has chardonnay, zin port, and other selections. Open daily. *276 Main Street; 209-728-1658.*

Black Sheep Winery   *map page 239, C-3*
Black Sheep was named by its owners, Dave and Jan Olsen, to signify their bold style of winemaking, which runs to small lots of premium varietals, including zinfandel, cabernet sauvignon, and cinsault. The winery, open daily, also puts out a white blend, True Frogs Lily Pad White, and a red True Frogs counter-part. *221 Main Street; 209-728-2157.*

Stevenot Winery   *map page 239, C-3*
One of the region's larger wineries, Stevenot makes quite a few varietals, includ-ing chardonnay, merlot, cabernet sauvignon, and petite sirah. Their style is super-ripe, concentrated fruit; the spicy, medium-bodied cabernet franc is full of berry flavors. In the last few years, the winery has also released a number of wines

An example of home winemaking hitting the (relative) big time.

A Great Drive in the Sierra Foothills

It's hard to do justice to the Lodi and the Foothills in a day, so you'll need to hone in on a particular area. The Shenandoah Valley AVA is particularly lovely, has plenty of delicious wine, and is manageable in a day's drive. Start in tiny Plymouth with late breakfast at the diner, and pack a picnic lunch from Amador Vintage Market (9393 Main Street; 209-245-3663). Drive 4 miles north on Highway 49 and turn right on Bell Road; after 1½ miles and sharp twists to the north and then the south, you'll find Story Winery on the left. After your zinfandel, continue on Bell for just under a mile to a sharp right-hand turn. Take the right to stay on Bell and go about 1½ mi to Shenandoah Road. Three-quarters of a mile after you turn left onto Shenandoah, take another left onto Steiner Road. In just over a mile, you will see Renwood Winery on the left; here you can pick up a cigar for later.

Taking a left back onto Steiner, you'll soon see Shenandoah Vineyards on your right. Browse the art gallery before continuing another scant quarter-mile on Steiner to Dobra Zemlja. Look carefully on your left for the winery sign; the narrow driveway leads through a fence and winds ½ mile to the winery, where you can have lunch at a picnic table in a eucalyptus grove. A left out of the driveway onto Steiner brings you to back to Shenandoah Road. Turn left and drive nearly 2 miles out to Sobon Estate, on the right. Its historic buildings and dusty museum are fascinating. Backtrack toward Highway 49 on Shenandoah, passing both of its intersections with Steiner (on the right now) and reaching Dickson Road in a little under 4½ miles. Turn right onto Dickson and pop over to Domaine de la Terre Rouge and Easton Wines. Back at Shendandoah Road, turn right and drive 3½ miles back to Plymouth. Cap your day off with dinner at Taste restaurant.

crafted in Spanish and Portuguese styles: two whites called Albariño and Verdelho and a rosé called Rosado. The tasting room, in downtown Murphys, is open daily. *458 Main Street; 209-728-3485.*

J. Lohr's hilltop vineyard at Paso Robles.

CENTRAL COAST WINERIES

Reaching from San Jose in the north to Santa Barbara in the south, the Central Coast's wine region lies along some 250 miles of rolling seaboard. Not too long ago this region was defined by its farmland and cattle and dairy ranches, and it's still largely agricultural. Since California's wine boom in the 1980s, however, much local agriculture has morphed into viticulture—cabernet sauvignon and chardonnay instead of strawberries and broccoli.

Central Coast winemaking came fully into its own in the past decade, with hundreds of wineries turning out premium vintages and earning a global reputation for excellent pinot noir, zinfandel, and chardonnay, among many other varietals. That status was affirmed in 2006, when two cabernet sauvignons from Ridge Vineyards, in the Santa Cruz Mountains, took the top honors at a re-creation of the famous 1976 "Judgment of Paris" tasting—the tasting that had put California on the international wine map 30 years before.

The climate along the Central Coast is mostly ideal for wine grapes, much like that in southern France, Italy, and Spain. Vines thrive on a diet of brilliantly sunny days and cool, often foggy nights; on aridly hot summers and gentle, wet (but not too wet) winters. Of course, the weather varies up and down this long strip of coastline raked by mountain ranges, and soil conditions differ from place to place. To recognize these variations in terroir, the Central Coast's five county appellations encompass some two dozen AVAs.

The same things that make the Central Coast a great place for winegrowing make it a beautiful place to visit. The ocean-edged landscape of open lowland is backed by forested peaks. Wild, ranched, or farmed, the land remains mostly rural, and in spring, wildflowers blanket the meadows. Some of the most scenic stretches of California's Highway 1 wind along the Central Coast. The road links small, pretty cities such as Carmel-by-the-Sea, San Luis Obispo, and Santa Barbara; relaxed beach towns such as Santa Cruz and Cambria; and spectacular landmarks such as Monterey Bay, Big Sur, and Hearst Castle. The speedier north–south route, U.S. 101, emerges from the congested Silicon Valley to cut straight through the heart of the fertile (if featureless) Salinas Valley. The freeway then connects the major dots of south Central Coast Wine Country: Paso Robles, Templeton, Edna Valley, Santa Maria, and the Santa Ynez Valley.

The wineries of the Central Coast still seem sleepier than those in Napa and Sonoma, but they can hop on weekends. You'll rarely find gridlock on the main roads, and tour buses are few and far between.

■ Santa Cruz Mountains

Palo Alto

Santa Cruz Mountains   San Jose

Santa Cruz   Santa Clara Valley

The Santa Cruz Mountains AVA, flanked by Silicon Valley suburbs and the Santa Clara Valley AVA on one side and beach towns on the other, lies only about 60 miles from San Francisco. The rugged area is cut by steep, redwood-studded canyons that shelter small vineyards and even smaller wineries. In all, there are less than 1,500 acres of vineyards and fewer than 60 wineries here, most of them tiny family operations.

This little appellation is one of California's oldest and most important. Wine grapes were first planted here in the 1850s, but most vineyards and wineries fell victim to Prohibition and competition from more prolific regions. In the 1970s, growing respect for high-quality California wine began to bring vintners back to the Santa Cruz Mountains, and now wineries such as Ridge and David Bruce turn out truly world-class pinot noir, cabernet sauvignon, and chardonnay.

The Santa Cruz Mountains may make excellent wine, but tough growing conditions mean that the AVA doesn't make a whole lot of it. The slopes are steep and rocky, with poor soil, and the weather is tricky. The range is also tall enough (2,000 feet to nearly 4,000 feet in elevation) to intercept weather systems drifting in from the Pacific Ocean. As a result, the AVA has two distinct growing climates: vineyards east of the ridge often bask in sunshine while sea fog chills those west of the ridge. On the cooler, wetter western face, fog slows the ripening of grapes, especially at lower elevations.

Visiting the wineries of the Santa Cruz Mountains requires some white-knuckle driving on twisting roads, but the scenery is gorgeous.

■ Woodside and Cupertino   *map page 264*
At the western fringe of the San Francisco Peninsula's inland suburbs, housing developments quickly give way to wooded foothills. Wineries only a few miles off I-280 perch far above the sprawl.

Thomas Fogarty Winery and Vineyards   *map page 264, A-1*
Pinot noir and chardonnay ripen slowly in these vineyards at the crest of the Santa Cruz Mountains. The results are intense and aromatic; a merlot redolent of berries, cocoa, and toast is particularly worth a try. Beyond the estate-grown wines, there are gewürztraminer, cabernet sauvignon, and other varietals from

In this mountain vineyard, leaves are pulled away from the fruit, maximizing the grapes' sun exposure.

Monterey County grapes. The multi-level winery (open Thursday through Sunday) takes in a lofty view over the Bay Area. *19501 Skyline Boulevard, Woodside; 650-851-6777.*

★ Ridge Vineyards *map page 264, A-1*
At 2,300 feet above sea level, aptly named Ridge Vineyards is famous for its sturdy, well-structured Monte Bello cabernet sauvignon. A 1971 bottle out-shone similar French and California vintages to win the 2006 "Judgment of Paris" tasting, a re-creation of the historic 1976 event, and a 2000 bottle topped the young wine category. The tasting room, where a wall of windows takes in the panorama, is open only on weekends. Fair warning for the drive: the road to the winery is winding to say the least. *17100 Monte Bello Road, Cupertino; 408-867-3233.*

■ Los Gatos *map page 264, A-1*
Highway 9 and Highway 17 cut roughly parallel north–south paths through the densely wooded Santa Cruz Mountains. Between them, several remote wineries work to capture the essence of the terroir.

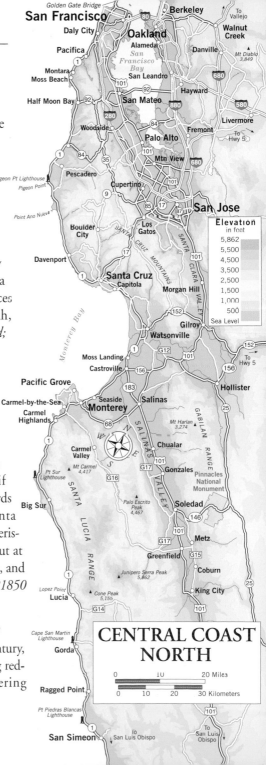

CENTRAL COAST NORTH

David Bruce Winery

map page 264, A-1

David Bruce Winery, founded in the early 1960s, was well respected long before the current crop of premium wineries came onto the local scene. Pinot noir is the soul of the operation and is made from local grapes as well as fruit sourced elsewhere in California. Each release is a little different from the next, but overall, the results are boldly elegant, with intense cherry flavors and a supple finish. The winery also produces first-rate chardonnay, zinfandel, syrah, and grenache. *21439 Bear Creek Road; 408-354-4214.*

Byington Vineyard & Winery

map page 264, A-1

The view from the manicured grounds of Byington's Italianate stone winery ranges across the slopes of the western Santa Cruz Mountains all the way to the distant Pacific Ocean—if there's no fog. From the estate vineyards comes an earthy pinot noir; the Santa Cruz Mountains chardonnay is characteristically zippy. After your tasting, hang out at the bocce court, umbrella-shaded tables, and outdoor grills (bring your own tools). *21850 Bear Creek Road; 408-354-1111.*

■ SANTA CRUZ *map page 264, A-1*
A seaside resort since the mid-19th century, Santa Cruz made its fortune by clearing redwoods from the mountains. Lumbering

wreaked havoc on the environment, but left behind open land where vineyards could be planted. Still a beach town, Santa Cruz is filled with surf shops, rinky-dink attractions, and coffeehouses catering to denizens of the University of California. A few wineries have tasting rooms in town, and many of the city's restaurants have wine lists well-primed with local vintages.

Bonny Doon Vineyard   *map page 264, A-1*

This iconoclastic winery's founder, Randall Grahm, grooves to the same different drummer followed by tie-died, surfy Santa Cruz. Fanciful labels bear punny names such as Le Cigare Volante and Syrah Le Pousseur. The winery grows its estate grapes biodynamically, in Soledad, Monterey County. And they've embraced the screw-cap instead of the cork. Here's your chance to taste oddball grapes such as

(previous pages) Cyclists skim along almost every road in Wine Country—even the steepest routes.

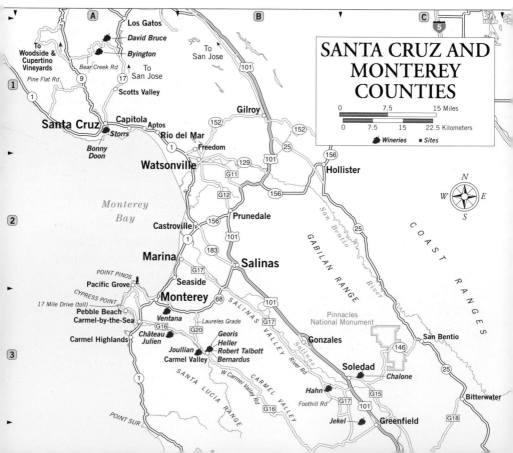

lemony, white erbaluce and robust, red madiran; Bonny Doon also does a solid job with more familiar viognier, mouvedre, and Rhône varietals. The tasting room often has a party atmosphere. *328 Ingalls Street; 831-425-4518.*

Storrs Winery   *map page 264, A-1*
Right in town, the Storrs tasting room is in a restored 1806 lumber mill, among shops and design studios. The winery carefully matches grape varieties to the microclimates in its Santa Cruz Mountains vineyards, focusing on chardonnay, pinot noir, and zinfandel. Apple and pear flavors burst from the chardonnay, balanced with slight minerality and toasty oak. *303 Potrero Street; 831-458-5030.*

■ MONTEREY COUNTY

When people think of Monterey, they commonly think of craggy coastline, sea otters, and maybe the Pebble Beach golf courses with their magnificent ocean views. When wine buffs think of Monterey, however, they conjure up inland valleys scored with row upon row of vines. Novelist John Steinbeck, a native of Monterey County, made the area's hardworking people famous in books such as *Cannery Row,* about Monterey's sardine-canning industry, and *Grapes of Wrath,* about migrant farm workers in the Salinas Valley during the Great Depression. The area's fortunes have improved since Steinbeck's day, but many locals still depend upon the generous land, sea, and climate for their livelihood.

A few coastal Monterey vineyards have ventured into cool-climate viticulture, but most of the county's grape-growers and wineries are concentrated in the Carmel and Salinas valleys. The Carmel Valley AVA runs southeast from Monterey Bay into the Santa Lucia Highlands AVA, whose mountains cut off the Salinas Valley from the Pacific Ocean. Almost 85 miles long and, on average, only 12 miles wide, the Salinas Valley is hemmed in on the east by the Gabilan Mountains. The Carmel and Salinas valleys get plenty of sun and cool sea breezes, and fog can roll in anytime, especially at night. Higher elevation distinguishes viticultural conditions in the Carmel Valley from those in the Salinas Valley. Over the undulating terrain of the Salinas Valley, which is split into five AVAs, pockets of warm or cold air and variable levels of sun and fog generate many microclimates in which grapes ripen unevenly.

A busy moment at the Bonny Doon tasting room.

Monterey County's first winery, Chalone, was established in 1962, on the slopes of the Gabilan Mountains, whose climate was far cooler and more changeable than that of the Salinas Valley floor. Other vineyards followed, but met with variable success because the region's terroir turned out to be complex. Nevertheless, the wine business boomed, especially in southern Monterey County, as growers started learning how and where to plant different grape varieties. Today, large quantities of Monterey grapes go into wine made in Napa, Sonoma, and elsewhere.

Either of the two **Taste of Monterey** shops is a great place to start a local wine-tasting tour. One is on Cannery Row in the city of Monterey, and the other is near the National Steinbeck Center in downtown Salinas (at the north end of the valley). You can taste wines from many of the county's wineries, some of which have no tasting rooms of their own. These include Lockwood Vineyard, whose noteworthy offerings include its chardonnay, cabernet sauvignon, and syrah; and Morgan, which produces chardonnay and pinot noir from organically farmed Santa Lucia Highlands grapes. The Cannery Row tasting room is open daily 11 to 6; the one in Salinas is open Monday to Thursday 11 to 5, Friday to Saturday 11 to 6, and Sunday 11 to 4. *700 Cannery Row, Monterey; 831-646-5446. 127 Main Street, Salinas; 831-751-1980.*

(above) Château Julien has the textbook winery look. (following pages) The hills surrounding Carmel Valley turn a rich green each spring; by summer many are golden.

■ MONTEREY   *map page 264, A/B-2/3*

This posh bay town is one of the California coast's main tourist destinations. Most visitors home in on Fisherman's Wharf, Cannery Row, the scenic 17-Mile Drive, and the Monterey Bay Aquarium—never suspecting that a rich wine region lies only a few miles inland from the bay.

Ventana Vineyards/Meador Estate   *map page 264, A-3*

Doug Meador, who arrived in Monterey County in the early 1970s, is a master in the art of cold-climate viticulture and a leader in the region's emergence as a wine producer. His most successful wines, made from locally grown grapes, are whites such as chardonnay, sauvignon blanc, and gewürztraminer; the off-dry (slightly sweet) riesling balances apricot flavors with mouthwatering acidity. Reds include grenache, cabernet franc, and syrah. The tasting room occupies an old stone house that's an easy five-minute drive east of downtown Monterey. *2999 Monterey-Salinas Highway; 831-372-7415.*

■ CARMEL VALLEY   *map page 264, B-3*

Winding out of the northern Santa Lucia Mountains at the almost too-pretty coastal town of Carmel-by-the-Sea, the Carmel River runs through the narrow Carmel Valley. The mountainside vineyards here are quite cool, so they produce more intense fruit with higher acid levels than do vineyards elsewhere in the county. Some of the wineries are hard to reach, so they operate tasting rooms in the more accessible lower valley. Many are in tiny Carmel Valley Village, about 13 miles southeast of Highway 1 via Carmel Valley Road.

Château Julien Wine Estate   *map page 264, A/B-3*

Taking its cue from French châteaux, this winery has a postcard prettiness. But the effect is more than just show: the wines made here from Monterey County grapes—sauvignon blanc, pinot grigio, chardonnay, gewürztraminer, merlot, cabernet sauvignon, syrah, sangiovese, and zinfandel—are first-rate. The views are captivating, and you can sip and snack at a cobblestoned picnic area. *8940 Carmel Valley Road; 831-624-2600.*

Heller Estate Vineyards   *map page 264, B-3*

Certified organic, Gilbert Heller's 120 acres of dry-farmed vineyards rely on underground springs for their water. The result is luscious wine that stands up well to aging (though the refreshing, dry merlot rosé is best young). Friendly servers in the simple Carmel Valley Village tasting room pour estate-grown wines such as chenin blanc, chardonnay, pinot noir, and cabernet sauvignon. Outside are a picnic area and a sculpture garden filled with work by Heller's wife, Toby. *69 West Carmel Valley Road; 831-659-6220.*

★ **Talbott Vineyards** *map page 264, B-3*
Using old-school Burgundian growing and producing methods, Robb and Cynthia Talbott make only small lots of impressive chardonnay and pinot noir. Voluptuous fruit and refined minerality characterize their various chardonnay bottlings; ripe cherry and subtle tannic structure define the pinots. *53 West Carmel Valley Road; 831-659-3500.*

Georis Winery *map page 264, B-3*
Georis makes cabernet sauvignon, merlot, and other wines from grapes grown on its 28 acres of vineyards. Opulent and tannic, the reds in particular have attracted a devoted following; they really are meant for aging. The tasting room, with plump leather chairs and a fireplace, is tucked in the back of an old adobe that it shares with Talbott Vineyards; there are tables on the garden patio. *4 Pilot Road, at West Carmel Valley Road; 831-659-1050.*

Joullian Vineyards *map page 264, B-3*
Though its vineyards lie far out in the hills, Joullian maintains its tasting room in Carmel Valley Village. The building itself is worth a look: modeled on Burgundian church architecture, it has a river rock exterior, arched windows, and lots of redwood and cypress inside. Except for the chardonnays, all of Joullian's wines are estate-grown. Try the creamy-tart sauvignon blanc and the smooth, mineral-cherry cabernet franc. *2 Village Drive; 831-659-8100.*

Bernardus Winery *map page 264, B-3*
Inspired by the vineyards of Bordeaux, Bernardus grows cabernet sauvignon and merlot high in the untamed hills above Carmel Valley. Marinus, a proprietary blend of the two, is the full-bodied signature bottle, full of black cherry and toast notes that lead to a long finish. Chardonnay grown elsewhere in Monterey County has a pineapple tang and appley sweetness. A couple of miles to the west, rustic-chic Bernardus Lodge houses an excellent California-French restaurant, Marinus. *5 West Carmel Valley Road; 831-659-1900.*

Harvesting grapes at Chalone.

■ SOLEDAD   *map page 264, C-3*
In the heart of the Salinas Valley, gritty Soledad is more famous for its vast produce farms and its state prison than for grapes, but it is the address of two Monterey County wine scene mainstays.

Hahn Estates   *map page 264, B/C-3*
Founded as Smith & Hook Winery in 1974, this former ranch along the east-facing slopes of the Santa Lucias is above the fog line and perfect for growing cabernet sauvignon. The winery, now called Hahn Estates, continues to produce noteworthy cabs, as well as meritage, chardonnay, syrah, and pinot noir. Hahn also continues to make pricier premium wines, such as a challenging cabernet sauvignon, under the Smith & Hook label. Tasting takes place in a low-slung house with views over the valley; outside, there's a wide deck with tables and umbrellas. *37700 Foothill Road; 866-925-7994.*

A Great Drive in Santa Cruz and Monterey

Since the Central Coast wine region covers such a large area, you'll need at least two days just to explore one or two counties. It's a quick hop down I-280 from San Francisco to the northernmost Central Coast AVA, the Santa Cruz Mountains. From I-280 in Cupertino, take Foothill Boulevard up to Montebello Road and make world-renowned Ridge Vineyards your first stop.

After trying the Ridge's outstanding cabernet, continue on the red wine trail to the David Bruce Winery. The quickest route is to go back to I-280, take it to Highway 17, and drive south into the mountains to Bear Creek Road. (In this case trying to take a scenic route isn't such a pleasure, since the roads between the two wineries are tortuous, steep, and slow.)

From David Bruce, continue on Bear Creek Road to reach Highway 9. Head south on this highway to reach Bonny Doon Vineyard, where you can taste wines made with less-familiar grapes. From Highway 9, wend west on Felton-Empire Road to Pine Flat Road, and you're there. That's enough driving for one day: spend the night in Santa Cruz.

On your second day, head south on Highway 1 to Monterey County. Stop in the town of Monterey for lunch (and perhaps a visit to Taste of Monterey to get a preview of local wines). Then continue south to Carmel Valley Road. Stop for the tour at Château Julien, then poke around the tasting rooms in Carmel Valley Village, making sure to drop in at Talbott Vineyards to try their pinot noir and chardonnay. Wind up with a night in Carmel-by-the-Sea.

★ **Chalone Vineyard**   *map page 264, C-3*
A Frenchman planted this vineyard with chenin blanc grapes in 1919—just in time for Prohibition—and other owners added chardonnay, pinot blanc, and pinot noir vines in the 1940s. By the early 1960s, the vines were barely alive, but Dick Graff resurrected them and began making some exceptionally fine wine, now including estate syrah and viognier. These are among the very few American wines grown in the revered limestone-based soil type on which Burgundy built its eminence. The on-site winery, added in 1974, remains the sole production facility in the Chalone AVA. Open only on weekends, the tasting room lies east of U.S. 101 on the road to Pinnacles National Monument, within sight of the dramatic remains of a prehistoric volcano. *Stonewall Canyon Road, off Highway 146; 831-678-1717.*

Oak-barrel aging at Chalone.

York Mountain   Paso Robles

Paso Robles

San Luis Obispo

Edna Valley

Arroyo Grande
Valley

Santa Maria
Valley

■ SAN LUIS OBISPO COUNTY

The Cuesta Ridge of the Santa Lucia Range divides San Luis Obispo County into northern and southern parts. The county's largest city, San Luis Obispo, sits in a pretty valley south of the Cuesta Grade, just a few miles inland from the ocean. A handful of AVAs, such as Edna Valley, shoulder in among the coastal ranges and valleys that stretch north and south of town. But the star of the show is without a doubt Paso Robles, California's fastest-growing AVA.

With more than 100 wineries, 25,000 acres of vineyard, and a surge of interest from the wine establishment, the Paso Robles AVA is booming. (Between 2002 and 2006, the number of wineries almost doubled.) It's also got something of a split personality. Starting from the eastern face of the Santa Lucia coastal range, only 6 miles from the Pacific Ocean, the AVA reaches 35 miles east, crossing the Salinas River into flatter rangeland. The river is a dividing line of sorts, acting as a psychic,

and to some extent climatic, boundary between Paso Robles' two distinct wine districts (see the East and West Paso Robles sections below).

Paso Robles experiences the widest temperature swings of any California AVA, especially on the east side, which is farther from the ocean. There, flatter topography allows for large-scale commercial viticulture, while the west side wineries are smaller and less accessible, tucked into hollows and perched on hillsides in the coastal mountains. North to south, Paso Robles has still more variations: the AVA tends to be warmest in the north, near San Miguel; coolest in its middle, where ocean air rushes through the Templeton Gap (a cleft in the Coast Range); and warm in the south. In tasting rooms and watering holes, the potential division of Paso Robles into two or more AVAs is a hotly debated topic, and in 2005 a group of west-side vintners launched a still ongoing effort to get approval for a separate AVA.

Paso Robles first gained fame for its grapes at the end of Prohibition. In the 1920s Polish concert pianist Ignace Paderewski, a major celebrity of his era, bought 2,000 acres here, planted petite sirah and zinfandel, and began winning prizes for his wine. Zinfandel remains one of Paso's strengths, joined by cabernet sauvignon in the 1960s and 1970s. Cab now accounts for a third of the AVA's grape tonnage, with merlot about one-fifth of the crop. In short, this is prime red-wine country.

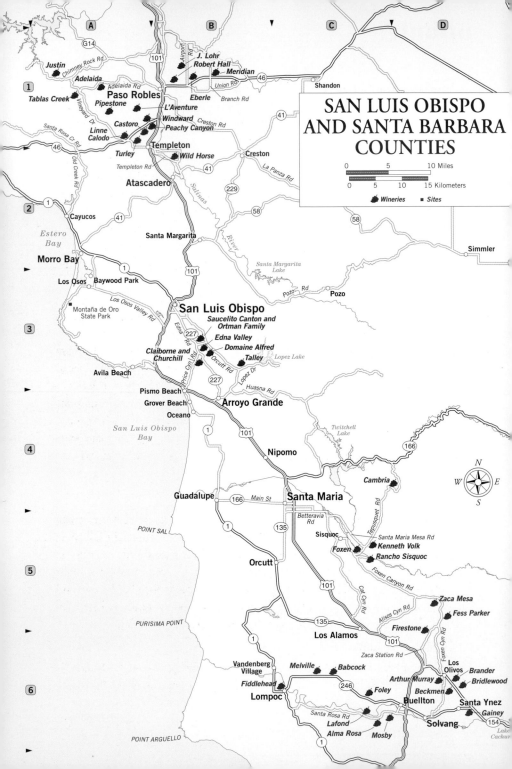

SAN LUIS OBISPO AND SANTA BARBARA COUNTIES

0   5   10 Miles

0   5   10   15 Kilometers

🍇 Wineries   ■ Sites

A   B   C   D

G14

Justin
Adelaida
Tablas Creek
Adelaida Rd
Paso Robles
Pipestone
Chimney Rock Rd
Vineyard Dr
101
Airport Rd
J. Lohr
Robert Hall
Meridian
Eberle
Branch Rd
Union Rd
46
Shandon

L'Aventure
Windward
Peachy Canyon
Creston Rd
41

Castoro
Linne
Calodo
Templeton
Turley
Wild Horse
Templeton Rd
41
Creston
La Panza Rd

Santa Rosa Cr Rd
46
Old Creek Rd
Atascadero
Salinas River
229

1

Cayucos
41
Santa Margarita
58
58
Simmler

Estero Bay

Morro Bay

2

Los Osos   Baywood Park
1
101
Santa Margarita Lake
Pozo Rd
Pozo

Los Osos Valley Rd
Montaña de Oro State Park
San Luis Obispo
Saucelito Canton and Ortman Family
Edna Valley
Domaine Alfred
Talley
Lopez Lake

3

Edna Rd
227
Claiborne and Churchill
Price Cyn Rd
Orcutt Rd
227
Lopez Dr
Huasna Rd

Avila Beach
Pismo Beach
Grover Beach
Oceano
Arroyo Grande

San Luis Obispo Bay
1
101
Nipomo

4

Twitchell Lake
166

Guadalupe
166   Main St
Santa Maria
Betteravia Rd
135
Cambria

W   N   E
S

POINT SAL
1
Sisquoc
Foxen
Kenneth Volk
Rancho Sisquoc
Santa Maria Mesa Rd
Tepusquet Rd

5

Orcutt
101
Foxen Canyon Rd

PURISIMA POINT
135
Cat Cyn Rd
Alisos Cyn Rd
Zaca Mesa
Fess Parker
Firestone
Los Alamos
101
Foxen Cyn Rd

Zaca Station Rd
Los Olivos
Brander
Bridlewood

Vandenberg Village
Melville   Babcock
Arthur Murray
Beckmen

6

Fiddlehead
1
246
Foley
Buellton
Santa Ynez
Gainey
154
Lake Cachuma

Lompoc
Santa Rosa Rd
Lafond
Alma Rosa   Mosby
Solvang

POINT ARGUELLO
1

But this is also an area of tremendous variety: close to 40 kinds of grapes are grown here. Rhône grapes have been so successful that the AVA has become a stronghold of the Rhône Rangers, an industry organization dedicated to promoting American-grown Rhône varieties such as grenache, marsanne, mourvèdre, roussane, syrah, and viognier. Italian grapes such as dolcetto and barbera, and Spaniards such as tempranillo and touriga, show great promise here too. A long growing season makes for high production, 65 to 75 percent of which is sold to wineries in Napa, Sonoma, and other areas.

The town of Paso Robles is well worth a visit too. Downtown Paso Robles got its start when its hot springs, long popular with local Native Americans and grizzly bears, prompted some enterprising early birds to build a big hotel in 1864. (These hot springs still bubble up at a temperature of 106 degrees Fahrenheit.) Paso then had a stint as "Almond City," because of the surrounding almond orchards. Since the 1970s, the trees have been uprooted to make way for vineyards. Though it's now firmly on the Wine Country map, Paso Robles still seems like a dusty agricultural town.

Spring and fall are the nicest times to visit Paso Robles; Edna Valley and Arroyo Grande are lovely year-round, especially in summer. On many weekends, special events and wine festivals—most notably, Paso's Hospice du Rhône, an international event attended by most of the major Rhône players from around the world—fill the streets, restaurants, and tasting rooms. Highway 46, which intersects with U.S. 101 and passes through downtown Paso Robles, is the main route to the AVA's east-side and west-side wineries. U.S. 101 links Paso in the north with San Luis Obispo in the south.

■ **EAST SIDE PASO ROBLES**   *map page 276, A/B-1*
The section of the Paso Robles AVA that's east of the Salinas River covers open, gently rolling land on loamy, nutrient-deficient soil. What little rain falls here drains away quickly, stressing the vines even further. Since the east side receives less of the ocean's moderating influence, it's generally hotter by day and colder by night than the west side. All of this adds up to great conditions for chardonnay and cabernet sauvignon, and not surprisingly, Paso's bigger producers operate here. Vast vineyards stretch to the horizon, occasionally sprouting grand wineries.

Meridian Vineyards   *map page 276, B-1*
This local heavyweight, established in 1988 by winemaker Chuck Ortman, is now part of the global company Foster's Group Limited. Meridian has exten-

sive vineyard holdings on the Central Coast: chardonnay comes from Santa Barbara County and the Edna Valley, while the east Paso Robles vineyards surrounding the hilltop winery provide cabernet sauvignon, syrah, and zinfandel. Limited release and reserve wines, sold only from the winery, can be sampled here. The picnic area, shaded by giant oaks, has sweeping vineyard views; catered lunches are available for a modest fee. *7000 Highway 46 East; 805-226-7133.*

Eberle Winery   *map page 276, B-1*

A bronze sculpture of a boar guards the entrance to this east-side institution. Gary Eberle, a founding father of the Paso Robles wine renaissance, has been making wine in the area since the 1970s. His barbera, cabernet sauvignon, chardonnay, viognier, zinfandel, sangiovese, syrah, and a "Côtes-du-Rôbles" blend are among the best the region has to offer, and his late-harvest muscat canelli is exquisite. You can bring your own food and picnic on a deck that has panoramic views of estate vineyards, and take one of the daily cave tours. *3810 East Highway 46; 805-238-9607.*

J. Lohr   *map page 276, B-1*

North of Highway 46, 6 miles east of town, this is one of the biggest producers in Paso Robles. They have several labels, from the inexpensive Painter Ridge and Cypress brands to the ultra-premium J. Lohr Cuvée series. In the middle is J. Lohr Estates, a well-regarded line that includes darkly fruity, spicy reds such as Seven Oaks Cabernet, Los Osos Merlot, and South Ridge Syrah. *6169 Airport Road; 805-239-8900.*

Robert Hall Winery   *map page 276, B-1*

Before settling on wine-making in 1995, Robert Hall tried his hand at construction, horse breeding, and a variety of other businesses. His winery, on a ranch above the Estrella Plain outside downtown Paso Robles, specializes in cabernet sauvignon, merlot, and zinfandel, although the viognier, orange muscat, and syrah are delectable, too. The three daily guided tours also take in the underground caverns—the largest of their kind on the Central Coast. There also are great bocce courts. *3443 Mill Road; 805-239-1616.*

Lazing on a sunny afternoon in East Side Paso Robles.

■ **WEST PASO ROBLES** *map page 276, A/B-1*
West of the Salinas River, the Paso Robles AVA gets hilly and wooded as it rises up the Santa Lucia slopes. Those mountains help bring down the rain, which is soaked up by generally calcareous (calcium carbonate–rich) soils. Marine air flows through the hills, keeping temperatures more moderate than on the east side. Zinfandel and Rhône varieties such as syrah do particularly well over here. Many of the wineries, which tend to be smaller than those on the east side, are family-operated, with cozy, casual tasting rooms. Once you leave Highway 46, the narrow back roads dip and climb as they wend their way through vineyards and forests.

Adelaida Cellars *map page 276, A-1*
On its hilltop ranch, with elevations of up to 2,300 feet, Adelaida grows pinot noir, cabernet sauvignon, syrah, and chardonnay. The cab and syrah from its Viking Estate vineyard are known for their ripe, fruity richness. From the tasting room, you can look through windows straight into the guts of the winery. From downtown Paso Robles, head west on 24th Street, which becomes Nacimiento Lake Drive. When the road forks, bear left on Adelaida Road. *5805 Adelaida Road; 805-239-8980.*

★ **Tablas Creek Vineyard** *map page 276, A-1*
In the far-west hills of Paso Robles, near the intersection of Adelaida Road and Vineyard Drive, Tablas Creek makes some of the area's finest wine. The vineyards are planted to Rhône varieties using vines imported from their partner, Château de Beaucastel, a highly regarded Châteauneuf-du-Pape *domaine* in the Rhône Valley. Organically grown and hand-harvested syrah, grenache, roussanne, viognier, and other grapes are blended or bottled as single varietals. With complex, multi-layered, and well-balanced aromas and flavors, the red and white versions of their signature Esprit de Beaucastel blend have classic Rhône style with a Central Coast twist. Twice-daily tours include a chance to graft your own grapevine. *9339 Adelaida Road; 805-237-1231.*

Justin Vineyards & Winery *map page 276, A-1*
Justin and Deborah Baldwin's winery has become one of Paso's better-known places, primarily thanks to the cult following for Isosceles, a hearty blend of cabernet sauvignon, cabernet franc, and merlot. Two other red blends, Justification and The Orphan, are rich and fruity. In addition to its tasting room, Justin has

Walnut trees at Pipestone Vineyards.

twice-daily winery tours, plus regularly scheduled blending classes. Deborah's
Room restaurant serves lunch on weekends and prix-fixe dinners nightly (reservations required). There's even an on-site B&B, Just Inn. Justin lies at the western end
of Paso Robles, 15 miles from town via lovely, winding roads. *11680 Chimney
Rock Road; 805-238-6932.*

Pipestone Vineyards *map page 276, A-1*
Sustainable viticulture gets an extra twist here; Jeff Pipes and Florence Wong
planted and maintain their vineyard according to feng shui principles too. At
this small, family operation tasting-room conversations with the owners, who do
almost everything themselves, provide an up-close, unvarnished look at wine-
making. Most often Jeff or Florence themselves are pouring in the simple tasting
room. Syrah, grenache noir, and viognier grown just outside go into full-bodied
wines. If the hearty, Rhone-style Chateauneuf du Pape hasn't sold out, grab a bottle
to drink with your picnic. Pipestone is open Thursday through Monday. *2040
Niderer Road; 805-227-6385.*

Linne Calodo   *map page 276, A/1-2*
These massive, mouth-filling wines take Paso Robles to Napa's outer limits, emulating the extreme styles that have brought some Napa boutique outfits a cult following. Ultra-ripe fruit explodes in red Rhône and zinfandel blends. Names like Problem Child and Slacker underscore the audacious approach. Another winner: the Outsider, which was released in the fall of 2009. Just north of Highway 46 West, the tasting room is open daily. *3030 Vineyard Drive; 805-227-0797.*

Windward Vineyard   *map page 276, A/B-1*
The Paso Robles AVA gained a reputation for superlative pinot noir starting in the early 1970s. Continuing that tradition of complex pinot noir wines are Marc Goldberg and Maggie D'Ambrosia, who in 1989 purchased 15 acres just north of Templeton in Paso Robles. These pinot devotees—pinot noir is the only wine they make—introduced their first vintage in 1993 and have had great success in recent years, fine-tuning their process to produce increasingly sophisticated wines. *1380 Live Oak Road; 805-239-2565.*

Bottles of L'Aventure's unusual blends.

L'Aventure *map page 276, A/B-1*

Trained in Burgundy and polished in Bordeaux, winemaker Stephan Asseo focuses on unconventional blends using Rhône varieties as well as cabernet sauvignon, zinfandel, and petit verdot. His signature, Optimus, varies from year to year but is reliably inky and soft, with flavors of leather, tobacco, tea, or chocolate. The tasting room is open Thursday through Sunday and by appointment. *2815 Live Oak Road; 805-227-1588.*

■ **TEMPLETON** *map page 276, A/B-1/2*

West of U.S. 101, Highway 46 rides the city line between Paso Robles to the north and Templeton to the south. It's a minor technicality as far as wine is concerned, because the wineries on either side of the road have a lot in common, regardless of which post office serves them. Tiny downtown Templeton, just east of U.S. 101, still looks like the set of a Hollywood western, its false-front businesses towered over by an outsize cattle feed elevator. The town hops on Saturday morning, when neighbors come to shop and gossip at a farmers' market that rings the picture-postcard village green.

Peachy Canyon *map page 276, A/B-1*

Peachy's main tasting room repurposes an 1888 schoolhouse sheltered by towering oaks. They built their name on zinfandel, and it is still their strong suit. You can taste several zins, including a rosé and a port-style dessert wine; expect a little spice, a little oak, and lots of concentrated fruit. Peachy Canyon also makes a viognier that is, well, peachy. The schoolhouse is less than two miles west of U.S. 101 off Highway 46. *1480 North Bethel Road; 805-237-1577.*

Castoro Cellars *map page 276, A/B-1*

A popular wine-touring spot off Highway 46 West, the large tasting room and grounds of this Mediterranean-style winery frequently hold concerts and other special events. Husband-and-wife team Niels and Bimmer Udsen founded Castoro in 1983 with the goal of making "dam fine wine" (*il castoro* is Italian for "beaver"). Their heady zinfandel, creamy chardonnay, and intensely aromatic merlot are very easy to drink; Castoro also makes quite a few other varietals from estate vineyards and locally bought grapes. *1315 North Bethel Road; 805-238-0725.*

★ **Turley Wine Cellars**   *map page 276, A-1*
A happy instance of a great second act—twice over. This old-vine zinfandel vineyard, planted in the 1920s, turned out decent wine for many years. With the help of his sister Helen, a renowned winemaker and consultant, Larry Turley (co-founder, in 1981, of Frog's Leap in the Napa Valley) bought and refurbished the winery and truly tapped its potential. In 1995 Helen left for her own winery, Marcassin in Sonoma, and Turley Wine Cellars has continued to thrill its cult following with zinfandels that are deep in color, intense in flavor, and full-bodied. The wines are hard to find, so a visit to the source is a rare opportunity. *2900 Vineyard Drive; 805-434-1030.*

★ **Wild Horse Winery & Vineyards**   *map page 276, B-2*
Wild Horse, founded in 1983, is off the beaten path but well worth searching out for the extraordinary quality of its wines. It's a local favorite for pinot noir, chardonnay, cabernet sauvignon, and especially a yummy, sophisticated merlot. Always experimenting with less familiar varieties, such as malvasia bianca, tempranillo, or verdelho, Wild Horse bottles consistently enjoyable wine. Some of the unusual varietals and reserves are available nowhere else but here. The tasting room, which overlooks vineyards planted on gently rolling hills, is east of U.S. 101 via Vineyard Drive and Templeton Road. The last part of the road is unpaved gravel. *1437 Wild Horse Winery Court; 805-788-6315.*

■ **SAN LUIS OBISPO**   *map page 276, B-3*
San Luis Obispo's wine roots reach back to the 18th century. It was founded in 1772 as a Spanish mission town and wine grapes have been grown here ever since. Since it's just a few miles from the ocean, SLO benefits from relatively moderate temperatures. It shares this good-for-grapes climate with two valleys that extend south of town, Edna and Arroyo Grande, each its own AVA. Edna Valley in particular is gaining momentum as a significant wine region.

Almost anywhere you stand in San Luis Obispo, you can see at least one of the conical peaks formed by volcanoes eons ago. A chain of these morros, as they are called, marches through Los Osos Valley from the sea, at Morro Bay a dozen miles northwest, to San Luis Obispo. Marine air and fog channeled down that valley feed into the east–west oriented Edna Valley. Once part of the sea floor, the valley

(opposite) Wine replaced the three "R"s at Peachy Canyon; their tasting room is in a 19th-century schoolhouse.

Wild Horse is off the beaten path but worth a visit for its unusual varieties.

is rich in marine mineral deposits, and its clay and loam topsoils are well-drained. It's good turf for grapes, especially chardonnay, pinot noir, and sauvignon blanc.

There are no wineries in SLO's bustling downtown, but a number of notable tasting rooms are a short drive away, in the Edna and Arroyo Grande valleys. The **San Luis Obispo Vintners Association** has good information about local wineries. *5828 Orcutt Road; 805-541-5868.*

To reach the Edna Valley from U.S. 101, take the Broad Street exit south. After it passes through San Luis Obispo, Broad Street becomes Edna Road. (The road is also marked as Highway 227.)

★ Claiborne and Churchill Vintners   *map page 276, B-3*

In an unusual winery built of straw bales (finished in stucco), Claiborne Thompson and Fredericka Churchill make Alsatian-style wines that are a departure for the Edna Valley. Their signature dry gewürztraminer and dry riesling are deeply aromatic whites, the gewürztraminer with a typical touch of spice and the riesling with a big dollop of acid-balanced fruit. Small batches of pinot gris and dry muscat round out the Alsatian list. *2649 Carpenter Canyon Road; 805-544-4066.*

Edna Valley Vineyard *map page 276, B-3*
Persuaded that the Edna Valley's singular soil is well suited for producing chardonnay and perhaps pinot noir, Dick Graff of Monterey County's Chalone Vineyard established this winery. The vineyards produce fine chardonnay, but success has been less easily achieved with the pinot noir. From the soaring picture windows of the tasting room, or from the picnic patio outside, you can look across the valley. *2585 Biddle Ranch Road; 805-544-5855.*

Saucelito Canyon Vineyard *map page 276, B-3*
Maybe this renowned old-vine zinfandel survived Prohibition because these vineyards are tucked so far up in the Arroyo Grande Valley. (The tasting room is easy to reach, in the heart of the Edna Valley.) Saucelito Canyon grows some of its grapes on 3 acres of vines planted in the early 1880s; their newer vines are more than a quarter-century old. Bill and Nancy Greenough acquired the land in 1974 and now make zins that combine the best of the old (subtle and complex) with the best of the not-so-old (fruity and bold) in wines that are full of berry flavors and have a silky, almost thick mouth feel. They also do some cabernet sauvignon and sauvignon blanc. *3080 Biddle Ranch Road; 805-543-2111.*

Ortman Family Vineyards *map page 276, B-3*
After a major success with Meridian Vineyards in Paso Robles, Chuck Ortman is turning his hand to a small, family venture. Now, with his son, Matt, he handcrafts vineyard-designated and blended chardonnay and pinot noir, among other varietals, sourced from the Edna Valley, Paso Robles, and Santa Rita Hills. Their chardonnay nicely balances pear and pineapple flavors with toasty vanilla, and the pinot noir has intense plum and berry notes touched with spice. *1317 Park Street; 805-237-9009.*

Domaine Alfred Winery *map page 276, B-3*
Established in the mid-1990s, this winery produces estate-bottled wines from its Chamisal Vineyard, which was planted in 1972. Domaine Alfred owner Terry Speizer re-planted in 1996 with pinot noir, syrah, and chardonnay. The pinot noir, a potion of black cherry, anise, and firm tannins, is the winery's strong suit. *7525 Orcutt Road; 805-541-9463.*

■ **ARROYO GRANDE** *map page 276, B-4*
Snaking back into the hills from the foot of the Edna Valley, the Arroyo Grande Valley has only a few wineries. Closest to the sea, the valley is frequently subject to

Saucelito Canyon Vineyard's mellow tasting room.

chilly fog, but higher up in the hills the microclimate is warm and sunny. Chardonnay and pinot noir grow well in the lower valley, while the upper valley yields potent zinfandel.

Talley Vineyards   *map page 276, B-3*
Vineyards of chardonnay and pinot noir, plus tiny plots of sauvignon blanc, syrah, sémillon, and cabernet franc, blanket Talley's mountain-ringed dell in the Arroyo Grande Valley. Crisp green apple, creamy peach, and spicy oak come through in the chardonnay; tannin keeps a firm grip on fruit in the pinot noir. Staff in the picture-windowed tasting room are friendly, and when you're done you can step outside for a look at the restored 1860s El Rincón Adobe, which used to house the visitor facilities. Drive south on Orcutt Road from the Edna Valley and head east (left) on Lopez Drive. Look for Talley Vineyards on the left after about a half mile. *3031 Lopez Drive; 805-489-0446.*

(opposite) A trail ride through Edna Valley vineyards.

■ SANTA BARBARA COUNTY

Though now an up-and-coming wine region, Santa Barbara County is still relatively new to the game—until the 1960s, it had no major commercial vineyards. After a few decades of steady growth, the region got a huge shot in the arm courtesy of Hollywood.

Long before the movies discovered Santa Barbara, things got off to a modest start. The Franciscan padres who colonized the region in the late 1700s planted grapes for sacramental wine. In 1884, a French immigrant planted 150 acres of French grapes on Santa Cruz Island. But none of those early vineyards survived. All was quiet until 1962, when Pierre Lafond of Quebec opened the Santa Barbara Winery downtown, a few blocks from the beach. It was an unpretentious place, making fruit wines as well as grape wines in its first years—the sort you'd take to the beach with a picnic. In northern Santa Barbara County, another hint of things to come appeared in 1964, when local farmer Uriel Nielson planted vines in the Santa Maria Valley. A few vineyards soon popped up in the Santa Ynez Valley.

The local industry really took off in the 1980s and 1990s. So many wineries were established in the Santa Ynez Valley that some locals feared the region might turn into another Napa Valley.

About 300 miles south of San Francisco via U.S. 101, Santa Barbara wine country is just 100 miles north of Los Angeles. Angelenos had long used Santa Barbara as a weekend and summer retreat, so it was only a matter of time before the county's wines started showing up at high-end restaurants in Santa Monica and Beverly Hills. In 2004, the hit movie *Sideways*, a comedy set in Santa Barbara wine country, brought tremendous attention to the region. Tourism and demand for local wines skyrocketed, and tasting rooms quickly filled up. Today, the sophistication that area wines have achieved is matched by wide recognition of the Santa Barbara name.

North of the city of Santa Barbara, a series of valleys and ridges runs roughly west–east from the coast into the mountains. These include the Santa Maria Valley, the Santa Ynez Valley, and the Santa Rita Hills, the county's three designated AVAs. The Los Alamos Valley, not officially recognized as an appellation as of this writing, is similarly aligned. The region's topography channels ocean air and fog through the valleys, creating one of California's cooler wine-growing climates.

Inland, days are warmer and sunnier and nights chillier than they are closer to the shore, where the sea moderates temperatures. A variety of soil types adds to the diversity that allows Santa Barbara County to grow quite a range of grape varieties.

U.S. 101 links Santa Maria in the north to Santa Barbara in the south, paralleled in the Santa Maria Valley by winery-studded Foxen Canyon Road. South of there, Highway 154 leads southeast into the heart of Santa Barbara wine country, through Los Olivos and Santa Ynez. Highway 246 runs east–west through the Santa Ynez Valley, between Santa Ynez and Lompoc, crossing the 101 at Buellton. Santa Rosa Road parallels 246 to the south, leading to other Santa Rita Hills wineries.

■ SANTA MARIA *map page 276, C-4/5*

Fogs frequently drift into the Santa Maria Valley from the ocean, making the western part of the AVA too cold for grapes (but perfect for many winter vegetables and early-season strawberries). Cool-climate grapes like chardonnay and pinot noir thrive on the warmer slopes east of U.S. 101 and north of the Santa Maria River. Heat-loving Bordeaux grapes do better in the eastern valley and in Foxen Canyon, which gets very hot in summer. Much of this fruit gets shipped to wineries throughout California.

Cambria Winery & Vineyard *map page 276, C/D-4*

On a benchland at the northern edge of the Santa Maria Valley, these vineyards lie only about 15 miles from the Pacific Ocean but are high enough above the valley floor to escape its fogs. Some of the vines at Cambria are part of the original Tepusquet Vineyard, planted between 1970 and 1971 by Uriel Nielson. Barbara Banke and her husband, Jess Jackson, of Kendall-Jackson fame, bought Tepusquet's premium acres in 1987 and renamed the winery. Cambria makes character-laden chardonnay and velvety-textured pinot noir. In addition to those wines, a viognier and a rich, spicy syrah, both from the Tepusquet vines, are produced here. *5475 Chardonnay Lane; 805-937-8091.*

Kenneth Volk Vineyards *map page 276, C-5*

A Central Coast wine pioneer and founder of Wild Horse Winery in Templeton, Ken Volk sold that business in 2003 and started this venture. He specializes in vineyard-designated chardonnay and pinot noir grown in Santa Barbara County and cabernet sauvignon and merlot grown in Paso Robles. Passionate about the effect of vintage and vineyard, Volk creates diverse results with each grape variety. One pinot noir release might be richly fruity, while another might be fragrantly refined. The simple tasting room pours this extraordinary wine daily. *5230 Tepusquet Road; 805-938-7896.*

Rancho Sisquoc Winery   *map page 276, C-5*

With its old ranch house and barn shaded by ancient trees, this is the region's most romantic winery. The vineyards here are warmer than those of the western Santa Maria Valley but cooler than those of the Santa Ynez Valley to the south. The tasting room, in a rustic wood building, might be pouring cabernet sauvignon, merlot, malbec, sauvignon blanc, chardonnay, pinot noir, and riesling, as well as California's only sylvaner, a crisp, fruity white. Turn onto the 2.5-mile-long driveway at the 19th-century San Ramon Chapel. *6600 Foxen Canyon Road; 805-934-4332.*

Foxen Vineyard   *map page 276, C-5*

A former blacksmith shop houses the tasting room on 2,000-acre Rancho Tinaquaic, which has been in Richard Doré's family since 1837. Only a few acres are planted to grapes, but Foxen has made a big name for itself by using grapes grown elsewhere in the county. Inky, peppery syrah; intense, citrusy chardonnay; and complex, cherries-and-cinnamon pinot noir are exceptional. Foxen buys some of its pinot noir grapes from Sea Smoke Vineyard, whose pinot starred in the movie *Sideways,* but the extremely limited releases are not poured in the tasting room. *7200 Foxen Canyon Road; 805-937-4251.*

■ LOS OLIVOS   *map page 276, D-6*

Heading south to Los Olivos, Foxen Canyon Road crosses the line from the Santa Maria Valley AVA into the Santa Ynez Valley AVA. As small as it is, the Santa Ynez Valley has several distinct climates. In the warmer vineyards east of U.S. 101, cabernet sauvignon, merlot, sauvignon blanc, and Rhône and Italian varietals do well. But there is no fixed rule: riesling and other cool-climate grapes do surprisingly well in certain niches of the valley.

Downtown Los Olivos has a few good restaurants and cafés along its several blocks. One very good reason to stop here is the **Los Olivos Tasting Room and Wineshop,** whose knowledgeable staff members pour the wines of many local wineries, including some—Hitching Post and Qupé among them—that aren't open to the public. *2905 Grand Avenue; 805-688-7406.*

Syrah, viognier, and the Z Gris blend are the specialties of ranchlike Zaca Mesa.

Zaca Mesa Winery   *map page 276, D-5*

With its tall working metal windmill out front and its barnlike buildings tucked into a small side canyon, Zaca Mesa might be mistaken for a cattle ranch. Chances are you won't even see the vineyards here, which rest high above the winery on a 1,500-foot-high mesa, where warm, sunny days and cool, breezy afternoons create ideal conditions for Rhône varietals. Among Zaca Mesa's signature wines are its syrah, viognier, and the much-lauded Z Three, a traditional Rhone-style blend made from grenache, mourvèdre, and syrah. The winery is a quiet place—the word *zaca* is the local Chumash tribe's word for "peaceful"— where you can picnic under the oaks or play a game of lawn chess. *6905 Foxen Canyon Road; 805-688-9339.*

Fess Parker Winery & Vineyard   *map page 276, D-5*

Wine Country meets the Alamo at this winery owned by the actor who starred as Davy Crockett in three 1950s movies and as Daniel Boone on a 1960s TV series. It is the region's hokiest tasting room (who else sells coonskin caps and other mountain-man paraphernalia?), but the wine is popular, well-priced, and has earned some good ratings from the critics. Ample fruit and oak are hallmarks in the easy-drinking chardonnay, viognier, and syrah. *6200 Foxen Canyon Road; 805-688-1545.*

Firestone Vineyard   *map page 276, D-5/6*
Firestone, Santa Barbara County's first estate winery (founded in 1972), is big and proud of it. It produces a variety of wines from its Santa Ynez Valley estate vineyards, most notably chardonnay, merlot, syrah, and late-harvest Riesling. The winery offers informative tours three times daily. It's stationed just where Foxen Canyon Road turns into Zaca Station Road. The winery also runs a tasting room in downtown Paso Robles (2300 Airport Road; 805-591-8050). *5000 Zaca Station Road; 805-688-3940.*

Andrew Murray Vineyards   *map page 276, D-6*
Andrew Murray is all about Rhône varieties. At his hands, estate-grown or sourced nearby, reds such as syrah and whites such as viognier turn into some of the region's finest wine. The roussanne-marsanne blend, Enchanté, and the syrah-grenache-mourvèdre blend, Espérance, reflect Rhône blending tradition and the California fondness for fruit and spice. The tasting room is in downtown Los Olivos. *2901 Grand Ave.; 805-693-9644.*

Brander Vineyard   *map page 276, D-6*
One of the Santa Ynez Valley's oldest wineries—it opened in 1981—Brander is renowned for its zesty, fresh sauvignon blanc. They offer several different styles, as well as some inventive blends that incorporate the grape. Most fun of all may be the Château Neuf de Pink, which blends sauvignon blanc with rosés of syrah, grenache, merlot, and sangiovese. Fittingly, the tasting room is in a cheery little pink château. *2401 Refugio Road; 805-688-2455.*

Beckmen Vineyards   *map page 276, D-6*
Family-owned Beckmen farms its 365-acre Purisima Mountain Vineyard biodynamically. Rhône-style wines made from the estate grapes include syrah, marsanne, grenache, and grenache blanc. The rosé of grenache has a bright spiciness, and the white blend, Le Bec Blanc, is peachy and round. Three picnic gazebos overlook the winery's duck pond. *2670 Ontiveros Road; 805-688-8664.*

(top) Fields of lavender amid oaks at Beckmen.
(bottom) Perusing the local wine selection at the Los Olivos Tasting Room and Wineshop.

■ **SANTA YNEZ** *map page 276, D-6*

Ranchers (and wannabe ranchers) look right at home in this fragment of the Old West in the heart of Wine Country. A saloon, a Victorian-style B&B, and assorted false-front shops line Santa Ynez's three-block-long downtown. A few miles west on Highway 246, between here and U.S. 101, is **Solvang,** the incongruous faux-Danish village created by immigrant farmers. The half-timbered, thatch-roofed tourist attraction is the place to stop if you are in the mood for some kitsch or smorgasbord.

Bridlewood Winery *map page 276, D-6*

This lushly landscaped winery, built to resemble an old Spanish mission, stands north of downtown Santa Ynez. Syrah is the specialty, and the style is tannic and dusty. Several versions are poured in the tasting room, as are viognier, pinot noir, and grenache. *3555 Roblar Avenue; 805-688-9000.*

Gainey Vineyard *map page 276, D-6*

Gainey's chardonnay, pinot noir, merlot, syrah, cabernet franc, and sauvignon blanc are consistently excellent, and in some years, there's also an exquisite late-

The ambience of Alma Rosa is decidedly rustic.

harvest riesling. The lush yet lively sauvignon blanc stands out; the warm, concentrated pinot noir fills the nose and mouth. People come to the Spanish mission–style winery in summer to enjoy concerts under the stars. At nearly any time of year, the well-groomed picnic area provides the perfect setting to have lunch or a snack and sip fine wine. *3950 East Highway 246; 805-688-0558.*

■ **BUELLTON** *map page 276, C/D-6*
West of U.S. 101 in Buellton and east of Lompoc, the cool vineyards of the Santa Rita Hills AVA (an appellation within the Santa Ynez Valley AVA) are influenced by marine air from the nearby Pacific. Pinot noir, the "heartbreak grape," thrives here. Grapes of the cabernet group ripen in warm pockets of the western hills. Buellton, a collection of motels and strip malls, lies west of Solvang at Highway 246 and U.S. 101. Three wineries of note can be found just south of Buellton, west off U.S. 101 on Santa Rosa Road, which parallels the Santa Ynez River. The wineries are all just south of the river.

Alma Rosa Winery and Vineyards *map page 276, C-6*
Alma Rosa's long driveway winds along a creek lined with sycamores and ends at a tasting room in the beat-up dairy barn of a family ranch. You couldn't ask for a more relaxed setting in which to try the pinot noir that started it all. Back in 1971, owner Richard Sanford introduced the Santa Rita Hills to the grape that has since made the AVA famous. Dark fruit flavors, juicy acidity, and refined tannins are common themes in Alma Rosa's pinot noir. The other trademarks here are chardonnay, pinot gris, and pinot blanc. *7250 Santa Rosa Road; 805-688-9090.*

Mosby Winery *map page 276, C-6*
At Mosby, you can explore the world of Cal-Ital wine—California's take on Italian wines such as pinot grigio, dolcetto, and cortese. The perfumy, floral traminer is a classic northern Italian white; the smoky, deep-ruby sangiovese evokes Tuscany. The vivid red carriage house of an 1853 adobe serves as the tasting room. The winery is just west of U.S. 101; look for the driveway in the sharp bend Santa Rosa Road takes west from the freeway. *9496 Santa Rosa Road; 805-688-2415.*

Lafond Winery and Vineyards *map page 276, C-6*
Pierre Lafond opened his large, modern winery and its equally large, modern tasting room in early 2001, just before the establishment of the Santa Rita Hills

AVA. Pinot noir, chardonnay, and syrah make up the portfolio, with the complex, concentrated pinot the main attention-getter. Bottles with Lafond's SRH label are an especially good value. *6855 Santa Rosa Road; 805-688-7921.*

■ **LOMPOC**   *map page 276, B/C-6*
A bedroom community for Vandenberg Air Force Base, Lompoc is surrounded by giant flower farms and produce fields. This a working town filled with dusty pickup trucks and cookie-cutter houses. Lompoc lies outside the Santa Rita Hills AVA on a stray loop of Highway 1 that leads west from U.S. 101; Highway 246 and Santa Rosa Road parallel it farther north and pass a number of the AVA's wineries.

It's no cutesy wine town, but Lompoc is now headquarters for several wineries in the Sobhani Industrial Park, on Chestnut Avenue behind the Home Depot. The complex has come to be known as the **Wine Ghetto,** and for the most part it consists of functional wine-making operations with no visitors facilities. Some of the wineries, however, have established tasting rooms that are open a few days a week; others welcome guests by appointment. You can visit Kathy Joseph's outstanding **Fiddlehead Cellars** (1597 East Chestnut Avenue; 800-251-1225) on Saturday, to taste her peachy, creamy, gorgeously acid-balanced sauvignon blancs and her plummy, elegant pinot noirs.

Foley Estates Vineyard & Winery   *map page 276, D-6*
Foley's estate-grown chardonnay and pinot noir show what a very cool climate, ocean fog, and rocky soil can do for a grape. Estate-grown Santa Rita Hills fruit goes into intensely fruity, golden chardonnay and earthy, berry-rich pinot noir. The big, spiffy tasting room, in a stone-and-stucco building with a tin roof, was built in 2005. *6121 East Highway 246; 805-737-6222.*

Babcock Winery & Vineyards   *map page 276, C-6*
A family-owned winery in the northern Santa Rita Hills about 9 miles west of U.S. 101, Babcock is known for chardonnay but also makes first-rate pinot noir, estate-grown pinot gris, syrah, and a red Bordeaux blend called Fathom. The acclaim won by Babcock's first wine, an estate-grown sauvignon blanc, has endured since the 1980s. *5175 Highway 246; 805-736-1455.*

(opposite) Foley Estates makes the most out of its relatively cool location.

A GREAT DRIVE IN PASO ROBLES

The west side of Paso Robles is a terrific area for a slower-paced, intimate winery experience. Starting from town, pack a picnic lunch and drive north, turning west onto 24th Street. As it leaves town, 24th Street turns into Nacimiento Lake Road; in about 1½ miles you'll reach a Y. Bear left onto Adelaida Road and drive 9 hilly, winding miles out to Tablas Creek for their morning tour. Next up: some knockout red wines at Justin Winery. Get back on Adelaida, drive 2 miles, and turn left at the T onto Chimney Rock Road. About 1½ miles along you'll find Justin, where you can tour, taste, and picnic.

To try some particularly hard-to-find wines at the source, head back to Adelaida, take a right onto Vineyard Drive, and cross Highway 46 into Templeton to reach Turley Wine Cellars. (Although Turley's just 10 miles away, the drive takes about 40 minutes since the roads are so twisty.) From Turley, continue on Vineyard, which turns into Templeton Road when it crosses U.S. 101, and after nearly 5 miles keep an eye out on your left for Wild Horse Winery Court, the half-mile driveway for Wild Horse. After sipping their merlot, backtrack on Templeton Road and, before you hit the 101, turn right onto Main Street. The street passes through Templeton's Old West–style town center, then picks up the freeway north of town.

If you've still got some juice, drive about 1½ miles north on U.S. 101 and take the first exit, onto Highway 46 West. Another 1½ miles brings you to Arbor Road (there's a big, white B&B on the corner); turn right and in about half a mile take a left onto Live Oak Road. On this road, you can stop by two wineries: Windward and L'Aventure. Finish your day by backtracking to Highway 101 and returning to downtown Paso Robles for dinner.

Melville *map page 276, C-6*
Earthy, herbaceous, firmly tannic, and darkly berry-flavored, Melville's pinot noir exemplifies the varietal's potential in the Santa Rita Hills. The grape grows all around the winery, a faux-Mediterranean villa with red-tile roofs. Inside, the airy space and tile floors of the rotunda-like tasting room offer respite from the baking sun. Melville also makes chardonnay and syrah. *5185 East Highway 246; 805-735-7030.*

The chef at work at Yountville's French Laundry. Reserve your table far in advance.

WHERE TO EAT
IN WINE COUNTRY

There is perhaps no place in the United States where you'll find food that's as consistently excellent as it is in California's Wine Country. In part you can thank the vintners and other folks in the wine industry, who spend years developing their palates—they bring a keen, appreciative attitude to the table. These winemakers know that there is no better way to show off their wines than with creative cooking, so they've encouraged a lively, top-notch food scene.

But we can't give the wine industry all the credit for those organic mâche salads. California's unique climate nurtures a rich variety of produce year-round, so Wine Country chefs are able to take advantage of ripe, local fruits and vegetables and artisanal products that simply aren't available elsewhere.

The Wine Country's top restaurants tend to serve what used to be called "California cuisine," which incorporates elements of French and Italian cooking and emphasizes the use of fresh, local products. If the restaurant scene here has a weakness, it's the absence of a greater variety of cuisines—a case of a good thing crowding others out. However, the number of immigrants from Central America who live here ensure that in almost any town you'll find some good, inexpensive spots selling tacos and other Latin American fare.

The Wine Country's restaurants, though excellent, can really dent your wallet. One way to avoid sticker shock is try restaurants at lunch, when prices are marginally lower. It also doesn't hurt to ask about a restaurant's corkage policy: some restaurants eliminate their corkage fee one night a week, or even every night, hoping to attract locals in the wine industry who would rather drink bottles from their own cellar than the restaurant's.

The sheer number of restaurants means you can always find an empty table somewhere, but it pays to call ahead for a reservation, even if only a day or two before you visit. For the big-name restaurants like Cyrus, Bottega, Martini House, and Farmhouse Inn, calling a few weeks in advance is advised, though you can often get in on short notice if you're willing to eat early or late. (For the famed French Laundry, reserve 2 months ahead to the day.)

The restaurant listings below are organized to reflect the geographical order of the preceding chapters, starting with the Southern Napa Valley, and then listed alphabetically within each town.

Prices for a main course at dinner:
$ = less than $10 $$ = $10–$20 $$$ = $20–$30 $$$$ = over $30
★ = Top Pick

Rustic French classics are served in a former boathouse at Angèle.

■ SOUTHERN NAPA VALLEY

■ NAPA   *map page 87*

★ **Angèle.** The Napa Valley's Rouas family (of Auberge du Soleil fame) created this French restaurant in a former Napa River boathouse that dates back to the 1890s. Although the main dining room is plenty romantic, in good weather ask for one of the even nicer tables outside. The kitchen dishes up refined versions of rustic French classics such as an onion and goat cheese tart with a frisée salad; beef bourguignon; and a classic French onion soup. The dessert list is short and very French (think pot de crème). *540 Main Street; 707-252-8115.* **$$$–$$$$**

BarBersQ. A far cry from a down-home ramshackle barbecue shack, this temple to meat in the middle of a shopping center has a clean, modern aesthetic, from the black-and-white photos on the wall to the brushed aluminum chairs. Still, the menu is full of 'cue favorites, like smoked baby-back ribs and a Memphis-style pulled pork sandwich, as well as supremely juicy fried chicken, served with mashed potatoes and collard greens. Outside seating (on a patio facing the parking lot) is available on fair days. *3900D Bel Aire Plaza; 707-224-6600.* $–$$

★ **Bistro Don Giovanni.** This warmly welcoming favorite of both locals and critics serves some of the best California-Italian food in the valley, delights such as milk-braised rabbit with Tuscan kale and house-made ravioli. Pizzas cooked in their traditional wood-burning fireplace are a specialty. Seats on the covered terrace are coveted in warm weather, but a fireplace and an impressive bar indoors mean that the restaurant is a good choice any time of year. *4110 Howard Lane; 707-224-3300.* $$–$$$

Celadon. Located downtown on the west bank of the Napa River, Celadon infuses California ingredients with a global flair. For instance, Maine crab cakes get paired with a grapefruit aïoli, while lamb shanks come with a Moroccan-inspired almond couscous. Small and large plates make this a good pick for a varying-appetite party. Exposed brick walls hung with vintage posters contribute to the elegant but fairly casual ambience. *500 Main Street; 707-254-9690.* $$$–$$$$

★ **Ubuntu.** Foodies from the Wine Country to New York City are abuzz over this Napa innovator, a "vegetable restaurant" that draws heavily on its own biodynamic gardens. Though vegetarian restaurants can sometimes seem ascetic—this one is even attached to a yoga studio, whose students can be faintly seen through translucent windows—Ubuntu is anything but. Each of the gorgeously composed plates reveals a unique combination of flavors, from the marcona almonds generously dusted with lavender sugar and sea salt, to the grits served with barbecued Brussels sprouts and a celery-root salad. The dining room strikes a New-Age-chic-meets-Wine-Country-rustic pose, with extremely high ceilings, parchment-color lamps, fieldstone walls, and a long communal table. Hours vary according to the season, since the restaurant is largely dependent on what the gardens are producing. *1140 Main Street; 707-251-5656.* $$$

ZuZu. Ocher-color walls, a weathered wood bar, a faded tile floor, and hammered-tin ceiling panels set the casual scene for a menu composed almost entirely of tapas. These little dishes, so perfect for sharing, and Latin jazz on the stereo help make this place a popular spot for festive get-togethers. Diners down *cava* (Spanish sparkling wine) or sangria with dishes such as white anchovies with endive, ratatouille, and salt cod with garlic croutons. Reservations aren't accepted, so expect a wait on weekends. *Bocadillos* (Spanish-style sandwiches) and empanadas available

PAIRING WINE AND FOOD

When the wine you're drinking and the food you're eating are a good match, both the wine and the food taste dramatically better. This sort of matchmaking, however, makes most people anxious. A laid-back "if you like it, they go together" philosophy has replaced the old "red wine with red meat, white wine with white meat" rule. If you're not yet familiar with a given wine, though, it can be difficult to decide on pairing. Principles that recommend matching hearty wine with hearty food, or fruity wine with spicy food, may not help if you're in uncharted wine waters. What if you can't remember whether viognier is full-bodied? What if you've never eaten rabbit before?

Don't be afraid to ask: the sommelier, your server, or the wine-shop clerk should be happy to help you out. If you're on your own, have some fun with it. Here are a few suggestions for pairing food with some popular varietals of California wine.

RED

Cabernet sauvignon: roast beef, steak, rack of lamb, venison, mushrooms, bittersweet chocolate.

Merlot: beef stew, lamb chops, pork loin, roast duck, pasta with meat sauce, parmesan and romano cheeses.

Zinfandel: hamburgers, braised beef, barbecue ribs, spicy sausages, dark chocolate.

Pinot noir: filet mignon, pork chops, rabbit, fowl, grilled "meaty" fish like salmon, tomato sauces, cherry pie.

Syrah: leg of lamb, smoked meat, dry sausage, winter vegetables, sharp cheeses, chocolate cake.

WHITE

Chardonnay: ham, veal chops, roast duck, lobster, crab, cream sauces, grilled vegetables, soft cheeses, crème brûlée.

Sauvignon blanc: chicken, turkey, mahi-mahi, shrimp, scallops, stir-fried vegetables, lemon tart.

Viognier: ham, spicy sausage, fried chicken, sea bass, red snapper, smoked fish, hearty vegetable soups, pecan pie.

Pinot gris: white-meat poultry, sole, flounder, Asian noodle dishes, spring vegetables, salads, sorbet.

Riesling: duck breast, trout, spicy Asian dishes, hot peppers, goat cheese, apple pie.

at lunch make it an inexpensive stop for a midday snack. *829 Main Street; 707-224-8555.* **$$**

■ YOUNTVILLE   *map page 78*

Ad Hoc. When superstar chef Thomas Keller opened this warm, low-key spot, with zinc-top tables and wine served in tumblers, he meant to run it for only six months, but locals were so charmed by the homey food that they clamored for the stopgap to stay. Now a single, seasonal fixed-price menu ($49) is served nightly, with an equally hearty meal served for Sunday brunch. The selection might include a juicy pork loin and buttery polenta, served family style, or a delicate *panna cotta* with a citrus glaze. *6476 Washington Street; 707-944-2487.* **$$$$**

★ **Bottega.** Celebrity chef Michael Chiarello has made a much-heralded return to the restaurant business with this lively trattoria that opened in 2008. The menu is simultaneously soulful and inventive, transforming local ingredients into regional Italian dishes with a twist. The antipasti in particular shine: house-made charcuterie or you can order olives grown on Chiarello's own property in St. Helena. Hearty main courses like braised short ribs could be served on a bed of spinach prepared with preserved lemons. The vibe is more festive than formal, with exposed-brick walls, an open kitchen, and paper-topped tables, but service is spot on. *6525 Washington Street; 707-945-1050.* **$$–$$$$**

★ **Bouchon.** Though considerably more casual than the French Laundry flagship restaurant, this spinoff bistro still showcases chef Thomas Keller's mind-boggling perfectionism. You could easily imagine you're in Paris sitting at the zinc bar drinking a kir royale or at the one of the velvet banquettes eating a classic steak frites, roast leg of lamb, or *croque madame*, a toasted ham and cheese sandwich topped with a fried egg. The restaurant's open and buzzing until 12:30 A.M.—a real rarity in the Wine Country. *6534 Washington Street; 707-944-8037.* **$$–$$$$**

Étoile. Housed at Domaine Chandon, this elegant stunner seems built for romance, with orchids on each table and views of the beautiful winery grounds from the large windows. After a few years off the radar of many local critics, the restaurant has soared lately under the young chef Perry Hoffman, who turns out sophisticated California cuisine. Starters like the poached lobster with radishes,

Home-style cooking is raised to the level of haute cuisine at Mustard's.

Asian pear, and pearl barley play with a variety of textures, and luxe ingredients like shavings of black truffle dress up a perfectly cooked beef tenderloin. The wine list naturally features plenty of Domaine Chandon sparklers, but it's strong in wines from throughout California as well. *1 California Drive; 888-242-6366.* **$$$$**

★ **French Laundry.** It's the most coveted reservation in all of California: chef-owner Thomas Keller serves nine courses of exquisite French food to his pilgrims. Yes, it costs a pretty penny to eat here—the menu is $250, not including wine—but that hasn't deterred the diners who speed-dial the restaurant two months to the day in advance of the day they are hoping to secure a table. Keller's signature "oysters and pearls," a sabayon of pearl tapioca with oysters and white sturgeon caviar, start the meal and set the tone for the feast to come. The setting—an old stone house that was once actually used as a laundry—is beautifully rustic rather than opulent, and the service is impeccable. *6640 Washington Street; 707-944-2380.* **$$$$**

★ **Mustard's Grill.** Busy and often noisy, Mustard's serves American comfort food with a local twist: baby-back pork ribs, Sonoma rabbit with herb butter and sweet corn tamales, as well as very good salads and soups. The food is a form of home cooking raised several notches. Service is fast and efficient, and though the staff seems always to be rushing about, no one ever rushes you. Make a reservation or you may have a long wait. *7399 St. Helena Highway; 707-944-2424.* **$$–$$$**

★ **Redd.** The sleek, minimalist dining room seems a fitting setting for chef Richard Reddington's up-to-date menu. Mixing culinary influences from California, Europe, and Asia, the food feels modern but never fussy. The rich glazed pork belly with burdock served in a pool of soy caramel is a prime example of the East-meets-West style, and seafood preparations—like a tuna and hamachi tartare and crispy calamari—are standouts as well. Many of the desserts put a novel twist on a classic: witness the butterscotch "sundae," a scoop of vanilla rum ice cream served with an airy butterscotch cream and salted butter shortbread. Service is enthusiastic if not particularly polished, but such refined cooking and elegant atmosphere are difficult to find at this price in the Wine Country. For the full experience, consider the five-course tasting menu ($75). Or for a quick bite, order small plates and a cocktail, and sit at the bar. *6480 Washington Street; 707-944-2222.* **$$$–$$$$**

■ NORTHERN NAPA VALLEY

■ RUTHERFORD *map page 107*

Auberge du Soleil. Possibly the most romantic roost for a dinner in all the Wine Country is a terrace seat at this restaurant in Napa's most expensive resort. Dramatic views over the vineyards below are almost matched by the quality of the cuisine, which puts a Mediterranean spin on top California ingredients. Service is as polished as you would expect at these prices, and the wine list is one of the most extensive around. *180 Rutherford Hill Road; 707-963-1211.* **$$$$**

■ ST. HELENA *map page 118*

★ **Gott's Roadside.** On summer days, the line at this 1950s-style, drive-in hamburger stand can be 20 people deep. "Hamburger stand," however, hardly does justice to the offerings here, which include not only a juicy bacon cheeseburger and garlic fries but also a super-popular rare ahi burger. Are you hankering for a bottle of wine from a local producer, or perhaps a root beer float instead? Here they've got the best of both worlds. *933 Main Street; 707-963-3486.* **$–$$**

Market. All-American favorites like meatloaf with mashed potatoes and macaroni and cheese are equal parts familiar and refined at this unusually welcoming spot in downtown St. Helena. Locally farmed produce and other choice ingredients elevate the homey dishes. Waiters and bartenders greet regular guests by name, and visitors are received just as warmly. Native fieldstone walls and a bar from the late 1800s that reportedly came from San Francisco's Palace Hotel make an attractive backdrop. *1347 Main Street; 707-963-3799.* **$$–$$$**

★ **Martini House.** Tucked into a side street of downtown St. Helena, this restaurant occupies the former home of the opera singer Walter Martini, a bootlegger during Prohibition. His 1923 Craftsman house was redesigned to great effect: three fireplaces glow in wintertime and lights sparkle in the garden in summer. Expect such dishes as sautéed foie gras, pork chops with crimini mushrooms and garlic sauce, Sonoma rabbit, and vegetarian tarts. The wine list includes many rare bottlings, and the specialty cocktails are excellent as well. *1245 Spring Street; 707-963-2233.* **$$$$**

Pizzeria Tra Vigne. Early in the evening families with kids flock to the outdoor tables at this casual pizzeria. Later on, young couples gather around the pool table. And at any time of day you'll find fabulous, crisp, thin-crusted pizzas, like the

unusual Positano, with sautéed shrimp and crescenza cheese. Salads and pasta round out the menu. Service is friendly, if not particularly speedy. *1016 Main Street; 707-967-9999.* **$–$$**

★ **The Restaurant at Meadowood.** Chef Christopher Kostow has garnered rave reviews (and two Michelin stars) for transforming seasonal local products (some grown right on the property) into elaborate, elegant fare. The "composition of carrots," constructed of the tiniest carrots imaginable and delicate shavings of chocolate, foie gras, and candied tangerine (it sounds odd, but it works) is just one example of Kostow's inventiveness, while the slow-cooked black cod with chorizo demonstrates an earthier approach. The chef's menu ($155), composed of eight or so courses, is the best way to appreciate the experience, but the gracious servers provide some of the best service in the valley even if you're ordering a less extravagant three-, four-, or five-course menu. *900 Meadowood Lane; 707-967-1205.* **$$$$**

Terra Restaurant. Brainchild of chef Hiro Sone, Terra is perfectly poised. Its 1884 fieldstone building balances comfort and elegance, with a candlelit dining room. The food is eclectic but not outré, drawing mostly from French and Italian cuisines, but with unexpected Asian twists that make Sone's dishes truly delightful. His signature dish, sake-marinated cod in a shiso broth, is justifiably popular, and the grilled duck with duck liver wontons manages an East–West harmony that other chefs vainly strive to achieve. Service here is unparalleled in the Napa Valley. *1345 Railroad Avenue; 707-963-8931.* **$$$–$$$$**

Tra Vigne Restaurant. It's hard to say whether this restaurant is most appealing in spring, when the wildflowers in the small vineyard out front are in full bloom, or on a rainy winter day, when the bright decor and friendly staff help mitigate the chill in your bones. The menu changes frequently, but butternut squash ravioli, braised short ribs, and truffle pizza have been among recent offerings. The wine list shuttles between California and Italy, with some obscure bottlings from small wineries. *1050 Charter Oak Avenue; 707-963-4444.* **$$–$$$**

Wine Spectator Greystone Restaurant. Though this cavernous restaurant is in Culinary Institute of America's St. Helena campus, rest assured that there are professional chefs rather than students behind the stoves. And, in fact, you can see those chefs at work in the open exhibition kitchen, unless you opt for one of the seats on the patio with vineyard views. The frequently changing Mediterranean-

(opposite) Sipping al fresco at Mumm in Napa. (following pages) Tra Vigne is one of the Wine Country's culinary meccas—and rightfully so.

influenced menu emphasizes local produce: the grilled hanger steak might be served with a Point Reyes blue cheese tart, and in summer you might find a Sonoma organic chicken with a salad of arugula and grilled corn. *2555 Main Street; 707-967-1010.* **$$$–$$$$**

■ CALISTOGA *map page 107*

All Seasons Bistro. Bistro cuisine takes a California spin in this cheerful sun-filled space, where tables topped with flowers stand on an old-fashioned black-and-white checkerboard floor. The seasonal menu might include seared scallops with a cauliflower purée or fettuccine puttanesca. Homey desserts include crème brûlée and rum-raisin bread pudding. You can order reasonably priced wines from their extensive list or buy a bottle at the attached wine shop and have it poured at your table. *1400 Lincoln Avenue; 707-942-9111.* **$$–$$$**

JoLē. This small space off the lobby of the Mount View Hotel feels casual, with servers in jeans and white shirts and jazz playing in the background, but the food is a cut above. The owners' "farm to table" philosophy means that you'll find lots of local ingredients in their California fare with a Mediterranean flair, like a lamb T-bone with a chickpea and chorizo stew. Just keep in mind that the small-plates format—and somewhat expensive wines by the glass—mean that the bill can add up quickly. *1457 Lincoln Avenue; 707-942-5938.* **$$$–$$$$**

★ **Solbar.** As befits a restaurant located in the spa and resort Solage, the menu here is divided into "healthy, lighter" dishes and "hearty" fare. But the food rises far above that at most hotels, and chef Brandon Sharp is making waves with his subtle and sophisticated take on Wine Country cooking. On the light side, a lemon-poached sole comes with baby artichokes and a bright Meyer lemon risotto, while a crispy poached egg served with house-cured lardo is a standout on the hearty side. Service is excellent, and in summer the patio is a festive spot for breakfast, lunch, or dinner. *755 Silverado Trail; 707-226-0850.* **$$$–$$$$**

■ CARNEROS DISTRICT *map page 159*

Boon Fly Café. This is one of the best—and one of the few—restaurants in the Carneros District. It looks like a traditional red barn on the outside, but has a cool, modern galvanized steel bar and tables inside. The small menu of three squares a day updates American classics. For instance, the reuben sandwich comes on artisan marbled-rye bread, and the braised short ribs come with broccolini and Pecorino cheese. *4048 Highway 121; 707-299-4872.* **$$–$$$**

■ SONOMA VALLEY

■ TOWN OF SONOMA *map pages 173 and 184*

★ **Cafe La Haye.** Though the tiny storefront half a block off Sonoma's Plaza might not catch your eye as you wander by, this spot is almost always packed with the food cognoscenti. It's a case of good things coming in small packages. The petite dining room, brightened by colorful art, looks into a minuscule kitchen. The menu's fittingly short, but each choice, such as pork tenderloin with white bean ragù, is notably good. The attentive, friendly service helps secure plenty of repeat customers. *140 Napa Street East; 707-935-5994.* **$$–$$$**

Della Santina's. The Della Santina family—Dan, Shirley, and son Robert—hails from Lucca, which explains their traditional menu of Tuscan favorites. (Some of the recipes were inspired by Dan's mother.) All the pastas are made in-house, while the roasted meats turn on a rotisserie. Don't miss the lasagna Bolognese. In summer everyone tries for seats on the brick patio; in winter, ask for a seat near the fireplace. *133 Napa Street East; 707-935-0576.* **$$**

★ **The Girl & the Fig.** Maybe it's the down-to-earth bistro cuisine, or the high quality of the service, or the stellar wine list focused on Rhône varietals from both France and California. Whatever the winning combination, owner Sondra Bernstein's The Girl and the Fig has succeeded marvelously in a location that was once a restaurant graveyard. The menu might include a flavorful white-bean and winter-kale soup, a fig and arugula salad (figs are included in many of the dishes), or red-wine-braised boar shoulder. There's an admirable selection of local and imported cheeses. *110 West Spain Street; 707-938-3634.* **$$$**

Swiss Hotel. On pleasant days, the front-porch tables here tend to be filled to the gills with locals and tourists watching life pass by on the plaza. Don't be put off by the crowd, though—there are many more tables in the garden out back. This is casual food; think burgers and pizza from the wood-fired oven. Salads, like the warm radicchio and frisée salad, are a bit more inventive. The restaurant's 19th-century bar is a favorite local hangout. To get in the spirit of things, ask for their signature secret-recipe drink, a Glariffee (a colder, sweeter variation of Irish coffee). *18 West Spain Street; 707-938-2884.* **$–$$**

■ **GLEN ELLEN** *map page 184*

★ **The Fig Cafe.** Pale sage walls, yellow tablecloths, and casual but very warm service set a sunny mood in this little bistro that's run by the same team behind Sonoma's The Girl & the Fig. The restaurant's eponymous fruit shows up in all sorts of unexpected places—not only in salads and desserts, but even in an aperitif (the bubbly-based "fig royale") and on thin-crusted pizzas piled high with arugula. The small menu focuses on California and French comfort food, like steamed mussels served with terrific crispy fries, and a braised pot roast served with seasonal vegetables. Moderate prices and a generous no-corkage policy make it a popular stop for locals. *13690 Arnold Drive; 707-938-2130.* **$$**

Garden Court Café & Bakery. A stone's throw from the post office, the "court," as locals say, serves something no other restaurant in Glen Ellen serves: casual, down-home food—served every day but Tuesday. Breakfasts include omelets and thick, fluffy pancakes; lunches provide sandwiches and homemade soups. Dinner is all about comfort food: fried chicken, pot pie, and more. *13647 Arnold Drive; 707-935-1565.* **$–$$**

Glen Ellen Inn. This cozy restaurant in a creekside house exudes romance, especially if you snag a seat on the patio, strung with tiny lights, or in the shady garden. The eclectic, frequently changing menu plucks elements from California, French, and occasionally Asian cuisines. For instance, you might try a ginger tempura calamari or a filet mignon with a cambozola (cow's-milk cheese) croquette. Desserts tend toward the decadent; witness the warm pecan bread pudding with a chocolate center that sits in a puddle of brandy sauce. The wine list is short but well chosen. *13670 Arnold Drive; 707-996-6409.* **$$–$$$**

■ **KENWOOD** *map page 184*

★ **Cafe Citti.** Locals love this no-frills Tuscan-style trattoria, and they don't mind ordering at the counter before taking one of the seats indoor by the fireplace or out on the patio. Plain fare such as roast chicken, focaccia sandwiches, and pasta with your choice of sauce (marinara, puttanesca, or pesto) is served with a variety of prepared salads displayed in the deli case. Everything is available to go, which makes this an excellent stop for picnickers. *9049 Sonoma Highway; 707-833-2690.* **$$–$$$**

Kenwood Restaurant & Bar. The menu changes constantly at Kenwood Restaurant, but you'll always find a great variety of French-inspired contemporary cooking, from a tender beef bourguignon to veal piccata on mushroom ravioli. The restaurant's at its best on warm afternoons and evening, when you can enjoy the view of the vineyards from the patio, but the Sugarloaf Mountains can be glimpsed through the French doors from the dining room as well. The wine list is very good, especially when it comes to local bottlings, and you can also order cocktails from the full bar. *9900 Sonoma Highway; 707-833-6326.* **$$–$$$**

■ NORTHERN SONOMA COUNTY

■ RUSSIAN RIVER REGION   *map page 197*

Applewood Inn and Restaurant. The woodsy dining room here is one of the most charming in Sonoma, especially on cold winter nights when fireplaces at both ends of the room are lit. The contemporary fare includes such dishes as roasted breast of Muscovy duck with rice, carrots, pearl onions, and five-spice parsnip purée. The wine list open-mindedly includes bottles from Sonoma, elsewhere in California, and Europe. *13555 Highway 116, Guerneville; 707-869-9093.* **$$$–$$$$**

★ **Farmhouse Inn and Restaurant.** Giant California bay trees shade this secluded inn holding one of Sonoma County's best restaurants. The dining room feels like a down-home Italian café, and a mural frieze depicting scenes of the owners' family history encircles the room. The short menu, however, isn't Italian at all. The dishes are simple but prepared with consummate skill. You might find Jerusalem artichoke soup; passion-fruit and habañero chili–glazed Niman Ranch pork chop; and Chef Steve Litke's signature dish: Rabbit, Rabbit, Rabbit, which changes seasonally but might be prepared with applewood-smoked, bacon-wrapped loin, roasted rack, and confit of leg with whole-grain mustard sauce. The wine list has some uncommon Sonoma County bottlings. Dinner is served from Thursday through Monday only. *7871 River Road, Forestville; 707-887-3300.* **$$$–$$$$**

John Ash & Co. John Ash was one of several trendsetting chefs who put Wine Country cooking on the culinary map. He no longer participates in the stylish restaurant he started, but under executive chef Tom Wiener the contemporary California dishes—which emphasize seasonal local meats, fish, and produce—are as good as ever (as is the Friday night schnitzel dinner). The wine list is large and reasonably priced. If it's nice out, ask for a seat on the patio, which has a lovely view of vineyards. *4350 Barnes Road, Santa Rosa; 707-527-7687.* **$$–$$$**

THE BEST PICNIC SPOTS

The Wine Country's known for its fancy restaurants—but how about the pleasures of eating a simple, hands-on meal outdoors, in the middle of all that gorgeous scenery? Some local parks are picnic-friendly but better yet, you can often have a picnic meal right by the vineyards. Many wineries have designated picnic areas, usually with shading trees, and some sell snacks as well. (Etiquette requires that if you use a winery's picnic grounds, you must buy wine there.) It's easy to find portable treats elsewhere along the way; the local markets and specialty food purveyors are stuffed with temptations. Following are a few suggestions for memorable picnics.

NAPA VALLEY
VIEWS PICNIC

For picnic supplies like bread, cheese, dry salami, and great olives, drop in at the Napa Valley Olive Oil Mfg. Co., at Charter Oak and Allison avenues in St. Helena, or try the splendid Dean & DeLuca store on St. Helena Highway, 1.5 miles south of downtown. Next, drive to Rutherford Hill Winery (take Allison to Pope Street, turn right on the Silverado Trail, left at Rutherford Hill) and enjoy the views across the Napa Valley from the shade of the olive grove while sipping a glass of merlot.

Picnicking at Chateau St. Jean.

Trail or Mountain Picnic

If you'd prefer to get a bit more exercise before indulging in that brie and those chocolate pastries, take your picnic supplies from St. Helena (*see above*) and make the short drive north to Calistoga, where the Oat Hill Mine Road is open to hikers and mountain bikers. Just north of Calistoga, a trailhead leads to up Mount St. Helena.

Adventure-Story Picnic

Pick up your supplies at Glen Ellen Village Market and then head west of town to Jack London State Historic Park. (Copy of *The Call of the Wild*: optional.)

Dry Creek Valley Picnic

On your way to Preston Vineyards, stop at the Dry Creek General Store for sandwiches and other picnic fixings. At Preston, if you're lucky, you'll find some house-made bread, olive oil, or even organic produce grown on the property for sale to add to your stash. Buy a bottle of refreshing sauvignon blanc to enjoy in the grassy yard.

Sonoma Picnic

In the town of Sonoma, stock up on almost everything you need at the Sonoma Cheese Factory on the north side of the plaza, then stop at the Basque Cafe for some sweet treats. Next, head for Gundlach-Bundschu Winery, where the views from up the hill are unbeatable.

Russian River Picnic

On the east side of Healdsburg's plaza, buy all the fixings for a picnic at the Oakville Grocery. Then drive on Westside Road to picnic at Rochioli Vineyards with a bottle of sauvignon blanc or pinot noir. (The views at Rochioli are much better than at neighboring Hop Kiln.)

Anderson Valley Picnic

In Boonville, the Boonville General Store has everything you need for an alfresco lunch. North of town, stop at Navarro, where the dry rosé and a dry gewürztraminer are perfect choices for a picnic on a hot day.

★ **Underwood Bar & Bistro.** The owners of the Willow Wood Market and Café took a major leap forward when they opened this upscale restaurant across the street. The dark wood of the bar contrasts with the stainless steel open kitchen in a place that might as well be in San Francisco. The tapas menu picks up favorite small dishes from Spain, Portugal, Italy, and France. On the main menu you might find fresh oysters or Moroccan lamb stew. But perhaps most important, Underwood is the only place in the West County where you can get French onion soup and a glass of wine at 11:30 P.M. on Friday and Saturday nights. *9113 Graton Road, Graton; 707-823-7023.* **$$–$$$**

Willow Wood Market and Café. The café half of this small-town spot serves simple but tasty soups, salads, and sandwiches. The brunches are *amazing*. Take a few minutes to poke around the quirky general store while you're waiting for your food. It's open for all three meals daily except Sunday, when it's closed for dinner. *9020 Graton Road, Graton; 707-823-0233.* **$$–$$$**

■ HEALDSBURG *map page 205*

Barndiva. Easily one of the hippest restaurants in all of Sonoma, Barndiva opened in 2004 and immediately made a splash with its sexy vibe, pricey specialty cocktails, and an inventive, if slightly difficult-to-decipher menu. The seasonal menu might include a pear, persimmon, fennel, and asiago salad; braised short ribs with horseradish mashed potatoes; and a duck shepherd's pie. From the outside, the restaurant resembles a brand-new barn, but inside, it's more big city than Mayberry, with dim lighting and well-dressed couples at the bar. There's also a lovely garden out back. *231 Center Street; 707-431-0100.* **$$–$$$**

Bear Republic Brewing Company. This wide-open hall of a brewpub on the Healdsburg Plaza is a local favorite for a casual lunch or dinner of burgers, chicken wings, or pasta. The beers are uncommonly tasty (if you like hoppy brews, try the Racer 5 IPA) and the service is friendly and fast. In warm weather, there's often a wait for the seats outdoors, but there's usually room in the spacious interior. This pub is for people who like to socialize and can be a welcome relief from the serious demeanor of some other local spots. *345 Healdsburg Avenue; 707-433-2337.* **$–$$**

A serving of Rabbit, Rabbit, Rabbit, the Farmhouse Inn's signature dish.

★ **Bistro Ralph.** The hallowed refrain of "fresh, simple, local" courses through this kitchen. They do as spectacular a job with shoestring potatoes as with ahi tuna. The menu shifts seasonally. In spring, for example, you might find the extraordinary grilled marinated asparagus. Also look for the grilled Columbia River sturgeon, Dungeness crab ravioli, and, with luck, Szechuan pepper calamari. Try to get a table in front of the restaurant for the best people-watching. *109 Plaza Street; 707-433-1380.* **$$–$$$**

Costeaux French Bakery & Cafe. This spacious pastry shop–café is a go-to standby for rich pastries, simple breakfasts (quiche, omelets), and lunches (salads, salmon niçoise). There's a large covered patio out front. *417 Healdsburg Avenue; 707-433-1913.* **$–$$**

★ **Cyrus.** When glamorous Cyrus opened in 2005, it was widely hailed as one of the first restaurants in Sonoma that could hold a candle to the French Laundry. The high praise is richly justified. Although the dining room borders on the overformal, with opulent window shades and a plastered cloister ceiling, it couldn't possibly detract from the phenomenal food and assured service. Chef Douglas Keane's fondness for extravagance is evident in the Champagne and caviar cart that arrives just after you're seated, his fondness for foie gras appetizers, and his liberal use of truffles in season. But even humble ingredients like chocolate, caramel sauce, and popcorn are transformed into a surprising and delightful dessert with a dollop of salty sorbet and a playful presentation. *29 North Street; 707-433-3311.* **$$$$**

Ravenous. Though the restaurant's look is simple, the menu's deliciously scattershot, ranging from the best hamburger in town to grilled flank steak with an avocado quesadilla to cannellini bean soup with corn and potato. There are some uncommon local bottlings on the carefully chosen wine list. *420 Center Street; 707-431-1302.* **$$–$$$**

Scopa. This restaurant might be narrow, but the food packs a punch. Chef-owner Ari Rosen cooks Italian comfort food: spicy Calabrese meatballs, tomato-braised chicken with soft polenta, and plump cannelloni. Scopa also makes pizzas, which you can order to go and eat on the plaza across the street. *109 Plaza Street; 707-433-5282.* **$$–$$$**

Zin Restaurant & Wine Bar. Concrete floors and large canvases on the walls create an industrial-chic mood here. Owners and childhood friends Jeff Mall and

Scott Silva planted their own garden to supply their restaurant with heirloom tomatoes, herbs, and peppers, which they match with the finest local meats and seafood. Nightly Blue Plate Specials change seasonally. You might see such dishes as buttermilk fried chicken with collard greens or maple roast turkey with "drunken" cranberry sauce and sage-sausage stuffing. Portions are generous (consider sharing). Of the roughly 100 bottles on the wine list, about half are zinfandels, naturally. *344 Center Street; 707-473-0946.* **$$–$$$**

■ GEYSERVILLE   *map page 210*

Diavola Pizzeria & Salumeria. Tucked away next to Geyserville's downtown tasting room is this outstanding and relatively casual restaurant. The specialty is pizza—not just any pizza, but thin-crust pizza cooked Neapolitan-style in an oven imported from Italy. Chef Dino Bugica also makes all of his own salamis and sausages, and the produce is sourced from local farmers. The wine list includes bottles from various regions of Italy as well as those made locally. *21021 Geyserville Avenue; 707-814-0111.* **$–$$**

Dining al fresco at the popular Bistro Laurent in Paso Robles.

■ Beyond Napa and Sonoma

■ Anderson Valley   *map page 226*

★ **Boonville Hotel.** Though the setting is pure Anderson Valley (concrete floors, rattan chairs), the food has a big-city flair at the area's most exciting restaurant. Organic meats and local produce—some from the garden just outside—drive the constantly changing menu. Though any cuisine is fair game, in general the kitchen tends toward comfort food, from a Dungeness crab salad to lamb burgers to osso buco with saffron potatoes. *14050 Highway 128; 707-895-2210.* **$$–$$$**

■ Lodi   *map page 239*

Wine and Roses Restaurant. Locals claim this as their special-occasion spot. The polished wood floors in the dining rooms reflect the soft light from a fireplace, and cushy upholstered chairs invite lingering conversations. Still, the overall atmosphere isn't too formal, and neither is the menu. For instance, you might try medallions of venison with mashed potatoes. *2505 West Turner Road; 209-334-6988.* **$$$–$$$$**

■ Sierra Foothills   *map page 239*

Taste. Unlike many wine regions, the Sierra Foothills have not been a destination for foodies—yet. This stylish little spot, unexpectedly located on the dusty main street of tiny, ungentrified Plymouth, immediately generated a buzz when it opened in 2006. The kitchen turns out an eclectic, modern menu using fresh, local produce; dishes range from phyllo-wrapped mushroom "cigars" to seared duck breast. There are limited hours, though; it's only open Thursday through Monday for dinner. *9402 Main Street, Plymouth; 209-245-3463.* **$$$**

■ Central Coast

■ Santa Cruz   *map page 264*

Soif. This French bistro may be named "thirst," but luckily it adjoins a wine shop. You can order dozens of wines by the glass, flight, or bottle from a lengthy list of selections from near and far. Small plates and mains arrive at the copper-top bar, a big communal table, or your private table. On weekends, the dinner-only

(opposite) Freshly baked bread at the St. Helena farmers' market, held on Friday mornings in Crane Park, behind the high school.

restaurant opens at 3:00 P.M. *105 Walnut Avenue, Santa Cruz; 831-423-2020.* **$$–$$$**

■ **MONTEREY COUNTY**   *map page 264*

★ **Marinus.** It's saying a lot to call a restaurant the best in the Monterey Bay area, but Marinus deserves the nod. The seasonal daily menu might include red abalone, pancetta-wrapped rabbit, or alder-smoked duck. Enjoy the discreet service in the serene dining room, or reserve the chef's table in the main kitchen and watch your meal in the making. Marinus is at Bernardus Lodge spa resort, surrounded by the vineyards of Bernardus Winery. *415 Carmel Valley Road, Carmel Valley; 831-658-3595.* **$$$$**

■ **SAN LUIS OBISPO COUNTY**   *map page 276*

Bistro Laurent. In an 1890s brick building on the Paso Robles town square, Laurent Grangien runs a handsome, welcoming French bistro. In the snug dining room and on the covered patio, choose from traditional dishes such as mussels gratin, rack of lamb, goat cheese tart, and onion soup; daily specials offer a modern twist. *1202 Pine Street, Paso Robles; 805-226-8191.* **$$–$$$$**

■ **SANTA BARBARA COUNTY**   *map page 276*

★ **Brothers Restaurant at Mattei's Tavern.** Beamed ceilings, hanging lanterns, and 19th-century photos evoke the history of this one-time stagecoach stop in the Santa Ynez Valley. Casual and unpretentious, Brothers serves up unabashedly rich dishes such as slow-roasted prime rib with garlic mashed potatoes, and the locally famous jalapeño cornbread. The menu changes every few weeks and the cedar wine cellar holds some hard-to-find vintages. In the bar, armchairs face a river-rock fireplace. *2350 Railway Avenue, Los Olivos; 805-688-4820.* **$$$–$$$$**

Wine Country lodgings encompass luxury resorts such as the Fairmont Sonoma Mission Inn & Spa as well as quaint B&Bs and chain accommodations.

WHERE TO STAY
IN WINE COUNTRY

With its endless vistas of lush vineyards, some of the world's best wineries, and top-notch restaurants in every little town, it's no wonder that California's Wine Country also racks up some of the country's finest hotels and B&Bs. All this luxury, however, comes at a high price: even a basic hotel room can cost $200 a night, and rates at the top hotels are considerably higher.

To make the most of your money, considering traveling sometime other than high season (April through October). Almost all hotels cut their prices, sometimes by up to 25 percent, outside the high season. Weeknight rates, versus weekend prices, also tend to be lower. If you're looking for a weekend reservation, watch out for the frequently imposed two-night minimum stays. Book well in advance—three months or more wouldn't be excessive for stays August through October—if at all possible. For last-minute bookings, consider the chain motels and hotels, some of which are listed at the end of this chapter.

The listings below follow the order of this book's regional chapters; within each regional section the hotels are alphabetized.

Prices designations for lodging, per couple

$ = less than $150 $$ = $150–$249 $$$ = $250–$400 $$$$ = $400 plus
★ = Top Pick

■ SOUTHERN NAPA VALLEY

■ NAPA   *map pages 78 and 87*

Blackbird Inn. Arts and Crafts style infuses this 1905 building, from the lobby's enormous fieldstone fireplace to the lamps that cast a warm glow over the impressive wooden staircase. The style is continued in the attractive guest rooms, with sturdy turn-of-the-20th-century oak beds and matching night tables. The spacious baths, however, are updated, most with spa bathtubs. The inn is within walking distance of Napa's historic downtown area. It tends to book up quickly, so reserve well in advance. *1755 First Street; 707-226-2450 or 888-567-9811.* **$$–$$$**

Milliken Creek. Though dating back to 1857, this onetime stagecoach inn purrs with modern luxury. Palm-frond ceiling fans, gauzy king-size canopy beds, and a khaki-and-cream color scheme suggest a posh hotel in British-Colonial Asia. You can enjoy the views over the tree-lined banks of the Napa River from almost everywhere: from your room's balcony over breakfast, from an Adirondack chair on the

The decor has changed greatly since the time when Milliken Creek was a stagecoach inn.

lawn, or from the treatment rooms of the intimate spa. *1815 Silverado Trail; 707-255-1197 or 800-835-6112.* **$$$$**

■ **YOUNTVILLE** *map page 78*

Bardessono. Although it bills itself as the "greenest luxury hotel in America," the rooms are anything but spartan, with luxurious organic white bedding, gas fireplaces, and huge bathrooms with walnut floors (large enough for a massage table, should you opt for an in-room massage). It's got all the high-tech touches you'd expect for a spot that opened in 2009—speakers for your iPod, a flat-panel TV, and fancy spa tubs—as well as a spa and 75-foot rooftop pool. *6526 Yount Street; 707-204-6000.* **$$$$**

Maison Fleurie. Rooms at this casual, comfortable inn, within easy walking distance of most of Yountville's restaurants, share a French country style (picture exposed brick walls and pastel trompe l'oeil paintings) but vary dramatically in size and amenities. The largest have a private entrance, deck, fireplace, and spa bathub;

for a much lower rate you can get a tiny but well-kept room—and save for a French Laundry meal instead. *6529 Yount Street; 800-788-0369.* **$$–$$$**

■ NORTHERN NAPA VALLEY

■ RUTHERFORD *map page 107*

Auberge du Soleil. Perched amid olive trees with stunning views down the hillside, the Auberge is renowned for its soigné ambience, attentive but unobtrusive service, and popular restaurant. Though prices are very high indeed, money-is-no-object travelers can enjoy lavish amenities, like flat-panel TVs, private terraces, and truly grand bathrooms—many with jetted soaking tubs. The spacious pool area and intimate spa, with its infinity hot tub perched on the hillside, seem fit for a superstar. The bar's terrace is the finest spot in the valley to enjoy a cocktail at sunset. *180 Rutherford Hill Road; 707-963-1211.* **$$$$**

■ ST. HELENA *map pages 107 and 118*

Ambrose Bierce House. America's favorite literary curmudgeon, Ambrose Bierce, lived here until 1910, when he became bored with the peaceful wine valley and vanished into Pancho Villa's Mexico, never to be seen or heard from again. The ambience at his namesake inn is blast-from-the-past Victorian—buttery yellow tones and a generally lacey feel—but the amenities in the four rooms and suites are strictly up-to-date. *1515 Main Street; 707-963-3003.* **$$–$$$**

El Bonita Motel. Only in the Napa Valley could the prices on rooms in a gussied-up classic motel start at nearly $200 a night in high season, but El Bonita nevertheless has a few things going for it, including its very convenient location between Rutherford and downtown St. Helena. There's even a sauna next to the hot tub and swimming pool, which is heated year round. *195 Main Street; 707-963-3216.* **$–$$**

Inn at Southbridge. Hidden away in a complex at the south end of town, this comfortable 21-room hotel is nonetheless ideally situated for exploring St. Helena: Pizzeria Tra Vigne is in the same building, Merryvale Winery is across the parking lot, and the restaurant Tra Vigne is next door. The rooms have an almost Scandinavian feel—clean and spare with light-colored wood details—though the overall effect is a tad corporate. (Indeed, corporate events are often held here.)

The staff are uncommonly helpful, and guests can enjoy the pool and extensive fitness facilities at the spa next door. *1020 Main Street; 707-967-9400 or 800-520-6800.* **$$$**

★ **Meadowood Resort.** You might feel you've arrived at a sprawling New England country estate when you drive into this resort. It's ideal for those who want to do more than drive and sip, as it's got a nine-hole golf course, a hiking trail through oak woods, a professional croquet course, seven tennis courts, two pools. Oh, and let's not forget the spa. . . . The 85 accommodations are arranged in gray clapboard bungalows all over the forested hillside. The extremely accommodating staff caters to your every whim, and the elegant (and expensive) restaurant on the property is one of the best in all the valley, perfect when you can't bear to leave this supremely comfortable resort. *900 Meadowood Lane; 707-963-3646.* **$$$$**

Wine Country Inn. A pastoral landscape of vine-covered hills surrounds this retreat, styled after the New England inns the owners used to visit. Rooms are comfortably done with homey furniture like four-poster beds topped with quilts, and many have a wood-burning or gas fireplace, a large jetted tub, and a patio or balcony overlooking the vineyards. A hearty breakfast is served buffet-style in the sun-splashed common room. *1152 Lodi Lane; 707-963-7077.* **$$$–$$$$**

■ **CALISTOGA**   *map page 107*

Calistoga Ranch. The sister property of Auberge du Soleil in Rutherford, this property trades in a different sort of luxury. Freestanding shingle cottages set in the forested hillside outside town look somewhat rustic from the outside, but inside they're anything but. There are cloud-like beds with crisp white bedding, DVD players, and luxe bathrooms with soaking tubs and outdoor showers. This indoor/outdoor alignment pervades the ranch. Each guestroom has a comfortable outdoor living room, and even the reception area and spa have outdoor seating next to fireplaces. Active types can hit the swimming pool, indoor/outdoor fitness center, and guided hikes. *580 Lommel Road; 707-254-2800.* **$$$$**

Indian Springs. This old-time spa has welcomed clients to its mud baths and mineral pool—supplied with mineral water from its four geysers—since 1871. Rooms in the lodge, though small, are beautifully done up a simple Zen style, with Asian-inspired furnishings. The larger cottages dotted around the property have kitchenettes or full kitchens, encouraging longer stays. A boccie ball court, shuffleboard, and croquet lawn provide entertainment when you're not indulging in various spa treatments or soaking in the toasty Olympic-size mineral-water pool. *1712 Lincoln Avenue; 707-942-4913.* **$$–$$$**

★ **Meadowlark Country House.** Simultaneously sophisticated and laid-back, this inn sits on twenty hillside acres just north of Calistoga, amid horse pastures, gardens, and forest. Each room has its own charms, like doors leading to a private garden, a fireplace, a deck with a mountain view, or a whirlpool tub for two. A clothing-optional pool, hot tub, and sauna is a rarity in these parts and tends to attract a younger, more relaxed crowd than some of the frillier B&Bs in the Wine Country. You're likely to meet the charming owners, Kurt and Richard, over the excellent breakfast (included in the room rate). *601 Petrified Forest Road; 707-942-5651.* **$$–$$$**

■ CARNEROS DISTRICT

Carneros Inn. Freestanding board-and-batten cottages with rocking chairs on each porch are simultaneously rustic and chic at this luxurious property. Inside, each cottage is flooded with natural light but still manages to maintain privacy worthy of a celebrity seeking to avoid the paparazzi, with windows and French doors leading to a private garden. Flat-panel TVs, ethereal beds topped with Frette linens, and spacious bathrooms with heated tile floors and outdoor showers may make it difficult to summon the will to leave the cottage and enjoy the hilltop infinity swimming pool and hot tub. *4048 Sonoma Highway; 707-299-4900.* **$$$$**

■ SONOMA VALLEY

■ TOWN OF SONOMA   *map pages 173 and 184*

El Dorado Hotel. Facing the Sonoma Plaza, this hotel was built in 1843 as the home of General Mariano Vallejo's never-quite-respectable brother, Salvador. It debuted as a hotel in 1851. Despite the building's long history, the spare rooms, with sleek four-poster beds and white bedding, are clearly 21st century. The rooms are generally small except for the newer ground-level suites beyond the pool and patio. *405 West First Street, 707-996-3220.* **$$**

The Fairmont Sonoma Mission Inn & Spa: pink, expensive, and popular.

Fairmont Sonoma Mission Inn & Spa. Pink and popular, this sprawling hotel has power in numbers: three pools, tennis courts, and two restaurants. Many come for the world-class spa, where you can soak yourself in warm mineral water or choose from a vast array of treatments. The rooms, though not always large, are always very comfortable, and some of the suites have large whirlpool tubs. *100 Boyes Boulevard, Boyes Hot Springs; 707-938-9000.* **$$$–$$$$**

The Lodge at Sonoma. This red-roofed, California mission–style complex near Sonoma's Plaza gives a nod to working travelers, with a business center and meeting rooms. More indolent visitors can sun themselves poolside or indulge in some spa time. Fairly spacious rooms carry on the unobtrusive mission style, with solid oak beds and paintings of California landscapes on the walls. *1325 Broadway; 707-935-6600.* **$$$**

■ GLEN ELLEN   *map page 184*

★ **Gaige House Inn.** This Queen Anne home, built in 1890 for the wealthy town butcher, is now an extremely stylish B&B, where modern paintings, Asian art objects, and gorgeous, greenhouse-quality orchids set it apart from the rest. Each room in the main house is different; yours might have a door onto the pool area or an enormous bathroom larger than some hotel rooms. Thirteen stand-alone spa suites kick the luxury up a notch, with enormous granite soaking tubs and, in some cases, sliding glass doors that lead to a patio overlooking the creek. Outrageously good three-course breakfasts are served either in the dining room or out on the terrace. Gaige House is exceedingly well run, yet the service never seems fussy. *13540 Arnold Drive; 707-935-0237.* **$$$–$$$$**

■ KENWOOD   *map page 184*

Kenwood Inn & Spa. This intimate inn in the heart of the Sonoma Valley brings a bit of Europe to the Wine Country. Crafted with the sensibility of a Mediterranean villa, the inn offers 29 rooms throughout five buildings. All of the buildings open onto courtyards, pools, and spa tubs; all of the rooms have private patios. The on-site spa offers a variety of treatments, and a special Jacuzzi room (try the wine bath) looks out on seemingly endless vineyards. Complimentary breakfast is served each morning in the on-site restaurant; the eatery also serves lunch and dinner à la carte. *10400 Sonoma Highway; 707-833-1293.* **$$$–$$$$**

■ NORTHERN SONOMA COUNTY

■ RUSSIAN RIVER REGION   *map page 197*

★ **Farmhouse Inn and Restaurant.** In a wooded glen right off River Road, this hostelry built in 1873 consists of 18 cottages, rooms, and suites half hidden by late-blooming roses and tall calla lilies. Although the setting is very woodsy, the interior is anything but rustic. All of the well-appointed rooms have whirlpool tubs and most even have private saunas. There's a swimming pool here, and the inn offers full spa services. Best of all, the Farmhouse Inn is home to one of the very best restaurants in Sonoma; don't even think about eating elsewhere if you're here on a night the restaurant is open, Thursday through Monday. *7871 River Road, Forestville; 707-887-3300.* **$$–$$$**

■ **HEALDSBURG** *map page 205*

★ **Camellia Inn.** Built in 1869 and surrounded by the namesake camellias, this Italianate nine-room inn is only a couple of short blocks from the shops and restaurants of Healdsburg Plaza. Several rooms have private entrances, whirlpool tubs, or gas fireplaces. The innkeepers are generous with their wine expertise—you might learn more about local wineries during happy hour on the swimming pool terrace than you will on many winery tours. The uncharacteristically modest rates for this pricey town attract loyal visitors that come year after year. Those on a budget should ask about the cozy room with the bathroom across the hallway that goes for about half what the others do. *211 North Street; 707-433-8182.* **$–$$**

Healdsburg Inn on the Plaza. This 12-room B&B occupies a former stagecoach stop built in 1900 (and shortly thereafter rendered obsolete by the automobile). The well-preserved architectural detailing is all in the grand Victorian style, but somehow the contemporary furnishings, such as modern Japanese-style lamps and whirlpool tubs, fit in smoothly. The special touches here include a full buffet breakfast and early-evening wine tastings. *112 Matheson Street; 707-433-6991.* **$$–$$$**

Honor Mansion. This 1883 Italianate inn has one of Healdsburg's most beautiful gardens. Tall trees shade an outdoor sitting area and a koi pond, and there's a swimming pool out back, near the putting green and tennis, bocce ball, and croquet courts. The 14 rooms, suites, and cottages, are outfitted with featherbeds and fresh flowers. The rates include a lavish full breakfast. Serious wine aficionados stay here, so you may even pick up some tips over morning coffee. *14891 Grove Street; 707-433-4277.* **$$–$$$$**

Hotel Healdsburg. Huge, overstuffed couches grouped around a fireplace warm up the minimalist concrete lobby of one of Sonoma County's most stylish hotels. Locals proudly point out that this looks like a New York or San Francisco establishment, and in one respect they are right: as in many urban hotels, the rooms here are on the small side. (For something roomier, ask for a suite.) Soothing earth tones and outrageously fluffy beds soften the sleek, modern look, most obvious in the green-tiled bathrooms, many with 6-foot-long bathtubs. Some rooms overlook the town plaza, one of the most pleasant urban spaces in the Wine Country. *25 Matheson Street; 707-431-2800.* **$$$$**

■ Beyond Napa and Sonoma

■ **Anderson Valley**   *map page 226*

Boonville Hotel. Blond wood wainscoting, walls painted in pale colors, and beds topped with down comforters make the rooms here resemble an IKEA catalog. Ten rooms are fairly basic, with no phone or TVs, but they are comfortable and attractive, with little touches like fresh wildflowers, and most have a balcony or view. The larger bungalow out back has a private entrance and yard, which makes it popular with couples on a romantic getaway. Ask about discounts on Tuesday and Wednesday nights, when the popular restaurant downstairs is closed and Boonville tends to be at its quietest. *14050 Highway 128; 707-895-2210. $–$$$*

■ **Lodi**   *map page 239*

Wine and Roses Country Inn. Set on 7 park-like acres, this 87-room hotel centers on a 1902 mansion and spreads out in several modern buildings. Rooms have a fitting spaciousness; many have a veranda and fireplace. Those in the spa wing have vibrant colors and plasma TVs. A new wing opened in 2009. The restaurant is a worthy destination even if you are not staying overnight. *2505 West Turner Road, Lodi; 209-334-6988. $$–$$$*

■ **Sierra Foothills**   *map page 239*

The Foxes Inn. In the center of Sutter Creek's well-preserved Gold Rush–era downtown, this 1857 Victorian somehow lacks the fussiness of many B&Bs. True, there are antiques and throw pillows, but the guest rooms are large, uncluttered, and bright. Bathrobes, CD players, and private bathrooms make the accommodations thoroughly comfortable. A full breakfast is delivered to your room on silver service. *77 Main Street, Sutter Creek; 209-267-5882. $$*

■ Central Coast

■ **Santa Cruz**   *map page 264*

Pleasure Point Inn. A popular romantic getaway, this modern B&B sits in a residential neighborhood right across the street from the ocean. The four rooms

(opposite) Guests can relax in minimalist style at the Hotel Healdsburg.

include such amenities as minibars and Wi-Fi; some have fireplaces. Lounge in the hot tub on the large rooftop sundeck overlooking the Pacific, or take a surfing lesson on the beach below. *23665 East Cliff Drive, Santa Cruz; 831-475-4657.* **$$$**

■ MONTEREY COUNTY   *map page 264*

★ **L'Auberge Carmel.** Twenty luxurious rooms, all with huge soaking tubs, radiate out from a sunny brick courtyard. The lobby lounge is a relaxing place to await your table in the intimate restaurant ($$$$), where the prix-fixe tasting menu offers up morsel after morsel of meticulously plated contemporary food. *Monte Verde at 7th Avenue, Carmel; 831-624-8578.* **$$$$**

■ SAN LUIS OBISPO COUNTY   *map page 276*

Garden Street Inn. This fully restored 1887 Italianate–Queen Anne B&B has 13 distinctive rooms filled with antiques. Yours might have a stained-glass window, a fireplace, or a deck. Each evening, wine and hors d'oeuvres are served in the intimate dining room and the library. The inn is the only lodging in lively, walkable downtown San Luis Obispo. *1212 Garden Street, San Luis Obispo; 805-545-9802.* **$$**

Summerwood Inn. Surrounded by gardens and the vineyards of Summerwood Winery, this B&B insulates you from urban life. The nine guest rooms have four-poster or sleigh beds, thick bathrobes, and gas fireplaces. Each opens onto a balcony or deck with vineyard views. The staff prepares breakfast to order, sets out Summerwood wines in the evening, and provides nightly turn-down service. *2175 Arbor Road, Paso Robles; 805-227-1111.* **$$–$$$$**

■ SANTA BARBARA COUNTY   *map page 276*

★ **Santa Ynez Inn.** Antiques and artifacts from the town's early days fill this posh Victorian-style inn built in 2002. The details ooze luxury: Frette linens, custom-made bathrobes, and DVD/CD entertainment systems. Most of the 23 rooms have gas fireplaces, double steam showers, and jetted tubs. The evening wine and hors d'oeuvres hour and full breakfast are outstanding. *3627 Sagunto Street, Santa Ynez; 805-688-5588.* **$$$**

THE BEST WINE COUNTRY SPAS

Looking for another way to indulge? In Wine Country, you'll never have to look far to find a spa that will massage, scrub, or soak you into a blissed-out stupor.

Spas in Napa and Sonoma generally offer the same treatments you'll find at spas everywhere—including a wide variety of massages, scrubs, and facials—with a couple of significant extras. First: the local mud baths. Since the Wappo tribe lived in the Napa Valley, folks have been slathering themselves with gooey volcanic ash. The town of Calistoga lays claim to a special blend of volcanic ash and mineral water that seeps up in local hot springs, but spas throughout the Napa Valley have devised various ways of using volcanic mud, from dabbing you with a paste of it to dunking you in vats of the stuff.

The other hot trend in Wine Country spas is the use of grape seeds and vines in treatments. The first "wine spa," Les Sources de Caudalie, opened in Bordeaux in 1999, and spas in California are increasingly incorporating some of the same techniques and ingredients. The result is a spa experience that simultaneously reflects the neighboring vineyards and takes advantage of the anti-oxidant properties of grape seeds.

SOUTHERN NAPA VALLEY

SPA VILLAGIO
Opened in 2008, this 13,000-square-foot spa with fieldstone walls and Mediterranean decor has all the latest gadgets, including multiple hot tubs and showers with an extravagant number of shower heads. Huge spa suites with flat-panel TVs and wet bars are suitable for groups. During the popular Hot Stone Massage, heated stones, slick with massage oil, are rhythmically stroked over your body. *6481 Washington Street, Yountville; 707-948-5050.*

NORTHERN NAPA VALLEY

HEALTH SPA NAPA VALLEY
This spa, associated with the adjacent Inn at Southbridge, plays down the fancy products prevalent at more luxurious places and concentrates instead on healing and rejuvenating the whole body in a sleek, understated environment. The well-organized layout includes small rooms that look out on a garden filled with bamboo plants and water features that create a soothing sound.

(opposite) A mud bath at Indian Springs (above) The resort in the mid-1940s.

A fitness room with treadmills, free weights, and other fitness equipment means you can get in a good workout before indulging in some pampering. (Book early for one of the popular private yoga and Pilates classes.) Among the treatments, go local with a grape-seed mud wrap, during which you're dabbed with a mixture of mud and crushed Napa Valley grape seeds, gently rubbed with exfoliating mitts, and finally wrapped in warm towels. (This is a more luxurious method than the mud bath dunk available at some other spas.) *1030 Main Street, St. Helena; 707-967-8800.*

Meadowood
The number of sports options available at this secluded resort explains the popularity of the Therapeutic Deep Tissue Massage, an intense experience valued by athletes for its ability to improve flexibility. Two different treatments, the Cabernet Crush and Vineyard Polish, incorporate grape-seed body polish to exfoliate the skin and infuse your skin with antioxidants. After your treatment, you can sit out on the porch drinking hot tea while browsing through the spa's bird-watching guide. *900 Meadowood Lane, St. Helena; 707-963-3646.*

Restorative Mud in Calistoga
The hot springs of Calistoga have attracted spa-goers since the 19th century, and the town is famous these days for its mud baths. The best choice in this category is **Indian Springs** (1712 Lincoln Avenue; 707-942-4913), where you're immersed in 100-percent volcanic ash for 10 minutes or so, after which you proceed through a regimen that

includes a mineral bath, steam, and a blanket wrap. Indian Springs, which has tidy little bungalows and lodge rooms for overnight stays, costs a lot less than Meadowood or Villagio, and you can go even further downscale at the motel-style **Calistoga Spa Hot Springs** (1006 Washington Street; 707-942-6269), **Golden Haven Hot Springs** (1713 Lake Street; 707-942-6793), and several other places where the treatments are similar to those at Indian Springs but the volcanic ash is mixed with peat.

SONOMA COUNTY

FAIRMONT SONOMA MISSION INN

The routine is seamless at the 40,000-square-foot Fairmont Sonoma Mission Inn's spa: fruit and water everywhere, an enormous centralized waiting room, and large locker areas.

This is easily the biggest and most extensively equipped of the Wine Country spas, with indoor and outdoor mineral water–soaking pools at varying temperatures, an outdoor whirlpool, steam and dry saunas, and even a dedicated Watsu pool. It's all very well done, but if you prefer a little solitude after your spa treatment, you may find the number of other spa-goers a bit daunting on summer weekends.

The long list of treatments includes all the spa mainstays—basic massage, aromatherapy massage, facials, salt scrubs, and herbal wraps—and more. There are also several twosome treatments, such as couples massage, couples yoga and Pilates, and a wine and roses package, in which you take a bath together while sipping sparkling wine and then are given a massage.

The highlight is the relaxing Bathing Ritual—an exfoliating shower, dips in warm and hot soaking pools, time spent in a eucalyptus steam room and a dry sauna, and a cool-down shower. You can spend as much time as you want in these areas before and after a treatment, and there are lounge chairs on the patio for relaxing in between. *100 Boyes Boulevard, Boyes Hot Springs, Sonoma; 877-289-7354.*

KENWOOD INN AND SPA

Vinotherapy treatments, which utilize grape seeds and vine extracts, have been popular in France for years, but the spa at the Kenwood Inn was one of the first to wholeheartedly embrace this approach to wellness here. Products such as red-wine extracts and chardonnay and Riesling oils are incorporated into many of their decadent treatments, such as the Harvest Sugar Scrub, a brisk exfoliating treatment that also uses milled grape seeds and sugarcane. A Swedish massage using grapeseed oil can be performed in the spa, in the privacy of your room, or, weather permitting,

In the lap of luxury at the Fairmont Sonoma Mission Inn.

on the spa's outdoor terrace. They also offer a wide variety of facials, using Arcona skin products.

Though their techniques may be French, the property calls Italy to mind. Persimmon and lemon trees shade several courtyards at the sprawling Tuscan-style villa, where guests of the hotel lounge in a number of pools, whirlpools, and saunas dotted throughout the property. (Spa guests have access to them for an additional fee.) *10400 Sonoma Highway; 707-833-1293.*

RAINDANCE SPA

The fountain in the reception room of this fairly small spa at the back of The Lodge at Sonoma is strewn with fresh roses, subtly scenting the air. Guests waiting for treatments lounge upstairs, in a room with a flickering gas fireplace—but if you come early, you can use the small swimming pool, mineral pool, and Jacuzzi just a few steps out the back door of the spa.

During the Lavender Luxury, an invigorating scrub with a fragrant salt mixture is followed by a slathering with lavender-scented shea butter. The treatment ends with a head and foot massage while you're wrapped in a warm cocoon. The signature treatment Encapsulated Wrapsody begins with an exfoliation using a body polish made from red grape seeds, followed by a mud wrap and a steam bath. A 50-minute massage caps the decadent experience. *1325 Broadway, Sonoma; 707-935-6600.*

(following pages) Sunny blooms in a Kenwood Inn courtyard.

■ CHAIN AND MOTEL LODGINGS

Calistoga
Calistoga Spa Hot Springs. *1006 Washington Street; 707-942-6269.*
Calistoga Village Inn & Spa. *1880 Lincoln Avenue; 707-942-0991.*
Golden Haven Hot Springs Spa and Resort. *1713 Lake Street; 707-942-8000.*
Hideaway Cottages. *1412 Fair Way; 707-942-4108.*
The Lodge at Calistoga. *1865 Lincoln Avenue; 707-942-9400.*

Geyserville
Geyserville Inn. *21714 Geyserville Avenue; 707-857-4343.*

Healdsburg
Dry Creek Inn. *198 Dry Creek Road; 707-433-0300.*
Travelodge. *178 Dry Creek Road; 707-433-0101.*

Napa
Chablis Inn. *3360 Solano Avenue; 707-257-1944.*
Inn at the Vines. *100 Soscol Avenue; 707-257-1930.*
Napa Discovery Inn. *500 Silverado Trail; 707-253-0892.*
Napa Valley Marriott. *3425 Solano Avenue; 707-253-8600.*
Napa Valley Redwood Inn. *3380 Solano Avenue; 707-257-6111.*
Napa Valley Travelodge. *853 Coombs Street; 707-226-1871.*
Wine Valley Lodge. *200 South Coombs Street; 707-224-7911.*

Rutherford
Rancho Caymus Inn. *1140 Rutherford Road; 707-963-1777.*

St. Helena
Vineyard Country Inn. *201 Main Street; 707-963-1000.*
Wine Country Inn. *1152 Lodi Lane; 707-963-7077.*

Santa Rosa
Americas Best Value Inn. *1800 Santa Rosa Avenue; 707-523-3480.*
Best Western Garden Inn. *1500 Santa Rosa Avenue; 707-546-4031.*
Hyatt Vineyard Creek. *170 Railroad Street; 707-284-1234.*
Santa Rosa Courtyard. *175 Railroad Street; 707-573-9000.*
Travelodge Santa Rosa Downtown. *653 Healdsburg Avenue; 707-544-4141.*

Sonoma
Best Western Sonoma Valley Inn. *550 West Second Street; 707-938-9200.*

The golden hills and green fields of a Napa Valley vineyard.

PRACTICAL INFORMATION

■ AREA CODES AND TIME ZONE

The area code for Napa, Sonoma, and Mendocino counties is 707; Livermore Valley, 925; Lodi and much of the Sierra Foothills, 209; Placerville, 530; Santa Cruz and Monterey counties, 831; San Luis Obispo and Santa Barbara counties, 805. All of California is in the Pacific time zone.

■ CLIMATE

The California climate generally follows a pattern of sometimes-heavy winter rainfall and summer drought accompanied by often stifling heat. Even in rainy season, most parts of the state enjoy numerous sunny days. In winter the hills are green, often strewn with wildflowers; in the heat and sun of summer the hills turn brown and dry. Summer days in coastal zones are often foggy, and fog rolls in many evenings throughout the year. Inland, temperatures can swing widely between day and night (in some places nights in the 50s often follow 100-plus-degree days), an effect that's moderated along the coast.

■ FEES

Many wineries charge tasting fees. The practice is especially prevalent at heavily visited wineries, at those that specialize in expensive premium wine, and in busy wine-touring zones. The charge to taste a set number of wines or everything that's being poured may be as little as $5 or as much as $30. There is sometimes an additional charge to taste the winery's more exclusive bottlings. The tasting price might include a winery tour, or an educational guided tasting. If not, the fee might be applied toward the price of any wine you buy from the winery. Sometimes you can take home your glass as a souvenir of your visit—check first with the tasting room staff.

■ GETTING THERE AND AROUND

■ BY AIR

San Francisco International Airport (SFO) is the area's largest airport and is served by most international and domestic airlines. The airport is 14 miles south of San Francisco. *Off U.S. 101; 650-821-8211; www.flysfo.com.*

Oakland International Airport (OAK) is served by many domestic carriers and some international airlines. The airport is closer to the Napa, Sonoma, and Livermore valleys than is SFO. *Hegenberger Road, off I-880; 510-563-3300; www. flyoakland.com.*

Charles M. Schulz Sonoma County Airport (STS) began receiving commercial air service in March 2007. Horizon Air flies to Santa Rosa from Los Angeles, Portland, Las Vegas, and Seattle. *2290 Airport Boulevard, off U.S. 101; 707-565-7243; www.sonomacountyairport.org.*

Sacramento International Airport (SMF) is served by many domestic carriers and some international airlines. This is the closest major airport to the Sierra Foothills and Lodi wine regions. *Off I-5, northwest of downtown; 916-929-5411; www.sacairports.org.*

Minetta San Jose International Airport (SJC), 2 miles north of downtown San Jose and served by 12 major airlines, is the closest large airport to the Santa Cruz Mountains and Monterey County. *Airport Boulevard, off Highways 85 and 87; 408-501-0979; www.sjc.org.*

Santa Barbara Airport (SBA), 8 miles from downtown and about 30 miles south of Santa Barbara County's wine region, is served by the feeder airlines of several major carriers. *500 Fowler Road, off U.S. 101; 805-681-4803; www.flysba.com.*

■ BY CAR

To reach the Napa and Sonoma wine regions from San Francisco, cross the Golden Gate Bridge and head north on U.S. 101, east on Highway 37, then north on Highway 121 into the **Carneros Region.** Continue on Highway 121 to Highway 29 north to reach the **Napa Valley.** To enter the heart of the **Sonoma Valley,** turn north from Highway 121 onto Highway 12.

To get to Sonoma County's **Russian River Valley** wineries, stay on U.S. 101 north to Highway 116 west. To reach the **Dry Creek** and **Alexander Valley** wineries of northern Sonoma County, stay on U.S. 101 all the way to Healdsburg. From the East Bay, head north on I-80, which has connections to Highways 37 and 29.

The **Anderson Valley** of Mendocino County can be reached from the Bay Area by taking U.S. 101 north and Highway 128 west. From coastal Highway 1, head east on Highway 128.

The **Livermore Valley** lies east of Oakland on I-580. Continue east on I-580 and turn north on I-5 to reach Highway 99 in **Lodi;** a short drive south from Sacramento on I-5 or Highway 99 will get you to Lodi as well. You can drive to Lodi straight from Napa on Highway 12 east. From Lodi, you drive into the **Sierra Foothills** on Highway 88, which intersects Highway 49. That north–south road will take you to most of the region's wineries. U.S. 50 east from Sacramento also hits Highway 49.

From the Bay Area, head south on I-280, Highway 1, or U.S. 101 to reach the Central Coast wineries. Highway 17 is the main artery through the **Santa Cruz Mountains**; Highway 1 and U.S. 101 sandwich most of the **Monterey, Carmel Valley**, and **Santa Lucia Highlands** wineries. U.S. 101 connects to the wine trails of San Luis Obispo and Santa Barbara counties: Highway 46 in **Paso Robles**, Highway 227 in the **Edna Valley**, Foxen Canyon Road in the **Santa Maria Valley**, and Highways 154 and 246 in the **Santa Ynez Valley**.

■ DRIVING TIPS

As you cruise down winding Wine Country lanes and highways, drive carefully. You may be on vacation, but the people who live and work here are not, so expect heavier traffic during rush hours (generally between 7 and 9 in the morning and 4 and 6 at night). Traffic can be especially bad on Friday and Sunday afternoons, when weekenders add to the mix.

Some drivers in the largely rural wine regions, especially workers in a hurry during the harvest and crush season, will cross double yellow lines before blind curves to get past slow drivers. For everyone's sake, pull over at a safe turnout and let them pass.

Don't overindulge when you go wine tasting, and don't drive if you've overindulged. Local cops always keep an eye out for drivers who have had one too many, especially on big festival weekends. If you can, bring a designated driver; if not, consider spitting when you taste.

■ HOURS

Winery tasting rooms are generally open from 10 or 11 A.M. to 5 P.M. Larger wineries may be open every day, but smaller ones may only open on weekends. Tuesday and Wednesday are the quietest days of the week for wine touring, when wineries are most likely to be closed or have limited hours. If you have a particular winery in mind, check their hours before you make the trek.

■ SHIPPING WINE

See "Buying and Shipping Wine" in the Visiting Wineries chapter.

■ General Visitor Information

Amador County. *877-868-7262; www.touramador.com.*
Calaveras County. *800-225-3764; www.visitcalaveras.org.*
California Travel & Tourism Commission. *877-225-4367; www.visitcalifornia.com.*
El Dorado County. *530-621-5885; www.eldoradocounty.org.*
Fodors.com. *www.fodors.com.*
Livermore Valley. *925-846-8910; www.trivalleycvb.com.*
Lodi. *209-365-1195; www.visitlodi.com.*
Mendocino County. *866-466-3636; www.gomendo.com.*
Monterey County. *877-666-8373; www.seemonterey.com.*
Napa Valley. *707-226-7459; www.napavalley.com.*
San Luis Obispo County. *800-541-8000; www.sanluisobispocounty.com.*
Santa Barbara County. *805 966-9222; www.santabarbaraca.com.*
Santa Cruz County. *800-833-3494; www.scccvc.org.*
Sonoma County Tourism Bureau. *707-522-5800; www.sonomacounty.com.*

■ Wine Tourism Information

Amador Vintners Association. *www.amadorwine.com.*
Anderson Valley Winegrowers Association. *www.avwines.com.*
Calaveras Winegrape Association. *www.calaveraswines.org.*
Carneros Wine Alliance. *www.carneros.com.*
El Dorado Winery Association. *www.eldoradowines.org.*
Livermore Valley Winegrowers Association. *www.lvwine.org.*
LocalWineEvents.com. *www.localwineevents.com.*
Lodi-Woodbridge Winegrape Commission. *www.lodiwine.com.*
Mendocino Winegrape and Wine Commission. *www.truemendocinowine.com.*
Monterey County Vintners & Growers Association. *www.montereywines.org.*
Napa Valley Vintners Association. *www.napavintners.com.*
Paso Robles Wine Country Alliance. *www.pasowine.com.*
San Luis Obispo Vintners Association. *www.slowine.com.*
Santa Barbara County Vintners Association. *www.sbcountywines.com.*
Santa Cruz Mountains Winegrowers Association. *www.scmwa.com.*
Sonoma County Vintners. *www.sonomawine.com.*
University of California Agricultural Database. *www.calagtour.org.*
WineCountry.com. *www.winecountry.com.*
Wine Road, Northern Sonoma County. *www.wineroad.com.*

■ WINE INFORMATION

Appellation America Online. *wine.appellationamerica.com.*
California Wines. *www.california-wine.org.*
Family Winemakers of California. *www.familywinemakers.org.*
Wine Institute. *www.wineinstitute.org.*
Winelovers Page. *www.wineloverspage.com.*

■ FESTIVALS AND EVENTS

■ JANUARY

Napa Valley Mustard Festival. Valley-wide art, wine, and food celebration of the blooming wild mustard. Late January–March. *707-938-1133; www.mustard-festival.org.*

Santa Cruz Wine Country Passport Program. On the third Saturday of the month, visit many wineries not usually open to the public. Also held April, July, and November. *831-685-8463; www.scmwa.com.*

Winter Wineland, Russian River Valley. Seminars, tastings, entertainment at about 100 wineries, many not otherwise open to the public. *800-723-6336; www.wineroad.com.*

■ FEBRUARY

Behind the Cellar Door, Amador County. Taste wines of the near future. *877-868-7262; www.amadorwine.com.*

President's Wine Weekend, Calaveras County. Barrel tastings, food pairings, live music. *209-728-9467; www.calaveraswines.org.*

■ MARCH

Lodi Spring Wine Show. Hors d'oeuvres, music, entertainment, and tastings of wines from more than four dozen wineries. *209-369-2771; www.grapefestival.com.*

Paso Robles Zinfandel Festival. More than 80 wineries, three days of winemaker dinners, seminars, special events. *800-549-9463; www.pasowine.com.*

Savor Sonoma Valley. Tastings, food, music, art at wineries. *866-794-9463; www.heartofsonomavalley.com.*

Wine Road Barrel Tasting Weekend, Northern Sonoma County. About 120 wineries participate. *800-723-6336; www.wineroad.com.*

The California golden poppy is the state flower and blooms from early spring through June.

World of Pinot Noir, Shell Beach. California producers gather in San Luis Obispo County to meet the public. *805-489-1758; www.worldofpinotnoir.com.*

■ **APRIL**

Passport to Dry Creek. A weekend of tastings and other events; sells out early in a lottery. *707-433-3031; www.wdcv.com.*

Santa Barbara County Vintners' Festival. Outdoor event with auction, hosted by local wineries and restaurants. *805-688-0881; www.sbcountywines.com.*

■ **MAY**

Hospice du Rhône, Paso Robles. World's largest Rhône variety wine festival, with winemakers of many countries. *805-784-9543; hospicedurhone.org.*

Paso Robles Wine Festival. Winery open-houses, winemaker dinners, outdoor tasting. *800-549-9463; www.pasowine.com.*

Pinot Noir Festival, Anderson Valley. *707-895-9463; www.avwines.com.*

Roll Out the Barrels, San Luis Obispo. Self-guided tour of Edna Valley wineries for tastings, food, music. *805-541-5868; www.slowine.com.*

Santa Cruz Mountains Wine Express, Felton. Rare chance to sample many area wines in one place and ride a steam railroad. *831-685-8463; www.scmwa.com.*

■ JUNE

Auction Napa Valley, St. Helena. Charity wine auction is world's largest. *707-963-3388; www.napavintners.com.*

Monterey Wine Festival. About 120 wineries at event sponsored by the American Restaurant Association. *800-422-0251; www.montereywine.com.*

Santa Cruz Mountains Vintners Festival. Two weekends of food, music, art exhibits, winery tours, and barrel tastings. *831-685-8463; www.scmwa.com.*

Taste of Alexander Valley, Alexander Valley. Cave and cellar tours, tastings, entertainment. *888-289-4637; www.alexandervalley.org.*

■ JULY

Central Coast Wine Classic, Shell Beach. San Luis Obispo and Santa Barbara county wineries raise funds for the arts. *805-544-1285; www.centralcoastwineclassic.org.*

Livermore Valley's Wine & Food Experience, Pleasanton. An evening of wine and food celebrates the valley's agricultural heritage. *925-447-9463; www.lvwine.com.*

■ AUGUST

Family Winemakers of California, San Francisco. Small family-owned wineries are showcased at world's largest tasting of California wines. *916-498-7500; www.familywinemakers.org.*

Shakespeare at Buena Vista, Sonoma. Every Sunday in August and September; bring a picnic, buy a bottle of wine, and enjoy the show. *707-252-7117; www.buenavistacarneros.com.*

■ SEPTEMBER

Valley of the Moon Vintage Festival, Sonoma. A blessing of the grapes, firemen's water fight, contests, wine, and food. *707-996-2109; www.sonomavinfest.org.*

Winesong, Mendocino Coast Botanical Gardens, Fort Bragg. The North Coast's top wine and food festival, with tastings and a charity auction. *707-961-4909; www.winesong.org.*

■ OCTOBER

Big Crush Harvest Festival, Amador County. Special events and a raffle at Amador County wineries. *209-245-6992; www.amadorwine.com.*

Harvest Fair, Santa Rosa. Grape stomping, wine tastings, livestock exhibits, and contests celebrate Sonoma County agriculture. *707-545-4200; www.harvestfair.org.*

Harvest Wine Weekend, Paso Robles. Winemaker dinners, barrel samples, seminars, barbecues, music, winery tours. *800-549-9463; www.pasowine.com.*

Pinot on the River, Russian River Valley. Weekend of pinot noir tastings and seminars. *707-723-0341; www.pinotfestival.com.*

■ NOVEMBER

Great Wine Escape Weekend, Monterey. Winery open houses, winemakers' dinners, and other events. *831-375-9400; www.montereywines.org.*

Harvest Celebration Weekend, Avila Beach. Music, food, and wine by the sea. *805-541-5868; www.slowine.com.*

Wine & Food Affair, Healdsburg. Wine tastings, food, music. *800-723-6336; www.wineroad.com.*

(following page) Try hot-air ballooning for a new perspective on the Wine Country.

G L O S S A R Y

For descriptions of specific grape varietals, *see* the Visiting Wineries chapter.

Acidity. The tartness of a wine, derived from the fruit acids of the grape. Acids stabilize a wine (i.e., preserve its character), balance its sweetness, and bring out its flavors. Too little or too much acid spoils a wine's taste. Tartaric acid is the major acid in wine, but malic, lactic, and citric acids also occur.

Aging. The process by which some wines improve over time, becoming smoother and more complex and developing a pleasing bouquet. Wine is most commonly aged in oak vats or barrels, slowly interacting with the air through the pores in the wood. Sometimes wine is cellared for bottle aging. Today, many wines are not made for aging and are drunk relatively young, as little as a few months after bottling. Age can diminish a wine's fruitiness and dull its color: whites turn brownish, rosés orange, reds brown.

Alcohol. Ethyl alcohol is a colorless, volatile, pungent spirit that not only gives wine its stimulating effect and some of its flavor but also acts as a preservative, stabilizing the wine and allowing it to age. A wine's alcohol content must be stated on the label, expressed as a percentage of volume, except when a wine is designated table wine (see below).

American Viticultural Area (AVA). More commonly termed appellation. A region with unique soil, climate, and other grape-growing conditions can be designated an AVA by the Alcohol and Tobacco Tax and Trade Bureau. When a label lists an appellation—Napa Valley or Chalone, for example—at least 75 percent of the grapes used to make the wine must come from that region.

Appellation. *See* American Viticultural Area.

Aroma. The scent of young wine derived directly from the fresh fruit. It diminishes with fermentation and is replaced by a more complex bouquet as the wine ages. The term may also be used to describe special fruity odors in a wine, like black cherry, green olive, ripe raspberry, or apple.

Astringent. The puckery sensation produced in the mouth by the tannins in wine.

AVA. *See* American Viticultural Area.

Balance. A quality of wine in which all desirable elements (fruit, acid, tannin) are present in the proper proportion. Well-balanced wine has pleasing nose, flavor, and mouth feel.

Barrel. A cylindrical storage container with bulging sides; usually made from staves of oak. A full barrel holds the equivalent of 240 regular 750-ml bottles.

Barrel Fermenting. The fermenting of wine in small oak barrels instead of large tanks or vats. This method allows the winemaker to keep grape lots separate before blending the wine. The cost of oak barrels makes barrel fermenting expensive.

Big Wine. A wine with considerable body, high alcohol, and strong aromas. A big wine is not necessarily a good wine; it may merely be coarse and heavy.

Blanc de Blancs. Sparkling or still white wine made solely from white grapes.

Blanc de Noirs. White wine made with red grapes by removing the skins during crush. Some sparkling whites are made only with red pinot noir and meunier grapes.

Blending. The mixing of several wines to create one of greater complexity or appeal, as when a heavy wine is blended with a lighter one to make a more approachable medium-bodied wine. Premium winemakers in California often label their blends with the percentages of different grape varieties used.

Body. The wine's heft or density as experienced by the palate. A full body makes the mouth literally feel full. It is considered an advantage in the case of some reds, a disadvantage in many lighter whites. *See also* Mouthfeel, below.

Bordeaux Blend. A red wine blended from varietals native to France's Bordeaux region—cabernet sauvignon, cabernet franc, malbec, merlot, and petit verdot.

Bottle Sizes. Metric sizes have replaced the traditional bottle sizes of gallon, quart, fifth, et al., though the old names linger:

Tenth . . . . .375 ml of wine

Fifth . . . . .750 ml (25.4 oz)
The most commonly used wine bottle

Magnum . . . . .1.50 liters (50.72 oz)

Double Magnum . . . . .3.0 liters
also called Jeroboam

Other, larger bottles include the approximately 9-liter Salmanzar and the Nebuchadnezzar, which holds 13 to 15 liters.

The renovated 19th-century Napa Valley Opera House is part of Napa's revitalization.

Botrytis. *See* Noble Rot, below.

Bouquet. The odors a mature wine gives off when opened. They should be pleasantly complex and should give an indication of the wine's grape variety, origin, age, and quality.

Brettanomyces. Also called Brett. A strain of yeast that gives wine a funky off-flavor. Winemakers try to keep Brett away from their wines, but some drinkers enjoy a mild Brett effect.

Brix. A method of telling whether grapes are ready for picking by measuring their sugars. Multiplying a grape's Brix number by .55 approximates the potential alcohol content of the wine.

Brut. French term for the driest category of sparkling wine (*see also* demi-sec, sec).

Burgundy. The English name for Bourgogne, a French region, and for the wine from that region. Inferior California red wines are sometimes mislabeled "burgundy."

Case. A carton of twelve 750-ml bottles of wine. A magnum case contains six 1.5-liter magnum bottles.

Cask. A synonym for barrel. More generally, any size or shape wine container made from wood staves.

Cellaring. Storage of wine in bottles for aging. The bottles are laid on their sides to keep the corks moist and prevent air leakage that would spoil the wine.

Chablis. A prime French wine-growing region making austere white wines. Inferior California wines and cheap pinks are sometimes mislabeled "Chablis."

Champagne. The northernmost wine district of France, where sparkling wine originated and where the world's only genuine Champagne is made. The term is often used inaccurately in America to denote sparkling wines in general.

Claret. A name sometimes applied to red wines made from Bordeaux varietals, notably the red Bordeaux blends of certain California premium wineries.

Clarity. The lack of suspended particles in a wine; a prerequisite of quality. Settled particles (*see* Sediment) are acceptable.

Cloudiness. The presence of particles that do not settle out of a wine, causing it to look and taste dusty or even muddy. If settling and decanting (*see* Decant) do not correct cloudiness, the wine has been badly made or is spoiled.

Complexity. The qualities of good wine that provide a multi-layered sensory experience to the drinker. Balanced flavors, harmonious aromas or bouquet, and a long finish are components of complexity.

Cooperage. A collective term used to describe all the containers in which a winery stores and ages wine before bottling. It includes barrels, casks, vats, and tanks of different materials and sizes.

Corked. Also, corky. Describes wine that is flawed by the musty, wet-cardboard flavor imparted by cork mold.

Crush. American synonym for harvest season, or vintage. Also refers to the year's crop of grapes crushed for wine.

Cuvée. Generally a sparkling wine, but sometimes a still wine, that is a blend of different wines and sometimes different vintages. Most sparkling wines are cuvées.

Decant. To pour a wine from its bottle into another container either to expose it to air or to eliminate sediment. Decanting for sediment pours out the clear wine and leaves the residue behind in the original bottle.

Demi-sec. French term that translates "half-dry" (in Italian, *abboccato*; in Spanish, *semi-seco*). It is applied to sweet wines that contain 3.5 to 5 percent sugar.

Dessert Wines. Sweet wines that are big in flavor and aroma. Some are quite low in alcohol; others, such as port-style wines, are fortified with brandy or neutral spirits and may be 17 to 21 percent alcohol.

Dry. Having very little sweetness or residual sugar. Most red, white, and rosé wines are dry, although some whites, such as rieslings are made to be off-dry, on the sweet side.

Estate Bottled. A wine entirely made by one winery at a single facility. The grapes must come from the winery's own vineyards within the same appellation (which must be printed on the label).

Fault. Any technically undesirable quality in wine. May refer to color, aroma, flavor, or qualities uncharacteristic of a grape variety.

Fermentation. The bio-chemical process by which grape juice becomes wine. Enzymes generated by yeast cells convert grape sugars into alcohol and carbon dioxide. Fermentation stops when the sugar is depleted and the yeast starves, or when high alcohol levels kill the yeast.

Fermenter. Any vessel, small or large (such as a barrel, tank, or vat), in which wine is fermented.

Filtering, Filtration. A purification process in which wine is pumped through filters to rid it of suspended particles.

Fining. A method of clarifying wine by adding crushed eggshells, isinglass, or other natural substances to a barrel. As these solids settle to the bottom, they take various dissolved compounds with them. Most wine meant for everyday drinking is fined; counterintuitively, fine wines are less often fined.

Finish. Also aftertaste. The flavors that remain in the mouth after swallowing wine. A good wine has a long finish with complex flavor and aroma.

Flat. Said of a wine that lacks acid and is thus dull; also of a sparkling wine that has lost its bubbles.

Fortification. A process by which brandy or natural spirits are added to a wine to stop fermentation and to increase its level of alcohol, as in the case of port-style dessert wines.

Forward. Describes the aromas and flavors that are the first to emerge when you smell or taste wine, as compared to more subtle qualities that appear later.

Fruity. Having aromatic nuances of fresh fruit—fig, raspberry, apple, et cetera. Fruitiness, a sign of quality in young wines, is replaced by bouquet in aged wines.

Fumé Blanc. A non-specific term for wine made with sauvignon blanc. Robert Mondavi coined the term originally to describe his dry, crisp, oak-aged sauvignon blanc.

Green. Said of a wine made from unripe grapes, with a pronounced leafy flavor and a raw edge.

Horizontal Tasting. A tasting of several different wines of the same vintage.

Late Harvest. Wine made from grapes harvested later in the fall than the main lot, and thus higher in sugar levels.

Lees. The spent yeast, grape solids, and tartrates that drop to the bottom of the barrel or tank as wine ages. Wine, particularly white wine, left on the lees for a time gains complexity.

Maderized. A term applied to a white or rosé wine that is past its prime and has become oxidized so as to smell and taste similar to Madeira, the Portuguese fortified wine.

Malolactic Fermentation. A secondary fermentation in the tank or barrel that changes harsh malic acid into softer lactic acid and carbon dioxide. Wine is sometimes inoculated with lactic bacteria, or placed in wood containers that harbor the bacteria, to enhance this process. Often referred to as ML or malo. Too much malo can make a wine flabby.

Meritage. A trademarked name for American (mostly California) Bordeaux blends that meet certain wine-making and marketing requirements and are made by member wineries of the Meritage Association.

Méthode Champenoise. The traditional, time-consuming method of making sparkling wines. *See also* the Champagne and Sparkling Wines box in the Northern Napa Valley chapter.

Mouth feel. Literally, the way wine feels in the mouth. Mouth feel, such as smoothness or astringency, is detected by the sense of touch rather than of smell or taste.

Must. The slushy mix of crushed grapes—juice, pulp, skin, seeds, and bits of stem—produced by the crusher-destemmer at the beginning of the wine-making process.

Neutral oak. The wood of older barrels or vats that no longer pass much flavor or tannin to the wine stored within.

New oak. The wood of a fresh barrel or vat that has not previously been used to ferment or age wine. It can impart desirable flavors and enhance a wine's complexity, but if used to excess it can overpower a wine's true character.

New World. Refers to wine production outside of Europe, as in the United States, and South America.

Noble Rot. *Botrytis cinerea,* a beneficial fungus that can perforate a ripe grape's skin. This dehydrates the grape and concentrates the remaining juice while preserving its acids. Botrytis grapes make sweet but not cloying wine.

Non-Vintage. A blend of wines from different years. Non-vintage wines have no date on their label. Wine may be blended from different vintages to showcase strong points that complement each other, or in order to make a commercial product taste the same from one year to the next.

Nose. The overall fragrance (aroma or bouquet) given off by a wine; the better part of its flavor.

Oak. The most popular wood for making wine barrels, generally grown in America, France, or Eastern Europe.

Oaky. Said of a wine that has been aged in new oak for too long and tastes more of the vanilla-like wood flavors than of the grape.

Organic viticulture. The technique of growing grapes without the use of chemical fertilizers, pesticides, or fungicides. *See also* the Organic

Wines box in the Carneros District chapter.

Organic wine. Wine that is produced from organically grown grapes and processed without the use of chemical additives such as sulfites.

Oxidation. Undesirable flavor and color changes caused to juice or wine by too much contact with the air, either during processing or because of a leaky barrel or cork. Most often occurs with white wine, especially if it is over the hill.

pH. Technical term for a measure of a wine's acidity. It is a reverse measure: the lower the pH level, the higher the acidity. Most wines range in pH from 2.9 to 4.2, with the most desirable level at 3.2 and 3.5. Higher pHs makes wine flabby, lower pHs make it tart.

Phylloxera. A disease caused by the root louse *Phylloxera vastatrix,* which attacks and ultimately destroys grapevine roots. The pest is native to the United States; it traveled to France with American grapevines in the 19th century and devastated non-resistant vineyards there.

Pomace. Spent grape skins and solids left over after the juice has been pressed, commonly returned to the fields as fertilizer.

Port-style wine. Fortified dessert wine made in the style of port. True port, or *porto,* comes only from Portugal.

Racking. Moving wine from one tank or barrel to another to leave unwanted deposits behind; the wine may or may not be fined or filtered in the process.

Reserve wine. Murky term applied by vintners to indicate a wine is superior in some way to others from their winery. The wine may come from a specific vineyard or be aged longer before release, among other possibilities.

Residual Sugar. The natural sugar left in a wine after fermentation, which converts sugar into alcohol. If the fermentation was interrupted or if the must has very high sugar levels, some residual sugar will remain, making a sweeter wine.

Rhône Blend. A wine made from grapes hailing from France's Rhône Valley, such as marsanne, roussanne, syrah, cinsault, mourvèdre, or viognier.

Rosé. Pink wine, usually made from red wine grapes. The juice is left on the skins only long enough to give it a tinge of color. After decades in the shadows, they're getting serious attention again.

Rounded. Said of a well-balanced wine in which fruity flavor is nicely offset by acidity—a good wine, though not necessarily a distinctive or great one.

Sec. French word that translates "dry" (in Italian, *secco*; in Spanish, *seco*). The term is generally applied within the sparkling or sweet categories, indicating the wine has 1.7 to 3.5 percent residual sugar. Sec is drier than demi-sec but not as dry as brut.

Sediment. Dissolved or suspended solids that drop out of most red wines as they age in the bottle, thus clarifying their appearance, flavors, and aromas. Not a defect in an old wine or in a new wine that has been bottled unfiltered.

Sourness. Experts use the term "sour" only for a spoiled wine that has a vinegary quality.

Sparkling Wines. Wines in which carbon dioxide is dissolved, making them bubbly.

Sugar. Source of grapes' natural sweetness. When yeast feeds on sugar, it produces alcohol and carbon dioxide. The higher the sugar content of the grape, the higher the potential alcohol level or sweetness of the wine.

Sulfites. Compounds of sulfur dioxide that are almost always added before

A tranquil vineyard.

fermentation during winemaking to prevent oxidation and to kill bacteria and wild yeasts that can cause off-flavors. Sulfites are sometimes blamed as the culprit in headaches caused by red wine, but the connection has not been proven.

Sustainable viticulture. A viticultural method that aims to bring the vineyard into harmony with the environment. Organic and other techniques are used to minimize agricultural impact to and to promote biodiversity.

Table Wine. Any wine that has at least 7 percent but not more than 14 percent alcohol by volume. The term is unrelated to quality or price—both super-premium and jug wines can be labeled as table wine.

Tank. A very large container, usually upright and cylindrical, in which wine is fermented and stored. Tanks are commonly made of stainless steel, though they may also be made of wood or concrete (the latter are usually straight-sided cubicles) and lined with glass.

Tannins. Naturally occurring but still somewhat mysterious compounds in grape skins, seeds, and stems, and in barrel oak, that produce a sensation of drying or astringency in the mouth and throat. A significant component of many red wines, tannins settle out as wine ages.

Tartaric Acid, Tartrates. The principal acid of wine. Crystaline tartrates form on the insides of vats or barrels and sometimes appear in the bottle or on the cork. They look like tiny shards of glass but they are not harmful.

Terroir. French word that translates as "soil." Typically used to describe the soil and climate conditions that influence the quality and characteristics of grapes and wine.

Varietal. A wine that takes its name from the grape variety from which it is predominantly made. California wines that qualify are almost always labeled with the variety of the source grape. According to U.S. law, at least 75 percent of a wine must come from a particular grape to be labeled with its variety name.

Vat. A large container of stainless steel, wood, or concrete, often open at the top, in which wine is fermented or blended. The term is sometimes used interchangeably with "tank."

Vertical Tasting. A tasting of several wines of different vintages, generally starting with the youngest and proceeding to the oldest. Vertical tastings may focus on wines from a single winery, on a single varietal, or another theme.

Vinifera. The wine grapes of Europe, all of which belong to the species *Vitis vinifera.* California wines are almost entirely produced from transplanted vinifera grapes; native New World grapes tend to have odd flavors.

Vinification. Winemaking, the process by which grapes are made into wine.

Vintage. The grape harvest of a given year, and the year in which the grapes are harvested. A vintage date on a bottle indicates the year in which the grapes were harvested rather than the year in which the wine was bottled.

Viticultural Area. *See* American Viticultural Area.

Viticulture. The cultivation of grapes.

Woody. Describes excessively musty wood aromas and flavors picked up by wine that has been stored in a wood barrel or cask for too long. Unlike "oaky," the term "woody" is always a negative.

Yeast. A minute, single-celled fungus that germinates and multiplies rapidly as it feeds on sugar with the help of enzymes, creating alcohol and releasing carbon dioxide in the process of fermentation.

WINERY WEBSITES

Southern Napa

Chimney Rock Winery	www.chimneyrock.com
Clos du Val	www.closduval.com
Darioush	www.darioush.com
Domaine Chandon	www.chandon.com
Far Niente	www.farniente.com
The Hess Collection	www.hesscollection.com
Mayacamas Vineyards	www.mayacamas.com
Opus One	www.opusonewinery.com
Plumpjack Winery	www.plumpjackwinery.com
Robert Mondavi Winery	www.robertmondaviwinery.com
Robert Sinskey Vineyards	www.robertsinskey.com
Silver Oak Cellars	www.silveroak.com
Stag's Leap Wine Cellars	www.cask23.com
Trefethen Vineyards	www.trefethen.com

Northern Napa

Alpha Omega	www.aowinery.com
Beaulieu Vineyard	www.bvwines.com
Beringer Vineyards	www.beringer.com
Cakebread Cellars	www.cakebread.com
Castello di Amoroso	www.castellodiamoroso.com
Caymus Vineyards	www.caymus.com
Charles Krug Winery	www.charleskrug.com
Clos Pegase	www.clospegase.com
Duckhorn Vineyards	www.duckhorn.com
Flora Springs Winery	www.florasprings.com
Freemark Abbey	www.freemarkabbey.com
Frog's Leap	www.frogsleap.com
Grgich Hills	www.grgich.com
Joseph Phelps Vineyards	www.jpvwines.com
Louis M. Martini	www.louismartini.com
Merryvale Vineyards	www.merryvale.com
Mumm Napa	www.mummnapa.com
Rubicon Estate	www.rubiconestate.com

Rutherford Hill Winery	www.rutherfordhill.com
St. Clement Vineyards	www.stclement.com
Saint Supery Vineyards	www.stsupery.com
Schramsberg Vineyards	www.schramsberg.com
Spring Mountain Vineyard	www.springmountainvineyard.com
Sterling Vineyards	www.sterlingvineyards.com
Stony Hill Vineyard	www.stonyhillvineyard.com
Terra Valentine	www.terravalentine.com

Carneros District

Artesa Winery	www.artesawinery.com
Bouchaine Vineyards	www.bouchaine.com
Cline Cellars	www.clinecellars.com
Domaine Carneros	www.domainecarneros.com
Gloria Ferrer	www.gloriaferrer.com
Madonna Estate	www.madonnaestate.com
Robledo Family Winery	www.robledofamilywinery.com
Saintsbury	www.saintsbury.com
Truchard Vineyards	www.truchardvineyards.com
Viansa Winery	www.viansa.com

Napa Valley Country Roads

Burgess Cellars	www.burgesscellars.com
Chateau Montelena	www.montelena.com
Ladera Vineyards	www.laderavineyards.com
Langtry Estate & Vineyards	www.langtryestate.com
Nichelini Winery	www.nicheliniwinery.com
Pope Valley Winery	www.popevalleywinery.com
RustRidge Winery	www.rustridge.com
Storybook Mountain	www.storybookwines.com

Sonoma Valley

Arrowood Vineyards & Winery	www.arrowoodvineyards.com
Bartholomew Park Winery	www.bartpark.com
Benzinger Family Winery	www.benzinger.com
Buena Vista Carneros Estate	www.buenavistacarneros.com
Chateau St. Jean	www.chateaustjean.com

Gundlach-Bundschu Winery	www.gunbun.com
Kenwood Vineyards	www.kenwoodvineyards.com
Kunde Estate Winery	www.kunde.com
Landmark Vineyards	www.landmarkwine.com
Ledson Winery & Vineyards	www.ledson.com
Matanzas Creek Winery	www.matanzascreek.com
Ravenswood Winery	www.ravenswood-wine.com
St. Francis Winery & Vineyards	www.stfranciswinery.com
Sebastiani Vineyards	www.sebastiani.com

Northern Sonoma County

Alderbrook Winery	www.alderbrook.com
Alexander Valley Vineyards	www.avvwine.com
Clos du Bois	www.closdubois.com
David Coffaro Vineyard & Winery	www.coffaro.com
Davis Bynum Winery	www.davisbynum.com
Dry Creek Vineyard	www.drycreekvineyard.com
Ferrari-Carano	www.ferrari-carano.com
Foppiano Vineyards	www.foppiano.com
Francis Ford Coppola Winery	www.franciscoppolawinery.com
Gary Farrell Winery	www.garyfarrellwines.com
Hop Kiln Winery	www.hopkilnwinery.com
Iron Horse Vineyards	www.ironhorsevineyards.com
J Vineyards and Winery	www.jwine.com
Korbel Champagne Cellars	www.korbel.com
Martinelli Vineyards & Winery	www.martinelliwinery.com
Porter Creek Vineyards	www.portercreekvineyards.com
Preston Vineyards	www.prestonvineyards.com
Quivira Vineyards	www.quivirawine.com
Rochioli Vineyards & Winery	www.rochioliwinery.com
Rodney Strong Vineyards	www.rodneystrong.com
Sausal Winery	www.sausalwinery.com
Seghesio Family Vineyards	www.seghesio.com
Simi Winery	www.simiwinery.com
Stryker Sonoma Winery	www.strykersonoma.com
Trentadue Winery	www.trentadue.com

Beyond Napa and Sonoma

Amador Foothill Winery	www.amadorfoothill.com
Berghold Estate Winery	www.bergholdvineyards.com
Black Sheep Winery	www.blacksheepwinery.com
Boeger Winery	www.boegerwinery.com
Charles B. Mitchell Vineyards	www.charlesbmitchell.com
Chatom Vineyards	www.chatomvineyards.com
Concannon Vineyards	www.concannonvineyard.com
Dobra Zemlja	www.dobraz.com
Domaine de la Terre Rouge	www.terrerougewines.com
Esterlina Vineyards	www.esterlinavineyards.com
Goldeneye Winery	www.goldeneyewinery.com
Greenwood Ridge Vineyards	www.greenwoodridge.com
Handley Cellars	www.handleycellars.com
Husch Vineyards	www.huschvineyards.com
Ironstone Vineyards	www.ironstonevineyards.com
Jessie's Grove Winery	www.jessiesgrovewinery.com
Lava Cap Winery	www.lavacap.com
Lucas Winery	www.lucaswinery.com
Madrona Vineyards	www.madronavineyards.com
Michael-David Winery	www.lodivineyards.com
Milliaire Winery	www.milliairewinery.com
Mitchell Katz Winery	www.mitchellkatzwinery.com
Montevina Wines	www.montevina.com
Navarro Vineyards	www.navarrowine.com
Peirano Estate Vineyards	www.peirano.com
Renwood Winery	www.renwood.com
Roederer Estate	www.roedererestate.com
Shenandoah Vineyards	www.sobonwine.com
Sierra Vista Vineyards & Winery	www.sierravistawinery.com
Sobon Estate Winery	www.sobonwine.com
Steven Kent Winery	www.stevenkent.com
Stevenot Winery	stevenot.comcastbiz.net
Thomas Coyne Winery	www.thomascoynewinery.com
Story Winery	www.zin.com

Vino Noceto	www.noceto.com
Wente Vineyards	www.wentevineyards.com
Woodbridge Winery	www.woodbridgewines.com

Central Coast Wineries

Adelaida Cellars	www.adelaida.com
Andrew Murray Vineyards	www.andrewmurrayvineyards.com
Babcock Winery & Vineyards	www.babcockwinery.com
Beckmen Vineyards	www.beckmenvineyards.com
Bernardus Winery	www.bernardus.com/winery
Bonny Doon Vineyard	www.bonnydoonvineyard.com
Brander Vineyard	www.brander.com
Bridlewood Winery	www.bridlewoodwinery.com
Byington Vineyard & Winery	www.byington.com
Cambria Winery	www.cambriawines.com
Castoro Cellars	www.castorocellars.com
Chalone Vineyard	www.chalonevineyard.com
Chateau Julien Wine Estate	www.chateaujulien.com
Claiborne and Churchill Vintners	www.claibornechurchill.com
David Bruce Winery	www.davidbrucewinery.com
Domaine Alfred Winery	www.domainealfred.com
Eberle Winery	www.eberlewinery.com
Edna Valley Vineyard	www.ednavalleyvineyard.com
Fess Parker Winery & Vineyards	www.fessparker.com
Firestone Vineyard	www.firestonewine.com
Foley Estates	www.foleywines.com
Foxen	www.foxenvineyard.com
Gainey Vineyard	www.gaineyvineyard.com
Georis Winery	www.georiswine.com
Hahn Estates	www.hahnestates.com
Heller Estate Organic Vineyards	www.hellerestate.com
J. Lohr Vineyards & Wines	www.jlohr.com
Joullian Vineyards	www.joullian.com
Justin Vineyards & Winery	www.justinwine.com
Kenneth Volk Vineyards	www.volkwines.com
Lafond Winery & Vineyards	www.lafondwinery.com

L'Aventure	www.aventurewine.com
Linne Calodo	www.linnecalodo.com
Melville Vineyards & Winery	www.melvillewinery.com
Meridian Vineyards	www.meridianvineyards.com
Mosby Winery & Vineyard	www.mosbywines.com
Ortman Family Vineyards	www.ortmanvineyards.com
Peachy Canyon Winery	www.peachycanyon.com
Pipestone Vineyards	www.pipestonevineyards.com
Rancho Sisquoc Winery	www.ranchosisquoc.com
Ridge Vineyards	www.ridgewine.com
Sanford Winery	www.sanfordwinery.com
Saucelito Canyon Vineyard	www.saucelitocanyon.com
Storrs Winery	www.storrswine.com
Tablas Creek Vineyard	www.tablascreek.com
Talbott Vineyards	www.talbottvineyards.com
Talley Vineyards	www.talleyvineyards.com
Thomas Fogarty Winery & Vineyards	www.fogartywinery.com
Turley Wine Cellars	www.turleywinecellars.com
Ventana Vineyards	www.ventanawines.com
Wild Horse Winery & Vineyards	www.wildhorsewinery.com
Windward Vineyard	www.windwardvineyard.com
Zaca Mesa Winery	www.zacamesa.com

INDEX

PHOTO CREDITS

Page 34 (third row, fourth from left), Trefethen Vineyards
Page 34 (bottom row, first from left), Heitz Wine Cellars
Page 34 (bottom row, middle), Stony Hill Vineyard (photograph by Emile Romaine)
Page 34 (bottom row, fourth from left), Gundlach-Bundschu

Visiting Wineries
41, Clos du Val Wine Company
46, wine aroma wheel copyright 1990,2002 A.C. Noble www.winearomawheel.com
Page 51 (top), Napa Valley Conference Bureau
Page 51 (second and third from top), Wild Horse Winery (Forrest L. Doud)
Page 51 (fourth from top), Napa Valley Conference Bureau
Page 51 (fifth from top), Panther Creek Cellars (Ron Kaplan)
Page 51 (sixth from top), Clos du Val (Marvin Collins)
Page 51 (bottom), Panther Creek Cellars (Ron Kaplan)
Page 53, Wild Horse Winery (Forrest L. Doud)
Page 61, Vineyard Soil Technologies

Southern Napa Valley
Page 81, Trefethen Vineyards
Page 85, Domaine Chandon
Pages 92–93, Opus One
Page 100, Oakland Museum of California
Page 101, Clos du Val (Marvin Collins)
Page 103, Hess Collection

Northern Napa Valley
Page 109, Wine Institute of California
Page 110, Kerrick James
Page 117 (left), Silverado Museum
Page 117 (right), Ambrose Bierce House
Page 124, Napa County Historical Society
Page 125, Merryvale Vineyards
Page 127, Wine Institute of California
Page 131 (top), Freemark Abbey
Page 131 (bottom), Stony Hill Vineyard
Page 133, Schramsberg Vineyards

Carneros District
Page 168, Artesa Winery